Motivation and Engagement in Various Learning Environments

Motivation and Engagement in Various Learning Environments

Interdisciplinary Perspectives

edited by

Margareta M. Thomson
North Carolina State University

INFORMATION AGE PUBLISHING, INC.
Charlotte, NC • www.infoagepub.com

Library of Congress Cataloging-in-Publication Data

A CIP record for this book is available from the Library of Congress
http://www.loc.gov

ISBN: 979-8-88730-538-7 (Paperback)
979-8-88730-539-4 (Hardcover)
979-8-88730-540-0 (E-Book)

Copyright © 2024 Information Age Publishing Inc.

All rights reserved. No part of this publication may be reproduced, stored in a
retrieval system, or transmitted, in any form or by any means, electronic, mechanical,
photocopying, microfilming, recording or otherwise, without written permission
from the publisher.

Printed in the United States of America

CONTENTS

Preface vii

Introduction ix
Margareta M. Thomson

1 Developing Students' Motivation for Science and STEM via
Role Models: An Interdisciplinary Program Intervention 1
Margareta M. Thomson, Irina Pop-Pacurar, and Oana Negru-Subtirica

2 Science-Related Beliefs and Attitudes of Parents: Building
Students' Interests and Career Aspirations 19
*M. Gail Jones, Katherine Chesnutt, Megan Ennes, Daniel Macher,
and Manuela Paechter*

3 Approaching STEAM via Inquiry-Based Responses
to Big Questions: How "Epistemic Insight" Changes Informal
Science Learning 29
Finley I. Lawson, Stefan Colley, and Berry Billingsley

4 Investigatory Approaches to the Teaching and Learning
of History: Using a Constructivist Inquiry-Based
Scientific Method 49
James Percival

5 Creativity and Design-Based Markerspaces Influences
on Student Motivation in Engineering Education 65
Micaha Dean Hughes

v

vi ▪ Contents

6 Teaching Science in Charter Schools: Facilities, Equipment, and Teacher Preparation 77
Pamela M. Huff and M. Gail Jones

7 Motivations for Technology Use Among Mothers of Young Children: Tech as a Tool for Self-Determination.............. 97
Catherine Noonan

8 Students' Perception of Scientists and Their Work: Stereotypes and Misconceptions..119
Margareta M. Thomson and Zarifa Zakaria

9 Examining Motivation Among Elementary-Aged African-American Students: A Review of Socio-Cognitive and Expectancy-Values Constructs.. 147
Quaneisha Smith, and Margareta M. Thomson

10 Research Experiences for Teachers in a Cognitive Apprenticeship Program: Motivations, Emotions, and Instructional Changes 161
Margareta M. Thomson

11 Case Study: The Process Behind Developing an Environmental Education Program 181
Hannah M. A. Rickets, K. A. I. Nekaris, Marco Campera, and Muhammad Ali Imron

12 Enhancing Students' Engagement in Learning Sciences Through Project-Based Science: Using Digital Technologies Support 213
Miriam Kenyeres and Irina Pop-Pacurar

About the Editor... 245

About the Contributors.. 247

PREFACE

The current volume includes research studies from various domains related to students' engagement and learning, parents' experiences, and teachers' involvement with interdisciplinary programs. Different perspectives are presented in this collection of work, namely those of students, teachers, and parents. A particular focus is placed on interdisciplinarity, and the current volume compiles research on motivation and engagement from domains such as Science Technology Engineering and Mathematics (STEM), Literacy, Design and Computer Science. Learning is a process that occurs across multiple domains and in various contexts, such as formal and informal education. Additionally, the current volume provides examples of studies discussing distinctive modalities in designing and implementing inquiry-based learning in formal and informal education, motivational strategies, and useful applications for K–12 instruction and educational programs. The volume appeals to a wide audience, including researchers, teachers, parents, students, and education specialists.

Motivation and Engagement in Various Learning Environments, page vii
Copyright © 2024 by Information Age Publishing
www.infoagepub.com
All rights of reproduction in any form reserved.

INTRODUCTION

The current volume includes research studies related to students' motivation and engagement, as well as parents' experiences, and teachers' involvement with novel interdisciplinary programs. Different perspectives are presented in this collection of work, namely students, teachers, and parents. Research shows that novel, inquiry-based activities lead to significant increase in student motivation and academic gains. Additionally, when teachers and parents experience themselves immersive interdisciplinary activities, they are agents of knowledge transmission, as their learning experiences are transmitted to students and motivate them to learn. Furthermore, these interactive interdisciplinary-focused activities, regardless of their form, such as formal or informal education, have the potential to help students identify with a career or professional path (Thomson et al., 2021). Most often, learning is associated with formal education, specifically the work completed in school, and the view that the typical learning outcomes acquired in school, consisting of knowledge and skills, can lead to the development of general or professional abilities. However, despite training for integration into various professions, the formal education system does not meet entirely all individuals' educational needs. Oftentimes, the individual must find other sources of personal enlightenment, and informal education is one of these sources. Informal education consists of any educational program organized by specialists outside the school system, which forms a bridge between the theoretical knowledge taught in school and the practical applications taking place outside of school.

Motivation and Engagement in Various Learning Environments, pages ix–x
Copyright © 2024 by Information Age Publishing
www.infoagepub.com
All rights of reproduction in any form reserved.

x ▪ Introduction

Providing immersive novel learning experiences for students, parents and teachers in an informal setting, provides the individual with options and desire to choose areas in which they are intrinsically motivated, seek personal and academic fulfillment and thus, become enthusiastically involved. Designing program and activities offered in a variety of contexts and domains, greatly enhances students' engagement and intrinsic motivation for learning. Ultimately, both the formal and informal educational activities aim at nurturing students' learning and motivation, and teaching students not only specialized knowledge and skills, but also guiding them into harmoniously developing interdisciplinary abilities. Key components aiming at developing interdisciplinary skills and abilities in students, such as communication, collaboration, critical-thinking, creativity, and intellectual curiosity are essential, and needed in the development of educational curriculum.

—Margareta M. Thomson

CHAPTER 1

DEVELOPING STUDENTS' MOTIVATION FOR SCIENCE AND STEM VIA ROLE MODELS

An Interdisciplinary Program Intervention

Margareta M. Thomson, Irina Pop-Pacurar, and Oana Negru-Subtirica

PROJECT OVERVIEW

Students' early experiences with Science Technology Engineering and Mathematics (STEM) are important for developing not just their STEM literacy but are also crucial in influencing their motivation for science and their domain identification with STEM careers. How students understand science and STEM, the work of scientists is partly influenced by how this information is presented to them, in both formal and informal contexts. Additionally, research shows that developing students' STEM motivation

Motivation and Engagement in Various Learning Environments, pages 1–18
Copyright © 2024 by Information Age Publishing
www.infoagepub.com
All rights of reproduction in any form reserved.

1

and literacy starts at an early age. To that purpose, a plethora of educational research and international reports focus lately on monitoring students' STEM achievements and career aspirations, as well as the composition of individuals pursuing STEM careers (OECD, 2014, 2016; NSF, 2017). Research shows that at large, the make-up of STEM workforce is comprised of men; women and individuals identifying with a minority group are underrepresented in most science and technology fields (Griffith, 2010; Nix, Perez-Felkner, & Thomas, 2015). Therefore, it is crucial to expose students to learning experiences in STEM that show diversity among scientists. Mentor scientists are acting a role-models for students, The interdisciplinary program intervention described in the current book chapter is based on collaborative research between researchers at a major university in the United States and a major university in Romania. The purpose of the current study was to develop and implement an innovative project with students in 6th and 7th grade enrolled in public schools in Romania aiming at increasing their motivation for STEM. The research project directed by the first author has been supported by the U.S. Fulbright Commission and took place over one academic year. Middle grades students from three public schools participated in the project, and a unique feature of the study was the focus on schools located in impoverished communities. This is important, given the fact that research findings show that typically economically disadvantaged students identify themselves as individuals from minority groups, and are most likely to be underrepresented in STEM domains or follow a STEM career path (Thomson et al., 2021).

The STEM program intervention focused on adopting an inquiry-based science instruction in order to foster student motivation for science, and identification with STEM domain. A distinctive feature of the interdisciplinary program was the *science mentorship approach*. Role model scientists were presented to middle grade students in order to illustrate how success can be achieved when *effort and persistence are valued*. Two types of role models were presented to students: (a) *mentor scientists in the classroom*, these were 10 mentor scientists who volunteered to teach biology during one semester to 6th and 7th grade students in the current research project, and (b) *historical figures scientists*, these were stories of eminent scientists that were included in students' biology curriculum to illustrate how these accomplished scientists overcome their intellectual and personal struggles. The overall purpose of the research project was to provide students with role model scientists, and to challenge students' views that scientific achievement reflects ability rather than effort. Providing students with these experiences—scientists in the classroom teaching the biology classes and introducing stories in students' biology classes about of how accomplished scientists overcame the challenges in their scientific endeavors, the research project aimed at helping students' understand the role of science and what scientists do, motivate students for science careers, and what is takes to become an accomplished scientist.

The current book chapter has two main goals, namely to: (a) describe the STEM research project and (b) describe the key factors that were influential in the project implementation (e.g., socio-cultural, educational, interdisciplinarity). The literature in the field is scarce when it comes to showing *how schools can develop and implement innovative interdisciplinary programs* in order to cultivate non-cognitive skills, such as growth-mindset and motivational strategies in a school community. Implementing such transformative programs have benefits for the students and school, as well as the wider community, as mentor scientists involved in the project supported various science projects and efforts in the community. There are no studies to the date on this topic with students from Romania, and the current book chapter addresses this gap in the literature. The STEM program implemented in Romania can be replicated in other countries, or in various contexts, where formal and/or informal learning occurs, such as K–12 schools, colleges, mentoring programs, and after-school programs.

THEORETICAL MODEL: MOTIVATIONAL FRAMEWORKS

The STEM program intervention described in the current book chapter is grounded on psychological principles from the Social-Cognitive Theory (Bandura, 1977) and the Implicit Theories of Intelligence (Dweck et al., 1995; Dweck, 2006).

Social-Cognitive Theory (SCT)

This learning theory proposed by Bandura (1977) holds the assumption that parts of an individual's knowledge acquisition are related to observing others within the context of social interactions, experiences, as well as the result of vicarious learning (e.g., learning about reinforcement from observing others). The SCT states that when people observe a model performing a behavior and the consequences of that behavior (via vicarious learning), they use this information to guide their own behaviors. Observing a model can prompt the learner to engage in the behavior they witness. Thus, individuals learn by watching others, observing the social context and behaviors in the surrounding environment (Bandura, 2008). These behaviors and cognitions act as primary factors that influence the learning process in a reciprocal triadic relationship.

Particularly, two main concepts from the SCT are central, regarding the current study, namely ***modeling*** and ***identification***. One assumption proposed by the SCT is that knowledge acquisition or learning is directly related to the observation of models. The models can be individuals we interact with in reality (e.g., interpersonal imitation) or fictional models (e.g., media sources). Effective modeling teaches typical rules and strategies for dealing with different situations. Additionally, modeling has a direct influence on building an individual's sense of identification. Identification allows the learner to distinguish similarities with the model and can lead the learner to follow through with the modeled action. The SCT states that individuals are more likely to follow behaviors modeled by someone with whom *they can identify*, such as certain demographic characteristics, personality traits, or similar lived experiences. The more commonalities or emotional attachments perceived between the observer and the model, the more likely the observer learns and reenacts the modeled behavior.

Implicit Theories of Intelligence

This model proposed by Dweck and colleagues (1995) and by Dweck & Leggett (1988) underlines the strong link between beliefs about intelligence, academic goals, and individual's performance. The way individuals perceive their intelligence affects their learning process, specifically their motivations, their academic goals and their actual performance. In the social cognitive framework outlined by Dweck and Legget (1988), explaining the processes through which individuals' motivation is driven by their implicit beliefs about intelligence, the authors propose two theories about implicit beliefs, as follows: *The Entity Theory*, and *The Incremental Theory*. Further, Dweck (2006, 2015) proposes that individuals holding an entity theory about intelligence may exhibit a fixed mindset, whereas those holding an incremental theory of intelligence may exhibit a growth mindset. An *entity theory view (associated with a fixed mindset)* is the belief that intelligence or talent are seen as unchangeable (e.g., fixed entities). An *incremental theory view (associated with a growth mindset)* is the beliefs that intelligence is changeable (malleable) and can be improved incrementally through effort. Cultivating an incremental view among students, particularly in STEM domain, is essential because it has the potential to develop motivation, cultivating persistence and effort in students, leading to improved academic achievement and identification with STEM domains (Boaler, 2013; Lin-Siegler et al., 2016, 2017; Perels et al., 2009). Research shows that students with an incremental view are more engaged academically, have mastery-oriented goals, and are more persistent (Blackwell et al., 2007, 2015; Cook & Artino, 2016; Dweck, 2008; Mangels et al., 2006).

METHODOLOGY

Study Context and Participants

Despite education reforms for the past 25 years implemented in Romania, student learning outcomes, as shown in recent European reports (i.e., OECD, 2014, 2016) need significant improvement. A large number of public schools are struggling with student enrollment and attendance; yet Romanian students at all levels, are expected to meet high global standards in literacy, mathematics and science despite the scarcity of STEM learning resources. More recent reform measures in Romania included changes to the structure of the overall educational system, but also to the curriculum in various disciplines, all being carried out in a European context concerned with assuring the quality of education.

The STEM program intervention described in the current book chapter was conducted in Romania as part of a research study funded by the United States Fulbright Commission. Three public schools participated in the study during Spring 2019 semester, and the STEM program intervention was implemented in all biology classes from these schools for the 6th and 7th grade students ($N = 326$ students). The student population in the three schools had similar demographics, and generally students came from low-income households (see Table 1.1). All schools followed a traditional science curriculum and the national standards for science teaching.

Study Design

The purpose of the study was to measure the effects of the interdisciplinary STEM program implemented, particularly regarding students changes in science motivation, domain identification with science, students' beliefs about intelligence and their views of academic success. A mixed-methods study design (QUANT+ Qual) was employed, both quantitative and qualitative data were collected.

TABLE 1.1 Participants' Demographics		
Demographic Category	Frequency	Percentage N (%)
Female	168	51.5%
Male	153	46.9%
Romanian	309	94.8%
Hungarian	4	1.2%
Other	11	3.4%

Survey

Paper and pencil surveys were distributed to all students in which quantitative and qualitative data were collected in a pre-posttest design. The survey was administered to students before the intervention (pretest) and after the intervention (posttest). Quantitative data were collected via Likert scale items and qualitative data was collected via open-ended items. Quantitative data collected inquired about student demographic data (i.e., gender, age, school grade), student motivation for science, student achievement beliefs, mindset and domain identification with science careers. Qualitative data consisted in individual responses (open-ended survey items) gauged students' reactions to the stories about struggling scientists.

Interviews

Individual interviews were conducted at the end of the STEM program intervention, following the posttest; these were face-to-face interviews with selected students from the pool of survey respondents (about 20% of survey respondents randomly selected). The interview questions inquired about students' experiences with the STEM mentorship program intervention, their level of motivation for science, and their views about intelligence and academic effort, and domain identification with science careers.

Procedures

This quasi-experimental study was implemented over a period of six weeks, as follows: T1 (week 1): pretest measures (survey); T2–4 (week 2, 3, and 4): STEM program intervention; T5 (week 5): posttest measures (survey), and T6 (week 6): qualitative data (interviews) with selected students. The STEM program intervention occurred during the week 2, 3, and 4. During this time, science instruction was taught differently for the control group compared to the treatment group. From each school, an even number of classes were assigned to the control group (i.e., 7 classes) and to the treatment group (i.e., 7 classes), described below.

Control Group

Condition T (Traditional teaching). This group of students received *traditional science instruction* taught by the biology teacher during week 2, 3, and 4 with an emphasis on teaching science knowledge. Regular science instruction was employed thus, with classroom science teachers in all schools following the standard curriculum for science.

Treatment Group

Condition M (Mentor Scientists). This group of students received *innovative science instruction* taught by the mentor scientists during week 2, 3, and 4 with an emphasis on inquiry-based learning. A team of two mentor

Developing Students' Motivation for Science and STEM via Role Models ▪ **7**

TABLE 1.2 Timeline and Measures

Survey time points	Actions/Events	Measures
Time 1	Week 1: pretest measures (survey)	All students take Survey #1: Likert scale items and open-ended items (e.g., Career motivation; Ability beliefs; Motivation for Science/Biology; STEM domain identification).
Time 2	Week 2: STEM program intervention	For treatment group: Mentor scientists teach the Biology lesson; Story #1 about struggling scientists is introduced to students.
Time 3	Week 3: STEM program intervention	For treatment group: Mentor scientists teach the Biology lesson; Story #2 about struggling scientists is introduced to students.
Time 4	Week 4: STEM program intervention	For treatment group: Mentor scientists teach the Biology lesson; Story #3 about struggling scientists is introduced to students.
Time 5	Week 5: posttest measures (survey)	All students take Survey #2: Likert scale items and open-ended items (e.g., Career motivation; Ability beliefs; Motivation for Science/Biology; STEM domain identification).
Time 6	Week 6: qualitative data (interviews) with selected students	Interview protocol

Note: Survey participants ($N = 326$) Grade 6 and 7 students from control and treatment group

Note: Interview participants ($n = 33$) are selected 6th and 7th grade students from the treatment group only (STEM program intervention).

scientists were assigned randomly to each class in the treatment group (condition M class). The team of mentor scientists worked together in planning and delivering the science instruction to the 6th and 7th grade students during their biology classes. Table 1.2 presents a summary of timeline and measures for data collection.

THE STEM PROGRAM INTERVENTION: A MENTORSHIP MODEL

The STEM program intervention was implemented in the research study for the treatment group only, Condition M (Mentor Scientists). The intervention featured a mentorship model in science instruction that took a more inquiry-based approach. Mentor scientists delivered the instruction to students demonstrating practices from scientific inquiry, as well as providing students with role model scientists. This way, middle grades students had the opportunity to learn science content and research skills directly from their mentor scientists. The intervention for the treatment group was particularly unique as the STEM mentorship program provided students with mentor scientists that were experts in both biology and education.

A unique aspect of the instruction in the treatment group were the motivational messages included in the curriculum taught. The motivational messages received by students featured two types of role model scientists, namely the *mentor scientists* (i.e., scientists that volunteered to teach the biology classes during the current project) and *historical* figure*s scientists* (i.e., stories about scientists who experienced struggles in life introduced to students). Each week, a different story was incorporated in the science instruction during the program intervention. The stories, similar in content and length, featured Maurice Hilleman, Marie Curie, and George Washington Carver, prominent scientists with great professional accomplishments, but with personal or intellectual struggles in their life. All stories emphasized the value of effort and persistence in achieving professional success in science related careers, over the individuals' talents or intelligence.

For their science teaching, all mentor scientists were responsible for planning their science lessons and activities under the guidance of the biology classroom teacher, and two faculty, university professors, experts in education and teaching leading the research project. Also, all mentor scientists were enrolled in a special course, under the direct supervision and guidance of a university professor, a science educator, and were trained in using inquiry-based science instruction, active learning and innovative teaching practices that were implemented in the STEM mentorship model program.

The mentor scientists were ten advanced biology graduate students with an expertise in life biology, scientific research, and K–12 teaching. All mentor scientists were in their last year of graduate studies, pursuing a dual graduate degree in biology and education, thus highly knowledgeable about the science curriculum and standards at the K–12 level.

SUMMARY OF KEY FINDINGS

The following section describes some of the key findings from the study, including survey results and interviews with selected students.

Key Survey Findings

A summary of the key findings from the survey are summarized below. Student responses from their pre-test to posttest revealed significant changes that occurred in students' motivation for science, in their views and attitudes about science, as a result of the STEM program intervention.

Pursuing a Career in Biology or Related Field

Students in the treatment group showed a significant increase in their scores from pretest to posttest ($p < .00$) regarding their answers about willingness to pursue a career in biology or related field. Additionally, students from the treatment group significantly differed ($p < .05$) in their views about following a biology career, or related field compared to students from the control group at the end of the STEM intervention program.

Motivation for Science/Utility Value for STEM Domain

For the students in the treatment group a significant increase ($p < .00$) in their scores from pretest to posttest was recorded regarding their motivation for science (i.e., their motivation from science increased from pre to posttest). Additionally, students in the treatment group showed significant differences ($p < .05$) in their scores at the end of the STEM intervention program, compared to the control group, with the treatment group scoring higher that the control group on their motivation for science survey items.

Beliefs About Effort

Students in the treatment group had a significant increase ($p < .00$) in their scores from pretest to posttest regarding their beliefs about effort. More precisely, they believe that by allotting more *effort* into their academic tasks, they will be achieving their goals and therefore succeed academically. This finding is in line with incremental views where effort is perceived as more important than talent in attaining goals or academic success. Additionally, students in the treatment group showed significant differences ($p < .05$) in their scores at the end of the STEM intervention program, compared to the control group, with the treatment group scoring higher that the control group on their beliefs about effort survey items.

These findings are important and encouraging and showed that students in the treatment group control group that received the STEM program intervention in which motivational messages via the program content (e.g., stories of struggling scientists, and providing role model scientists for students) had an impact on their views.

Key Interview Findings

Individual interviews conducted with 33 students from the treatment group inquired about students' opinions and their experiences in the STEM program intervention, their motivation for science and interest in science careers, or science related career, and their views about the role of effort and intelligence in achieving academic success. The findings revealed that students generally talked about three major themes, namely: *Growth mindset, Motivation for science,* and *Scientists as role models.*

Regarding their thoughts about *growth mindset,* students expressed the importance of cultivating a mindset that promotes an incremental view, meaning they expressed that effort is crucial in achieving their goals, rather than talent or innate intelligence. Students also expressed views such as 'persistence and effort' are important in attaining goals, despite challenges and setbacks that one might encounter in life. One student said: "If I work and don't give up, yes [I can achieve my goals]."

As related to students' views about their *science motivation,* most comments were related to students' experiences in the STEM program intervention and expressed the value of this experience that provided them not only with new science knowledge, but also with applied science knowledge. One student noted: "I find it interesting that you can save lives using [science] knowledge," while another student commented on the utility value and science career related interests: " If I were a doctor, I could apply this [science] information better...Yes, it helps me understand nature and what is happening in the human body."

And most importantly, students talked about *scientists as role models,* particularly how the scientists, both the mentor scientists and the stories about struggling scientists that were introduced in their biology lessons, helped them see scientists as models they could follow. Students talked about their science related career aspirations and if they can see themselves becoming scientists. One student commented: "I liked the texts [stories] that were given to us. It was interesting, about people who managed to build a career in this field [science]," while another student captured the powerful message from the stories: "Yes, I can—because they [scientists that struggled] can prove us that even if you are poor or you do not have enough money you can continue to go on, doing what you like—and this is very important in life."

INFLUENTIAL FACTORS IN STUDY IMPLEMENTATION

The following section describes several factors that that were influential to our study design and implementation. These factors underline particularly the social, cultural, economic and educational context in Romania, and are related to: (a) Gender bias and STEM careers; (b) Socio-Economic Status bias and STEM careers; (c) Partnership between university and K–12 schools; and (d) Interdisciplinary collaborations. Similar factors could be taken into consideration by researchers and practitioners that wish to design and implement educational programs aimed generally at developing students' STEM motivation and identification with STEM careers.

Gender Bias and STEM Careers

The Romanian culture is often described as being guided by traditional values, with high levels of conservatism and hierarchy values (Gavreliuc, 2012). This implies that traditional gender roles are clearly set out through family gender socialization and career guidance in families and in schools that oftentimes orients girls toward social sciences, and boys toward sciences. This is linked to the development of vocational interests according to gender stereotypes, with males being encouraged to have stronger realistic interests and females having stronger social interests (Iliescu, Ispas, Ilie, & Ion, 2013). Students entering high school in Romania are assigned to one of the three educational tracks: *vocational*, *technology*, and *theoretical*. National reports show that girls are overrepresented in teaching, arts, and humanities high schools and boys in STEM fields (National Institute of Statistics, 2018).

Additionally, national data from university enrollments (National Institute of Statistics, 2018) shows an overrepresentation of girls in fields focused on educational sciences, social sciences, journalism, and information, and health and social work (National Institute of Statistics, 2018). Some college programs with core STEM curriculum have mainly male students, this being the case for engineering and construction, or information and communication technologies. These trends indicate that a cultural bias toward STEM careers exists in Romania, but the nuanced results show that some progress has been made in reducing this bias.

Socio-Economic Status Bias and STEM Careers

Another aspect of the Romanian context is related to student identity, grounded in socio-economic status and ethnic membership that act as gateway to university enrollment. Tuition fees are low or waived for specific categories of students, such as students from the rural areas, Roma[1] students which are minority ethnics, groups generally composed of individuals with a lower socio-economic status compared to the average Romanians. Despite the fact that there are state-provided financial aid programs for students with low socio-economic status (European Commission Education and Training Monitor Romania, 2018) and these facilities contribute to the massification of higher education, socially disadvantaged youth still struggle to carve a professional path that require a university degree (Tight, 2019).

Youth who pursue STEM-oriented programs in college are a pre-selected sample, who performed above average in high-school and who have the socio-economic support to pursue higher education. Because of this, one of the core recommendations for Romania made by the Council of the

12 • M. M. THOMSON, I. POP-PACURAR, and O. NEGRU-SUBTIRICA

European Union (2018) was to "improve upskilling and the provision of quality mainstream education, in particular for Roma and children in rural areas" (p. 3). These categories on under-privileged youth have very limited access to STEM education and very high levels of school dropout (ECET-MR, 2018). Therefore, the special places allocated each year to Roma and students from rural areas for entrance in university bachelor studies do not solve the baseline issue of poverty and marginalization.

Partnerships Between Universities and K–12 Schools

For the current project an important factor that facilitated the study implementation was the partnership between the K–12 schools and the local university. The teacher preparation program that was our main collaborator strongly emphasizes the importance of establishing and maintaining a strong partnership between university and K–12 schools, precisely the between the partner K–12 schools and faculty liaison (e.g., the methodologist, a faculty appointed as the main coordinator for the practical stages of teachers training). Traditionally, the K–12 teachers that host preservice teachers in their classrooms, named 'mentor-teachers' are also formally enrolled in the Science Teacher Training Program at the local university based on clear agreements and assignments within a long-term partnership school-university. They are teachers well trained professionally and most important, most of them are *certified* mentors due to the Mentor Training programs they attended over time.

A successful partnership between universities and K–12 schools provides teacher training programs with opportunities to provide preservice teachers with *meaningful field experiences* (Pop-Pacurar & Barna, 2004). One common critique in Romania's teacher preparation program is the scarcity of field experiences and the reduced number of preservice teachers' exposure to innovative instructional programs emphasizing inquiry-based learning. Thus, traditional teaching and coursework is the typical instruction in K–12 settings, which prospective teachers have experienced themselves as students and thus are in need to experience different models of classroom teaching (Pop-Pacuarar & Biris-Dorohoi, 2015).

In the Unites States for instance, field experiences over an entire teacher preparation program (e.g., four years) can ran up to 900 hours (Thomson et al., 2019). The field experiences consist in a unique combination of coursework in methods, micro-teaching and observational learning. A schedule of field experiences is provided ahead for preservice teachers along with course assignments that are encouraging them to visit schools, develop lesson plans with their mentor teachers, and practice their own teaching. Supervision from a university faculty (i.e., field experience

Developing Students' Motivation for Science and STEM via Role Models ▪ **13**

supervisor) and a university liaison is provided for prospective teachers during their field-based assignments. This way, prospective teachers are guided and supported at multiple levels in their development as teachers. Most helpful, would be to have prospective teachers placed into schools that have successful instructional models in place, or schools that are willing to develop such programs.

Interdisciplinary Collaborations

A strong component of the current project and the mentorship program intervention was the interdisciplinary collaboration and community-based feature. The research faculty involved in designing and implementing the research study had strong teaching and research experiences, all being trained to work with K–12 students and teachers, in addition to teaching education and related fields courses in higher education. The range of expertise among faculty involved in the project varied across several disciplines, such as Teacher Education, Psychology, Educational Psychology, Biology and Science Education, and thus, all brought a myriad of interdisciplinary views and valuable knowledge into the project. One notable fact- all Romanian research faculty and all mentor scientists involved in the project volunteered to participate and to support the project's implementation. Bringing together members of the local community to participate in creating innovative programs and working collectively with schools to solve educational problems is immensurable valuable.

CONCLUSION AND IMPLICATIONS

Implications related to designing and employing STEM programs similar to ours, are numerous and beneficial for both research and practice. First, *new research avenues* can be proposed to investigate the impact of such programs in different countries, cultures or learning contexts. Second, *more research and practical applications* regarding students' *non-cognitive variables* (i.e., motivational beliefs, mindset, STEM motivation), which are generally understudied, can be conducted. Third, *generalizability*—the STEM program and various components of the program described in the current book chapter can be replicated in various informal or formal learning settings.

Some of the lessons we learned as we worked on designing and implementing the STEM program were related to: (a) *Providing research-based instructional models*, more exactly providing training for teachers and prospective teachers with effective instructional models that are grounded on research; (b) *Providing research experiences*, namely, providing hands on experiences, actual research opportunities for teachers and prospective teachers; (c) *Providing gender role models for K–12 students-* providing role model scientists for the K–12 students and addressing cultural bias in STEM; (d) *Addressing issues of socio-economic status* as related to STEM careers and opportunities for pursuing a career in science.

Providing Research-Based Instructional Models

Research shows that teachers' and prospective teachers' past instructional experiences serve oftentimes as models for their own instructional choices when they become teachers (Thomson, 2016). Traditional teaching often fails to link theory to practice and is out of touch with the real-world complexities and demands of school leadership" (Darling-Hammond, Meyerson, LaPointe, & Orr, 2010). Providing teachers and preservice teachers with knowledge about effective research-based instructional models and how instructions is grounded in psychological principles (e.g., Social-Cognitive Theory, Achievement Theory, Growth Mindset, Resilience) help build a strong teaching foundation. However, theory alone is not enough as teachers and prospective teachers will most likely ask themselves how are these models going to work in practice? Practicing and implementing elements of such models is important and having the opportunity to see an innovative program based on effective psychological concepts and principles in action is vital. Finding research mentors who have experience with similar programs and who are willing to answer questions about the benefits and pitfalls of various instructional models, about the implementation and costs, and about existing research, would help teachers and future teachers learn from the expertise of others.

Providing Research Experiences

In addition to content and pedagogical knowledge, it is important to provide teachers and prospective teachers with immersive research experiences. In the teacher preparation programs it is important to include experiences that provide rich engagements for prospective teachers to learn about research and research-based practices. In order to conduct successful research studies in schools and test innovative STEM programs, it would be extremely helpful if teachers had previous knowledge and exposure to research. In the the Biology and/or Biology teaching area, just becoming a university graduate student cannot provide one with knowledge and skills for research, or lifelong skills. Therefore, one goal of teacher preparation is to prepare future teachers for a continuous process of professional development, including training in research. While the idea of expecting each trainee to become a "researcher" is not realistic, it is crucial thou to ensure that each prospective teacher can be trained *to think and act as a reflective teacher* and understand research-based practices.

Teachers' research skills could be developed considering at least two approaches: action research and case-study research. Taking a reflective practitioner approach to teacher training proposed by Della Fish (1995) is opposite to competency-based teacher training, in which teaching it perceived as an "occupation" rather than a "profession." However, case-study research can be more relevant to prospective teachers and easier to implement as both versions seek change in professional's practice. Thus, any efforts in teacher preparation to support prospective teachers' exposure to research is crucial, as teachers will be able to understand and hopefully implement research-based practices in their classroom afterwards.

Providing Gender Role Models for K–12 Students

In order to better understand and actively challenge the cultural bias towards STEM careers, providing scientists models for K–12 students that address the cultural bias in STEM seems crucial. In our STEM program implementation, ten mentor scientists volunteered and all had strong experiences and background in research, in addition to being prospective biology teachers. A unique feature of our STEM program was that nine of the ten mentor scientists were female scientist, and only one mentor was a male scientist. This is notable, given the fact that research (NIS, 2018) show that the majority of scientists are man, while women are underrepresented in STEM.

In addition to offering gender appropriate models to students to challenge the gender bias in STEM, future studies could focus on longitudinal designs that investigate how students' gendered attitudes towards specific STEM careers (e.g., engineering versus natural sciences) change during educational transitions (e.g., from high-school to university) and as a function of direct work experiences. In this manner researchers can directly tap into how girls and boys differentially process information that indicates that their intelligence is malleable and hence they can learn STEM contents. Existing longitudinal studies with Romanian adolescents indicate that girls tend to be more involved in their vocational development compared to boys (e.g., Negru-Subtirica, Pop, & Crocetti, 2018; Negru-Subtirica & Pop, 2016). So, it may be that present-day adolescent girls actively work toward reducing the gender bias regarding career advancement.

Addressing Issues of Socio-Economic Status

Another aspect notable for interventions like ours is to understand more deeply how the socio-economic status of students, particularly students from ethnic minority groups, like Roma students limits their pursuing of STEM careers. Such understandings require more qualitative research paired up with quantitative data in order to map how disadvantaged youth negotiate their perceptions of intelligence with the limitations of their environment. To date, mindset interventions focused to a lesser extent on youth from high-poverty communities, where communities are closed, in that STEM careers, for instance, might not even have a cognitive representation in the cognitive map of occupations of these young people. Therefore, interviews with and participative observation of Roma youth and youth from rural areas would shed light on how they envision their capacities to learn and change their intelligence. Overall, for impact beyond individual schools, changes are required at a system level, such as a new approach into teacher training programs, teacher professional development and training for school administration. For a program based on social-cognitive and motivational concepts and principles, to become embedded in schools, elements of these models must be part of the whole school community, involving the school administration, the teacher and student body, as well as parents.

NOTE

1. Roma population (different than Romanian population) is one of the minority ethnic groups living in Romania, and has been historically marginalized.

REFERENCES

Bandura, A. (2008). Social cognitive theory of mass communication. In J. Bryant & M. B. Oliver (Eds.), *Media effects: Advances in theory and research* (pp. 94–124). Routledge.

Blackwell, L. S., Trzesniewski, K. H., & Dweck, C. S. (2007). Implicit theories of intelligence predict achievement across an adolescent transition: A longitudinal study and an intervention. *Child Development, 78,* 246–263.

Blackwell, L., Rodriguez, S., & Guerra-Carrillo, B. (2015). Intelligence as a malleable construct. In S. Goldstein, D. Princiotta, & J. A. Naglieri (Eds.), *Handbook of intelligence* (pp. 263–282). Springer.

Boaler, J. (2013). Ability and mathematics: The mindset revolution that is reshaping education. *FORUM, 55*(1), 143.

Cook, D. A., & Artino, A. J. (2016). Motivation to learn: An overview of contemporary theories. *Medical Education, 50,* 997–1014.

Council of the European Union. (2018). *Council Recommendation of 13 July on the 2018 National Reform Programme of Romania and delivering a Council opinion on the 2018 Convergence Programme of Romania.* Available at: http://data.consilium.europa.eu/doc/document/ST-9448-2018-INIT/en

Darling-Hammond, L., Meyerson, D., LaPointe, M., & Orr, M. T. (2010). *Preparing principals for a changing world: Lessons from effective school leadership programs.* Jossey-Bass.

Dweck, C. S., Chiu, C. Y., & Hong, Y. Y. (1995). Implicit theories and their role in judgments and reactions: A word from two perspectives. *Psychological Inquiry, 6*(4), 267–285.

Dweck, C. S., & Leggett, E. (1988). A social-cognitive approach to motivation and personality. *Psychological Review, 95*(2), 256–273.

Dweck, C.S. (2006). *Mindset: The new psychology of success.* Random House.

Dweck, C. S. (2008). *Mindsets and math/science achievement.* Carnegie Corp. of New York–Institute for Advanced Study Commission on Mathematics and Science Education.

Dweck, C. S. (2015). Growth. *British Journal of Educational Psychology, 85*(2), 242–245.

Dweck, C. S. (2016). What having a "growth mindset" actually means. *Harvard Business Review.* Online article. Available at: https://hbr.org/2016/01/what-having-a-growth-mindset-actually-means.

European Commission Education and Training Monitor Romania. (2018). Available at: https://ec.europa.eu/education/sites/education/files/document-library-docs/et-monitor-report-2018-romania_en_0.pdf

Gavreliuc, A. (2012). Continuity and change of values and attitudes in generational cohorts of the post-communist Romania. *Cognition, Brain, Behavior, 16,* 191–212.

Iliescu, D., Ispas, D., Ilie, A., & Ion, A. (2013). The structure of vocational interests in Romania. *Journal of Counseling Psychology, 60,* 294–302.

Lin-Siegler, X., Ahn, J., Chen, J., Fang, F., & Luna-Lucero, M. (2016). Even Einstein struggled: Effects of learning about great scientists' struggles on high school students' motivation to learn science. *Journal of Educational Psychology, 108*(3), 314–328.

Lin-Siegler, X., Ahn, J. N., Chen, J., Fang, F-F. A., & Luna-Lucerno, M. (2017). Stories of struggle: Teaching the value of effort and persistence in science. *American Educator, 41*(1), 35–38.

Mangels, J.A., Butterfield, B., Lamb, J., Good, C., & Dweck, C.S. (2006). Why do beliefs about intelligence influence learning success? A social cognitive neuroscience model. *Social Cognitive Affective Neuroscience, 1,* 75–86.

National Institute of Statistics [NIS]. (2018). *The educational system in Romania. Synthetic data. The 2016–2017 school/university year.* Available online at: http://www.insse.ro/cms/ro/content/sistemul-educa%C5%A3ional-%C3%AEn-rom%C3%A2nia-date-sintetice-1

Negru-Subtirica, O., & Pop, E. I. (2016). Longitudinal links between career adaptability and academic achievement in adolescence. *Journal of Vocational Behavior, 93,* 163–170.

Negru-Subtirica, O., & Pop, E. I. (2018). Reciprocal associations between educational identity and vocational identity in adolescence: A three-wave longitudinal investigation. *Journal of Youth and Adolescence, 47,* 703–716.

OECD. (2014). *Education at a Glance 2014: OECD Indicators.* Paris: Organisation of Economic Cooperation and Development.

OECD. (2016). *PISA 2015 Results: Excellence and Equity in Education,* (Volume I). PISA, OECD Publishing.

Perels, F., Merget-Kullman, M., Wende, M., Schmitz, B., & Buchbinder, C. (2009). Improving self-regulated learning of preschool children: Evaluation of training for kindergarten teachers. *British Journal of Educational Psychology, 79,* 311–327.

Pop-Pacurar, I., & Barna, A. (2004). Mentoring in Biology. Cooperative learning in pre-service teachers training. In Chiș, V., & col. (Eds.), *Education 21*(1), Series Sciences of Education /13 (pp. 349–369). Cluj-Napoca: Casa Cartii de Stiinta.

Pop-Pacurar, I., & Biris-Dorhoi, E.S. (2015). Implementing active techniques in teaching-learning process: a case study throughout mentoring student-teachers at Babes-Bolyai University. Proceedings from the 2nd International Multidisciplinary Scientific Conference on Social Sciences and Arts, Albena, Bulgaria. Book 1 *Education and Educational Research, 2,* 485–492.

Tight, M. (2019). Mass higher education and massification. *Higher Education Policy, 32,* 93–108.

Thomson, M. M. (2016). Metaphorical images of schooling: Beliefs about teaching and learning among prospective teachers from United States displaying different motivational profiles. *Educational Psychology, 36*(3), 502–525.

Thomson, M. M., Huggins, E., & Williams, W. (2019). Developmental science efficacy trajectories of novice teachers from a STEM-focused program: A longitudinal mixed-methods investigation. *Teaching and Teacher Education, 77,* 253–265.

Thomson, M. M., Gray, D., Walkowiak, T., & Alnizami, R. (2022). Developmental trajectories for elementary novice teachers: Teaching efficacy and mathematics knowledge. *Journal of Teacher Education, 73*(4) 338–351.

CHAPTER 2

SCIENCE-RELATED BELIEFS AND ATTITUDES OF PARENTS

Building Students' Interests and Career Aspirations

M. Gail Jones, Katherine Chesnutt, Megan Ennes, Daniel Macher, and Manuela Paechter

BACKGROUND

Parents play an important role in the development of their children's science interests in- and out-of-school as well as their career aspirations. This chapter describes how science-related attitudes and beliefs of parents can shape interests, engagement with science, and science career goals of youth and how these parental beliefs can be measured. This work is built on a study of youth in grades 3–4 and their parents. The study was situated in a science capital and family habitus framework that examined expectancy value variables related to science interests and career aspirations. Parents completed an assessment, and the results suggest the use of a 7-factor structure to measure parent attitudes toward STEM and the value of science as a career for themselves and for their child. Reliability levels were high for all scales. The

Motivation and Engagement in Various Learning Environments, pages 19–27
Copyright © 2024 by Information Age Publishing
www.infoagepub.com
All rights of reproduction in any form reserved.

findings demonstrate we can reliably measure parental science achievement value, future science task value for their child, childhood science experiences, childhood career aspirations, and prior experiences with science.

There is increasing evidence that the family plays a critical role in the development of students' interests and career aspirations (e.g., Howard & Reynolds, 2008; Johnson & Hull, 2014). Within science education, researchers have shown that family engagement with science is linked to students' perception of science as a future career (e.g., Jones et al., 2021). To better understand how family engagement influences the interests and career aspirations of youth, the present study examined factors that are related to parents' perception of the future value of science. By understanding parents' perceptions of science, we can design and build more effective educational programs to enhance interest and engagement with science for youth.

Researchers have shown that parent involvement in education and youth can contribute to higher school achievement (Lee, 1993; Sui-Chu & Willms, 1996), fewer behavioral problems at school (Lee, 1993), lower dropout rates (McNeal, 1999), higher grades in school (Muller, 1993) and enhanced aspirations to attend college (Cabrera, & La Nasa, 2000). Understanding the influences of the family on career interests and aspirations is particularly crucial in the fields of science, technology, engineering, and mathematics (STEM) where there are significant discrepancies in course enrollment and career aspirations for many minority groups (National Science Foundation, National Center for Science and Engineering Statistics, 2017). However, there is limited research that examines how family engagement and attitudes in STEM influence students' interests (e.g., Aschbacher et al., 2010; Ferry et al., 2000; Gilmartin et al., 2006).

Archer et al., (2012) applied the concepts of science capital and family habitus ("the ways and settings in which families operate... [that] encompass[es] values and everyday practices" p. 886) to measure factors that were associated with youth science aspirations. They found that the attitudes of the parents were key to the formation of youth's science career aspirations. A study by Maltese and Cooper (2017) reported that when parents were involved in STEM-related experiences, their children were more likely to choose a STEM field than students whose parents were not involved. The influence of parental beliefs and expectations on the development of interests and career aspirations is an understudied area and this study begins to fill this gap by proposing a new tool to assess parental experiences, expectations for their child, and science achievement value.

A recent study of middle school students (Jones et al., 2021) used expectancy value theory to examine factors that influence engagement and science career aspirations. This study used structural equation modeling with a sample of 1,015 students and the authors reported that exposure to STEM practitioners, tool access, and STEM experiences were associated with higher science achievement value (a measure of students' science self-efficacy and self-concept) and perceptions of family science achievement value (a measure of a student's perceptions of whether and how their family values science). These two factors were predictive of future science task value. Future science task value includes the utility (usefulness) of engaging in STEM in the future. This variable is associated with STEM interests and career aspirations. Other researchers have shown that task value can predict an individual's expectation of success in a particular field (Eccles & Wigfield, 2020). The study by Jones et al. (2021) conducted in the context of science, found evidence that a student's perception of the value the family places on science was a key factor in determining the students' interests and career goals. These findings led us to develop the assessment described here to measure parents' science capital (access to experiences and science-related tools) and the family habitus for science (the degree to which the family sees science as something they do).

SCIENCE CAPITAL AND HABITUS

Science capital is made up of the resources- social, economic, and cultural- that individuals have related to science (Archer et al., 2015). These resources can impact how a family thinks, values, identifies, talks about, or engages with science which in turn impacts how children view themselves in relation to science (Archer et al., 2012). These values, dispositions and behaviors related to science are frequently described as a family's science habitus (Archer 2012). Guided by their science habitus, whether or not a family chooses to engage in science experiences as well as the types of experiences they choose to engage in can influence the science interest and career aspirations of children (Archer et al., 2012). One way to measure science interests and career aspirations is through expectancy value theory (e.g., Eccles & Wigfield, 2002; 2020).

RESEARCH QUESTION

In previous studies, we developed and validated assessments (*NextGen Scientist Survey*) to measure expectancy value factors for elementary and middle school youth (Jones et al., 2020; Jones et al., 2022). Expectancy value theory (e.g., Eccles & Wigfield, 2002; 2020) suggests that individuals will engage in science if they value science and see benefit for engaging in science. The theory suggests that the subjective value of engagement in an activity is related to utility value, attainment value, intrinsic value, and costs associated with the engagement. Utility value is associated with the perception that the engagement will help the student achieve a goal. Attainment value is related to how the student perceives the activity will give them value such as prestige. Intrinsic value is associated with satisfaction that one gets from doing the activity and finally costs are the perceived sacrifices or costs that are experienced from this engagement (such as not engaging in a different activity).

In this chapter we build on these studies of expectancy value theory by examining parent expectancy value factors. Here we describe the development of a new parent assessment that parallels the assessments developed for children and middle school youth. The research question explored in this study was: *What is the factorial structure of the NextGen Scientist Survey-Parents?* Being able to assess the expectancy value factors for parents and youth can inform the field about how parent's values and expectations are related to those held by their children. Furthermore, this assessment documents science capital and family habitus variables that can contribute to expectancy values.

METHODS

In order to examine the structure of the survey we conducted a confirmatory factor analysis of the data. The constructs for the survey were congruent with the research literature on expectancy value, science capital, and family habitus. Expectancy value theory explores how cultural stereotypes, caregiver's beliefs and behaviors, prior experiences, youth perceptions of caregiver's beliefs, youth interpretations of their experiences, youth sense of self, memories, values, and expectations of success influence an individual's goals and performance (e.g., Eccles & Wigfield, 2002). Constructs emerging from expectancy value that guided this study included parental beliefs about science, science experiences, self-concept, self-efficacy, and future science expectations. The constructs that emerged from Archer and colleagues' (2012, 2015) research on science capital and family habitus included access to science tools, knowledge of individuals who engaged in STEM, and science experiences.

Data Sources

The parent version of The *NextGen Scientist Survey* was designed to be a parallel version of the previously validated *NextGen Scientist Survey Middle School* (Jones et al., 2020) and the *NextGen Scientist Survey Elementary* (Jones et al., 2021). The final survey was established after review by an expert panel and a pilot study with 5 parents.

The final *NextGen Science Survey- Parents*, consisted of 39 items that are assessed on a 5-point Likert scale for the degree to which the respondent identifies with science and has self-efficacy for science (12 items), whether or not they had experiences with science as a child (4 items), their childhood career considerations (3 items), experiences in science communication (7 items), their active science experiences as an adult (5 items), their experiences with science tools (4 items), and whether they see STEM as a future career for their child (4 items; see Table 2.2 for items).

Sample and Descriptive Statistics

Parent participants were contacted at afterschool programs sponsored by a non-profit group for youth in grades 3–5 who are from groups historically underrepresented in science located in several communities in a southeastern state of the United States. Altogether, 277 parents participated, 226 female/women (81.6%) and 49 male/men (17.7%; 2 missing values); 148 White (53.4%), 94 Black (33.9%), 17 Hispanic (6.1%), 4 Asian (1.4%), and 14 Other (5.1%). The parents indicated they lived in rural (39.4%), suburban (35.0%), and urban (25.3%) areas.

Analyses and Results

Confirmatory factor analysis (CFA) resulted in a 7-factor solution that best fit the data (see Strijbos et al., 2021). RMSEA and SRMR are within the desired boundary. CFI has an adequate fit value (see Table 2.1).

Table 2.2 shows the final factor solution for the 7-factor model. The seven factors show acceptable to good reliability with Cronbach's α between $.629 \leq \alpha_i \leq .935$. Item to factor loadings and fit indices were satisfactory (Table 2.1). The first factor, *Science Achievement Value*, had twelve items and asked parents to rate their self-efficacy for science and if they think their family sees them as a science person. The second factor, *Future Science Task Value*, had four items and asked the parents if they would recommend careers in science or technology to their child. Factor three, *Childhood Science Experiences*, included four items and asked parents to indicate if they had access to science tools and toys when they were a child or knew anyone who

TABLE 2.1 Fit Indices for CFA-Model									
Model	*n*	AIC	BIC	χ^2	df	χ^2/df	CFI	RMSEA	SRMR
1	275	24709.850	25223.431	1276.853	677	1.8860	0.902	0.057	0.056

24 ▪ M. G. JONES et al.

TABLE 2.2   NextGen Scientist Survey–Parents: Factors, Sample Items, and Item Loadings β

Items, Factors, Cronbach's α	Item Loading β_i
Factor 1 *Science Achievement Value* ($\alpha = 0.935$)	
I see myself as a science person	0.822
I think my family sees me as a science person	0.783
Factor 2 *Future Science Task Value for My Child* ($\alpha = 0.901$)	
I would recommend a career for my child that involves science	0.862
I would recommend a career for my child that involves technology	0.881
Factor 3 *Childhood Science Experiences* ($\alpha = 0.629$)	
When I was a child, I had access to science tools and toys (science kits, books, tv, etc.)	0.725
When I was a child, I knew someone who worked in science, technology, engineering, or math fields	0.570
Factor 4 *Childhood Career Considerations* ($\alpha = 0.782$)	
When I was a child, I considered a career in engineering.	0.864
Factor 5 *Science Communication Experiences* ($\alpha = 0.904$)	
Talked about science-related topics with other people.	0.854
Talked with your child about science	0.764
Factor 6 *Active Science Experiences* ($\alpha = 0.740$)	
Gone to a museum, zoo, aquarium, or planetarium	0.615
Used binoculars or a telescope	0.696
Factor 7 *Science Tool Experiences* ($\alpha = 0.737$)	
Used a ruler, measuring tape, or measuring stick	0.785
Built, repaired, or taken things apart	0.698

worked in a STEM field. The fourth factor, *Childhood Career Considerations*, had three items and this factor investigated whether parents considered a career in technology as a child. Factor five, *Science Communication Experiences*, asked parents if they watched science on television as a child or talked with their own child about science and included seven items. The sixth factor, *Active Science Experiences*, asked parents to indicate if, in the past year, they had gone to a museum, zoo, aquarium or planetarium or gone on a nature walk in the last year and this factor included five items. Finally, parents were asked in the final four factor items, *Science Tool Experiences* questions such if during the last year they had used a thermometer to measure temperature or built, repaired, or taken things apart.

SIGNIFICANCE OF THE STUDY

The CFA shows that the *NextGen Scientist Survey- Parents* has seven factors that have been shown to influence future task value for science. The instrument allows for the measurement of self-efficacy and academic identity (*Science Achievement Value*), parent perceptions of future career options for their child (*Future Science Task Value for My Child*), measures of prior childhood experiences (*Childhood Science Experiences*), careers the parent considered when a child (*Childhood Science Experiences*), experiences reading and discussing science (*Science Communication Experiences*) and finally, the scales *Active Science Experiences* and *Science Tool Experiences* assessed the parent's experiences with science as well as using science-related materials. All of these items assess elements of science capital that have been shown to contribute to career aspirations and interest in science (Archer et al., 2012).

The parent assessment is similar to the elementary youth assessment that found a five factor structure that included *Science Achievement Value, Future Science Task Value, Perceptions of Family Science Achievement Value, Tangible Science Experiences* (such as planting seeds or using a telescope), and *Intangible Science Experiences* (such as watching science on television or looking up science information online). The current survey has seven factors because the items are not completely parallel. Parents were asked about their own values, perceptions, and desires for their child. The experiences in the parent survey were split into three types that included science tools, science communication, and active science experiences.

IMPLICATIONS

This study demonstrates that we can reliably measure components of science capital and family habitus that contribute to interests and career aspirations for science. This examination of parent perceptions and factors adds a unique opportunity to begin to track how parent expectancy value factors might contribute to the future science task value of their children. By beginning to examine the weights of factors and influences over time, we can begin to design more effective educational programs for youth and their families as well as explore new ways to honor cultural capital while building social capital. With the growing recognition of the role of the family in the development of interests and career aspirations this instrument can open up new studies to examine different factors related to the development of youth and parental expectations across generations.

REFERENCES

Archer, L., Dawson, E., DeWitt, J., Seakins, A., & Wong, B. (2015). "Science capital": A conceptual, methodological, and empirical argument for extending bourdieusian notions of capital beyond the arts. *Journal of Research in Science Teaching, 52*(7), 922–948.

Archer, L., DeWitt, J., Osborne, J., Dillon, J., Willis, B., & Wong, B. (2012). Science aspirations, capital and family habitus: How families shape children's engagement and identification with science. *American Educational Research Journal, 49*(5), 881–908.

Aschbacher, P. R., Li, E., & Roth, E. J. (2010). Is science me? High school students' identities, participation, and aspirations in science, engineering, and medicine. *Journal of Research in Science Teaching, 47*(5), 564–582.

Bourdieu, P. (1984). *Distinction: A social critique of the judgement of taste.* Harvard University Press.

Cabrera, A. F., & La Nasa, S. M. (2000). Overcoming the tasks on the path to college for America's disadvantaged. *New Directions for Institutional Research, 2000*(107), 31–43.

Eccles, J. S., & Wigfield, A. (2002). Motivational beliefs, values, and goals. *Annual Review of Psychology, 53*(1), 109–132.

Eccles, J. S., & Wigfield, A. (2020). From expectancy-value theory to situated expectancy-value theory: A developmental, social cognitive, and sociocultural perspective on motivation. *Contemporary Educational Psychology, 61*, 101859.

Ferry, T. R., Fouad, N., & Smith, P. (2000). The roles of family context in a social cognitive model for career-related choice behavior: A math and science perspective. *Journal of Vocational Behavior, 57*, 348–364.

Gilmartin, S. K., Li, E., & Aschbacher, P. (2006). The relationship between interest in physical science/engineering, science class experiences, and family contexts: Variations by gender and race/ethnicity among secondary students. *Journal of Women and Minorities in Science and Engineering, 12*(2–3).

Howard, T. C., & Reynolds, R. (2008). Examining parent involvement in reversing the underachievement of African American students in middle-class schools. *Educational Foundations, 22*, 79–98.

Johnson, U. Y., & Hull, D. M. (2014). Parent involvement and science achievement: A cross-classified multilevel latent growth curve analysis. *The Journal of Educational Research, 107*(5), 399–409.

Jones, M. G., Chesnutt, K., Ennes, M., Macher, D., & Paechter, M. (2022). Measuring science capital, science attitudes, and science experiences in elementary and middle school students. *Studies in Educational Evaluation, 74*, 101180.

Jones, M. G., Chesnut, K., Ennes, M., Mulvey, K. L., & Cayton, E. (2021). Factors predicting future science task value. *Journal of Research in Science Teaching, 58*(7), 937–955.

Jones, M. G., Ennes, M., Weedfall, D., Chesnutt, K., Cayton, E., (2020). The development and validation of a measure of science capital, habitus and future science interests. *Research in Science Education, 51*, 1549–1565. DOI: 10.1007/s11165-020-09916-y

Lee, S. A. (1993). Family structure effects on student outcomes. In B. Schneider & J. S. Coleman (Eds.), *Parents, their children, and school* (pp. 43–75). Westview Press.

National Science Foundation, National Center for Science and Engineering Statistics. (2017). *Women, minorities, and persons with disabilities in science and engineering: 2017*. Special Report NSF 17–310. www.nsf.gov/statistics/wmpd/

Maltese, A. V., & Cooper, C. S. (2017). STEM pathways: do men and women differ in why they enter and exit? *AERA Open, 3*(3), 1–16.

McNeal, Jr., R. B. (1999). Parental involvement as social capital: Differential effectiveness on science achievement, truancy, and dropping out. *Social Forces, 78*(1), 117–144.

Muller, C. (1993). Parent involvement and academic achievement: An analysis of family resources available to the child. In B. Schneider & J. S. Coleman (Eds.), *Parents, their children, and school* (pp. 77–113). Westview Press.

Plasman, J. S., Gottfried, M., & Williams, D. (2021). Following in their Footsteps: the Relationship Between Parent STEM Occupation and Student STEM Course taking in High School. *Journal for STEM Education Research, 4*(1), 27–46.

Strijbos, W., Pat-El, R., & Narciss, S. (2021). Structural validity and invariance of the feedback perceptions. *Studies in Educational Evaluation, 68*, 100980.

Sui-Chu, E. H., & Willms, J. D. (1996). Effects of parental involvement on eighth-grade achievement. *Sociology of Education*, 126–141.

CHAPTER 3

APPROACHING STEAM VIA INQUIRY-BASED RESPONSES TO BIG QUESTIONS

How "Epistemic Insight" Changes Informal Science Learning

Finley I. Lawson, Stefan Colley, and Berry Billingsley

The collation of this edited volume highlights the "challenging" environment of STEAM engagement work with children and young people. By its very nature, if the question "how do we engage more young people in STEM?" was easily answered an entire volume dedicated to the question would be superfluous. So it is in recognition that the barriers to engagement are varied, and that the aims of formal and informal opportunities don't always align that this chapter has been written through a collaboration between researchers and university outreach professionals with the aim of providing an accessible overview of some of the moving parts in STEAM outreach, and sharing how, through collaboration, we have changed English secondary school students' attitudes and aspirations towards STEAM.

Motivation and Engagement in Various Learning Environments, pages 29–48
Copyright © 2024 by Information Age Publishing
www.infoagepub.com
All rights of reproduction in any form reserved.

This chapter examines the impact that that an "epistemically insightful" approach to informal science learning (ISL) can have on students' attitudes, aspirations, and perceptions of STEAM. The chapter draws on practitioner research and the use of innovative pedagogy to challenge the knowledge application versus knowledge generation dichotomy prevalent in ISL.

Before progressing with the detail of the chapter it is necessary to set out the chapter's scope. Firstly, whilst we discuss a research-engaged approach to Higher Education (HE) widening participation (WP) activities this chapter doesn't report in detail on the research methodology or findings (although we do make use of some of the evidence we have collected).[1] Secondly, this chapter sits somewhere between a theoretical discussion and a practical "how to" guide. The Inspiring Minds project discussed received sustained funding through the Office for Students (OfS) which enabled us to tackle multiple barriers through a single opportunity, and we are aware that not everyone will be able to address all of these within their own informal practice, however we hope that through the discussion of what works, teachers, practitioners, parents can make use of our findings to support STEAM activities with the children and young people in their care.[2] Finally, whilst this chapter begins by looking at some of the existing literature on children and young people's engagement with STEAM (particularly in relation to HE) this is by no means exhaustive; however, it does provide context for the space into which Inspiring Minds was developed and highlights that the challenges we address regarding informal science learning (ISL) are global and not simply relevant to our local context. Inspiring Minds was designed as a sustained engagement program for secondary school students in year 10 (age 14/15). Run over six Saturday sessions each cohort of 60–75 students received interactive lectures delivered by academics and were supported in the lectures and the development of their own research questions and skills by student ambassadors as they completed a Bronze CREST award. The sixth session is a public showcase event where students work is shared with parents and guardians, the university community, and their schoolteachers. To date the project has engaged 493 students in a total of 11,832 hours of direct contact engagement, of whom approximately 92% of students were from POLAR 3 Quintile 1[3] wards and 85% achieved a Bronze CREST Award.[4]

Finally, this chapter examines the impact and relevance of innovative pedagogy—epistemic insight—for ISL. Therefore, before progressing further it is necessary to briefly set out what is meant by this approach and how it differs from other approaches to interdisciplinary teaching. As identified by Billingsley et al. (2018) an epistemically insightful curriculum (whether formal or, as in the case of Inspiring Minds, informal) is framed around three key learning areas firstly, the nature of science in real world contexts and multidisciplinary arenas; secondly, ways of knowing and how they interact; and thirdly, the relationships between science and religion. The Inspiring Minds program was designed to explicitly address the first two. For the Inspiring Minds scholars, the use of epistemic insight was designed to develop their understanding of the nature, power, and limitation of science, in relation to disciplines in the wider humanities, and within the context of "Big Questions"[5] at the interface of science, religion and society.

Epistemic Insight refers to students' *knowledge about knowledge* and whilst it may bring metacognition to mind the two should not be confused. For instance, where metacognition is, according to a recent study "thinking about thinking" (Perry, Lundie, and Golder 2019, 485) that is "a second order or higher-order thinking process which involves active control over cognitive processes" (Mevarech and Kramarski 2014, 36); an *epistemically insightful* approach to learning is one in which the boundaries between and distinctiveness of disciplines is investigated. For students, this not only highlights for students the relationships between science and other disciplines within their curriculum (as we discuss further later) but also develops their understanding of how knowledge is formed and how some questions (which are referred to as Big Questions) cannot be answered by science in isolation by require a multidisciplinary approach. In other words, "focusing on epistemic insight . . . engenders a pragmatic approach to helping students make better sense of the message they receive in different subjects about scholarship and how claims are tested" (Billingsley and Hardman 2018). It is about moving beyond topic-based work (that highlights the content taught within curriculum subjects) to developing students' understanding of the methods, questions, and norms of thought of disciplines and the interaction between them.

SETTING THE STAGE—THE CHALLENGES AND OPPORTUNITIES OF INFORMAL SCIENCE LEARNING

There is agreement within the UK and internationally that our economy and workforce will be increasingly dependent on STEM-related opportunities and skills. However, there is a lack of agreement on the best ways to improve diversity and recruitment into these fields. It would be naive to think that any one solution would work for all students (or indeed for all sectors) however this alone is no reason to maintain the status quo and hope that the situation will be resolved. The barrier to STEM engagement at post-16 and consequently HE is in fact a dual challenge of engagement and lack of science capital for the most under-represented. For example students from "economically disadvantaged backgrounds" are said to have poorer science attainment than their more advantaged peers, with the divide appearing as early as Key Stage 1 (age 5–7 years; ASE 2018), and continuing through to

GCSE choices where they are three times less likely to take triple science at GCSE level (Archer et al. 2016, 302) therefore influencing the opportunities open to them in STEM at post-16 and in HE.

The *Growth Through People* report highlights the pressing need that in order to "create new pathways into work we need to start much earlier" (UKCES 2014, 20), thus it isn't simply enough to target under-represented groups at key transition points (GCSE and post-16, and University choices in the UK), rather there is a need to transform their experience of STEM education much earlier, this is further supported by the evidence provided to the UK All Party Parliamentary Group on Inclusion and Diversity in STEM (ASE 2020). Whilst the work discussed here focused on year 10 students, and therefore is arguable occurring "too late" the pedagogy and approaches discussed work equally well with students earlier on the in their secondary schooling and indeed, when appropriately scaled, for students as young as year 3 (aged 7/8).

Whilst it is arguable that there are many possible potential educational barriers along this pipeline (e.g., attitudes to learning, attainment, classroom resources), the greater barriers are those considered "social" of "cultural" (science capital, visibility of diversity, appearance of relevance) and it is the direct targeting of these that tends to be the main concern of university WP work—focusing on providing inspiring "contact" with STEM opportunities that aims to provide "one-off" opportunities (think STEM fairs/ activity days/ taster sessions etc). When not driven by an exposure model, STEM "outreach" based in universities is often instead driven by an educational demand produced by schools and colleges for activities that focus on *knowledge application* or, more often, *knowledge generation. Knowledge application* refers to students being able to use knowledge they already have, whereas *knowledge generation* refers to students creating new knowledge (with the newness being relative to the student).

However, if we are to overcome the findings by Barmby et al. (2008) that in English year 7–9 students (ages 11–14) their attitude towards science declines as they progress through secondary school, then the greatest opportunity provided by ISL is that it doesn't have to be constrained by curriculum content or a focus on imparting specific career information. Rather the opportunity is provided to build students' science capital and understanding of the "wider relevance" to 'help foster students' interest in and perceived utility of science, which may then encourage aspirations towards science careers" (Sheldrake, Mujtaba, and Reiss 2017, 171).There is evidence to suggest that conveying the wider relevance of science can help foster students' interest in and perceived utility of science, which may encourage aspirations towards science careers (Sheldrake, Mujtaba, and Reiss 2017), and that contextualizing science education within real-world problems can help students' motivation and enable them to deepen their understanding of the nature of science and scientific practices (Allchin 2013).

As already noted a compartmentalized curriculum, particularly within English secondary school means that students experience of STEM can be fragmented, there are limited opportunities, if any, to consider the relationship between science and history for example in understanding historic events, or where the boundary of science/technology is able to provide us with information about what is (or could be) possible but requires engagement with philosophy to consider whether it *should* be used/created etc. Opportunities to link between STEM and the arts within curriculum time are even more limited, for example the chance for students to consider the role of detailed scientific drawings within the development and communication of scientific knowledge, or how graphic and computer models/visualization are often used to examine and explain complex scientific theories. Whilst there are understandable barriers within already pressured curriculum time it is these wider links and opportunities that should be rich territory for the ISL provider.

Before students can see themselves as a potential STEM scholar who can and should consider STEM-related opportunities at HE, it is first necessary to themselves as confident scholars with the critical thinking skills and epistemic insight to engage with, and contribute to, the "science" discussion(s). It is in this space, creating critical confident thinkers, who understand the broader place of science in society, and are aware of the breadth of interactions between science, technology, arts, and humanities that ISL has an opportunity to excel. In doing so it can reach children and young people who think science isn't "for them," until they are able to experience it in a format that doesn't echo their experience to date. It is to what this "novel" experience looks like that we shall now turn. The next sections will discuss a few of the identified barriers to engagement in STEM and nature and rationale of the curriculum design for Inspiring Minds—just because activity is informal it doesn't mean that it can't benefit from a structured and progressive approach. Finally, we will conclude by looking at the role evaluation and (informal) practitioner research can and should play in assessing the impact of ISL.

DRESSING THE STAGE—WHY LOCATION MATTERS AND HOW TO MITIGATE SOME OF THE BARRIERS TO SUSTAINED ENGAGEMENT

University outreach departments are often located within the marketing and recruitment departments within the university, this, alongside funding metrics can drive an outreach approach that focuses on reaching the greatest numbers of students, often for "one-off" interventions and with the aim of reaching those that have the potential to be graduands. More sustained activity tends to target "gifted and talented" pupils within lower participation areas where the potential (access to university/recruitment) gains are greatest and whilst understandable this approach can lead to a reinforcement of STEM and/or HE as being "not for" those students who are most disadvantaged or least likely to progress. A clear example of this conflict is provided by Gartland (2016) when she notes of the institutions participating in her research that for one "the Aimhigher target group coincides relatively closely with the target group for student recruitment' whereas for the other 'an elite Russell Group institution, [...] the target group for Aimhigher hardly overlaps at all with the target group for recruitment" (Gartland, 2016, 1. 1414) this kind of perceived conflict between the "recruitment" and "outreach" roles of the university can create challenges in reaching the most underserved populations. One of the ways to start to mitigate the potential conflict between recruitment and outreach is to work as part of a wider partnership. This allows the participating institutions/groups to recognize the cumulative value of multiple interactions, meaning that an activity in institution A may engage a student with STEM, or creative industries, but it's at institution B that they find a campus[6] that connects with them and allows them to see their potential place. It is this collaborative attitude that lies at the heart of the Kent and Medway Progression Federation (KMPF) approach "towards ensuring that every young person in our area who has the potential to benefit from higher education (HE)—particularly those currently under-represented—is aware of the opportunities available and can make an informed choice about their future" (KMPF 2022).[7] Identity and community can be key contributing factors to students from underrepresented groups "taking the chance" on HE and greater collaboration (alongside detailed monitoring of engagement through HEAT) allows for an approach that is targeted on the student experience first, and then understanding how to maximize reach rather than the other way round. Whether or not you are able to work as part of a broader partnership one of the key means to providing a (soft) recruitment aspect to outreach activities, alongside working with the most underserved is through locating them on campus and combining this with consistent, and intensive interaction with student ambassadors. Although based in the United States, Elise Swanson et. al. (2021) provide a valuable case study that highlights the importance of location for the impact of outreach activities. However, delivery of events on campus gives rise to two key challenges (a) the additional time required out of curriculum activity when planned during the school day (b) the cost/ability to travel to campus (an issue for both schools and individuals) impacts on both in-curricular and extra-curricular activities, especially for students and/or universities in rural locations. When delivered within curriculum this requires a further commitment from the school to spread the "delivery" of the opportunity outside the curriculum subject that is being addressed-for Inspiring Minds students may have to miss an English and Geography lesson in addition to the Science lesson to travel to and from campus. To maximize reach (working with 60–75 students per cohort) we worked with multiple schools, to have organized delivering six four-hour sessions across multiple school timetables would have been completely infeasible.

For those working with single institutions it may be more feasible to organize delivery on campus during curriculum time, however the feasibility of this relates back to issues associated with student selection. Multi-session interventions targeting "gifted and talented" students or working with selective schools are more likely to be able to access curriculum time that spans beyond a single lesson, because of the perception that these students are able to "catch up" on missed learning. For Inspiring Minds, we are deliberately targeting students from the lowest participation rates, and in partnership with schools' working with students across the ability spectrum. This meant that significant numbers of IM scholars, the "cost" of missing curriculum time would have been too prohibitive and would have (potentially) led to the deselection of the precisely those students we were looking to engage. This highlights the balance that needs to be struck when designing outreach activities between the breadth of students participating and cost of transport (either individual or institutional) when selecting the location and timing of activities.

Therefore, to gain the benefits[8] from locating on campus it was decided to host the sessions on a Saturday (avoiding loss of curriculum time) and to provide transport from each school to the university campus. This meant that students we able to either use their normal method of transport to school to join the bus or get dropped off by parents/carers, with the activities taking place on Saturday morning/over lunchtime the timing also means that students' attendance at Inspiring Minds didn't impact on other family activities (e.g., siblings with sports' practice etc). The additional advantage of this approach meant that the duration of the session could be designed to match the structure of the sessions rather than having to match/adapt the curriculum aims to fit the time schools could make available.[9]

When the issue and impact of campus-based activity is examined alongside the work of Helen Colley et. al. (2003) and Gartland (2016) there emerges a picture of the importance of both location and the "attributes of learning" within the outreach activities for the development of impactful ISL. The attributes of learning and role of structure and location become important in the creation of an effective learning environment. As noted by Colley et. al the boundary between "informal" and "formal" learning experiences is a contested one. In the context of this chapter "informal" is being used as shorthand for "extra-curricular" but also to refer to aspects (or attributes) of the ISL program that distinguish the opportunity from students' "formal" learning within the school curriculum. "Location" is being used both in relation to physical location (on campus) and the learning environment created on campus. For those with lower science capital, and less like to participate in HE the more their experience of STEM is going to be limited to interactions through the curriculum, this means that they have less opportunity to interact with STEM in entirely non-formal settings (conversations with family, cultural visits etc). Thus, for this group of students who aren't currently being met by the compartmentalized content-heavy curriculum delivering ISL in a "neutral" venue immediately removes the preconceptions (and any misperceptions) about the content and expectations of STEM learning.

After identifying 20 attributes of in/formality across the literature, H. Colley draws them together under four broad clusters: process, location and setting, purpose, and content. Within this section we will draw on the first two (purpose and content are examined in "Going Live"). STEAM outreach activities tend to either provide an incredibly structured learning process (i.e., those activities aimed at increasing students' content knowledge) or sit at the "other-end" of the spectrum—focused on increasing student engagement where the learning process is more "incidental." In aiming to provide a counterpoint to the formal school process the Inspiring Minds program consciously straddles the formal and formal "processes" identified by H. Colley. Each session was divided into two parts the first was an academic-led interactive session. These were led by an academic through an interactive workshop format—core subject content was didactively delivered regular application opportunities that were student-led and supported through student ambassadors working with small groups. The second part led facilitated students' submission of a project for a science CREST Award (usually a marker of a formal learning process) however in sharp contrast to the formality of a summative assessment the "process" was entirely student-led with student groups supported to choose their own questions to investigate, develop their own methodology, and decide on the kind of final output (academic poster, film, experimental model, artifact). Furthermore, whilst overseen by academic and outreach staff, the students' knowledge acquisition is facilitated by the group's ambassador who works with them across the academic and CREST sessions and throughout the program. The relationship development forms a core part of the learning process, and the learning becomes even more "informal" yet impactful when the CREST research is supported by ambassadors from outside the STEM faculties, where the process to design/build a robot or irrigation system (for example) is collaborative with ambassadors and students working together to discover what works.[10]

By selecting topics for investigation that fall "outside" the National Curriculum in England, the academic-led workshop sessions are designed to provide all the students with the "new" knowledge they need to engage with the topic, and importantly, highlight the links between the STEM "issue" and how answers to the question are being informed by arts and humanities disciplines. Students are actively supported by ambassadors to investigate these relationships and then apply this knowledge to both the session and their own research project where students provide a STEM+ response to a question drawing out the limitations of a single disciplinary response and the importance of multidisciplinary investigation where STEM interacts with society. The development of a learning environment that differs from school is both intended to prevent pre-conceptions about what is going to "happen" in the setting and serves a secondary purpose of introducing students to the learning opportunities within a HE context and forefront activities that develop their agency as learners, helping students to see themselves as co-creators in the learning process empowered to examine their own interests within the scaffolding and boundaries of a planned curriculum—preventing an "anything goes" format—allowing agency whilst maintaining a common learning goal. The importance of developing students' epistemic agency is at the heart of the epistemic insight pedagogy and, in the Inspiring Minds context, is intended to positively develop students' self-perception of their STEM ability and potential to progress to HE.

Using the "neutral" location of the university campus supports the program to transgress expectations and alongside a "university" experience that centers learner agency also serves a secondary function of supporting the recruitment (broadly understood) function of STEM outreach. Within the program change of location is also used to demark the different learning activities with academic-led sessions addressing the cohort as a single group and ambassadors and their group finding their own learning spaces within the library building with academics and outreach staff "visiting" each group. Students, through their ambassadors, are supported to develop their time management of the project with limited interim deadlines prior to the showcase session and whilst there is a shared learning goal—the completion of the CREST award—there aren't formal "learning objectives" for what skills or knowledge should be acquired (beyond the award assessment criteria).

We hope that this discussion helps to highlight that it is possible to develop ISL activities that contain "formal" learning objectives, delivery methods, assessment, or curricula. The "informality" can be developed in contrast to the "expected" learning experience and equally, particularly in the case of sustained ISL, through the inclusion of student-led activity where students are supported to apply their new learning within a context of their choosing. The next sections will examine the rationale and impact

38 • F. I. LAWSON, S. COLLEY, and B. BILLINGSLEY

of involving the whole university community (including those outside your own institution) followed by an explanation of the epistemic insight pedagogy that underpinned the program and how this provides an innovative approach to STEAM outreach.

CASTING—MAKING USE OF A DIVERSE TEAM, AND WHY YOU SHOULDN'T TRY TO GO SOLO

The role of the student ambassadors has been implicitly acknowledged in the previous section; however, it will be examined in more detail here alongside the role of the whole university in creating an impactful ISL experience. Gartland (2015a, 2015b, 2016) has investigated the role of student (and faculty) ambassadors as role models and providers of STEAM outreach. Her work provides accessible discussions and scholarship around many of the issues we have raised in this chapter, however the following discussion departs markedly from Gartland's work since most ambassadors working on the Inspiring Minds program came from outside the Faculty of Science, Engineering and Social Science—the majority came from the Faculty of Arts, Humanities and Education with a smaller number from the Faculty of Medicine, Health and Social Care. Across the program a significant number of ambassadors came from creative industries, literature/creative writing, nursing, and primary teaching degrees, with student ambassadors from Science and Engineering joining the program for the most recent cohorts. This balance in part reflects historical low participation rates from natural and engineering sciences in the student ambassador program, but also speaks to the breadth of appeal of the sessional content as ambassadors were aware at recruitment that the program was STEAM outreach activities.

The program invested in a high ambassador to participant ratio (on average one ambassador to five to seven students). Use of a high ratio and commitment from ambassadors to the complete program was designed to facilitate relationship building between students and the university community, with each group having their "own" ambassador it provided opportunity during the sessions for students to ask questions about university life once they had started to build a relationship, of those across the first five cohorts that responded to a re-engagement survey in 2021 (16% of the IM population[11]) 60% said that the experience would have been further improved by opportunity to keep in contact with their ambassador and the university after taking part, and 87% said it would have been improved through opportunities to meet more ambassadors from across the university. This points towards the impact that ambassadors (and forming relationships) have on participants, something only possible through sustained engagement, and also highlights that the relationship is potentially more important than the subject specialism of the ambassadors provided the academic content and support is available to the students when it is needed with 64% reporting at re-engagement that participating had positively impacted their experience in science lessons (ranging from greater understanding of specific content, to increased confidence and engagement, and self-reported improvement in attainment). We believe that these impacts are directly tied to the role of ambassadors and something that wouldn't be possible to achieve through delivery of the sessions within a lecture format or through research projects only supported by academic and outreach staff.

This brings us to the next community players involved in sessions—academic staff from across universities. The initial session design arose from collaborations between academics and outreach practitioners, for example a session designed in collaboration with an artist and a social science academic exploring the symbolism and messages in "portraiture" through art history, and the use (and data) included in digital portraiture (e.g., social media profiles). These engagements provided students an opportunity to meet scholars from a range of HE institutions and importantly the academics were chosen for both their subject knowledge and experience of working with school students. This meant that they were able to produce sessions that deeply engaged with STEAM from unexpected angles. Where the collaboration came in to its own was through the role of outreach practitioners in shaping the delivery, interaction and resources presented to the students. This meant that the academics weren't expected to be experts in how to engage school students in a manner that didn't replicate either HE lectures or school teaching, and outreach practitioners weren't expected to be experts in all the topics being examined. The digital and printed resources were quality checked, designed, and printed through the university central team (having been looked at through a "marketing lens") and this ensured that whilst the topics may have felt disparate the common format and visual design ensured they were presented as a cohesive group.

Finally, the production of a Showcase event where students shared their final outputs provided opportunity for the university, school, and home communities of the participating students to come together. Hosting the event on campus and inviting the parents into the same space provided opportunity to create shared family experiences, often with younger siblings also attending. The invitations to schoolteachers and leaders provided opportunity for their work outside the curriculum to be formally recognized by the school and often creating positive conversations between students and teachers about what they had been able to achieve. The invitations to academics who had delivered, and the wider university staff involved in STEAM subjects created further opportunities for students to interact with university staff and have their work recognized. Throughout the showcase the students were supported by their ambassadors, again highlighting the importance of this link.

The combination of academics, ambassadors and outreach staff is perhaps most explicitly linked to ISL within the HE outreach sector, however the principals apply to other groups bringing "experts" into their STEAM (and other) activities—the message is this—don't be hesitant to be explicit about collaboration on delivery and resource production, you know the children and young people you work with that is the expertise you bring and it is just as important as the disciplinary expertise brought by the academic or guest speaker. Michelangelo reportedly said "The greater danger for most of us lies not in setting our aim too high and falling short; but in setting our aim too low, and achieving our mark" this is often true in education—for Inspiring Minds students dealt with complex issues that are tacked at sixth form and university level, over a two-hour session, we were ambitious in the content we presented, but we also carefully structured the sessions and, as will be discussed in the next session, chose topics that didn't rely on prior (curriculum) knowledge but instead posed questions that everyone could have an opinion on and supported students to examine the power and limitations of science to inform the question and how the STEM interacted with the arts and humanities. This approach, alongside the work of the whole community fostered relationships, students' epistemic agency and built their STEM identity and self-confidence. For students with little or no science capital the development of confidence, and epistemic agency lie at the heart of changing their perception that STEM is not "for them."

GOING LIVE—HOW TO SHIFT STUDENTS' EXPECTATIONS OF STEM THROUGH EPISTEMIC AND PRACTICAL INQUIRY

The pedagogy and curriculum underpinning Inspiring Minds, we believe, lies at the heart of its success. The framing of STEAM within real-world contexts, relevant to the students engaging with the project provides the entry-point that means even students who said "I wouldn't have come if I had realized it was about science"[12] often left the project more excited by and engaged with STEM than when they started and this carried through into statistically significant shifts in their self-awareness and future participation in STEM, as well as their understanding of the relevance of STEM for society (see Lawson, Colley, & Harvey, 2021).

Epistemic Insight is a pedagogical approach that cultivates intellectual virtues of epistemic curiosity and humility. The cultivation of these virtues occurs within an epistemically insightful learning environment. Epistemic Insight is teachable, assessable, and transferable across learning settings through the cultivation of epistemic curiosity and teaching of critical thinking skills that can be expressed through students' epistemic humility (e.g., ability to recognize the power and limitations of individual discipline's capacity to inform our thinking about complex or real-world problems). In this context it is particularly notable in students' ability to distinguish between the information science can provide about X and the necessity to draw on arts and humanities to inform he implementation or application of the science in society. As part of developing intellectual virtues epistemic insight provides students with transferrable skills and contextual learning that can be transferred between humanities and science disciplines and between the informal Inspiring Minds setting and the formal classroom learning. In this way an epistemically insightful approach aims to move beyond the knowledge application Vs knowledge generation dichotomy often seen within ISL and instead provide students with a broader set of skills that empowers them to recognize the differing norms of thought and questions that frame disciplinary responses to questions. This enables students to examine and understand disciplinary boundaries and in doing so recognize the change that occurs when a question or issue is carried across those boundaries.

A breadth of research undertaken by Billingsley and her team (Billingsley, 2017; Billingsley & Ramos Arias, 2017; Billingsley et al., 2018; Billingsley & Hardman, 2018; Billingsley & Nassaji, 2019) has highlighted the current compartmentalization of the curriculum alongside other pressures and barriers within the UK educational system systematically dampens student's interest in Big Questions. When this is understood in connection with research on the importance of science capital (Wellcome, 2017) students from low participation backgrounds are far less likely to have opportunity to develop their understanding of science in real-world and multidisciplinary contexts.

The Inspiring Minds' curriculum was designed to not only offer and evaluate sustained outreach engagement to improve HE uptake, but also to implement and trial ISL that develops students' understanding of the power and limitations of scientific knowledge as part of a wider research project. The power and limitations of science (sometimes called "epistemic humility") is both a curriculum objective in science KS4 and a central aspect to the development of epistemic insight. Further research by Billingsley et al. has highlighted the current compartmentalization of the curriculum alongside other pressures and barriers within the UK education systematically dampens student's interest in Big Questions. It has been argued (Craven, Hand, & Prain 2002; Schwartz, Lederman, & Crawford 2004; Şeker & Welsh 2005) that teaching about the nature of science needs to be explicit, and whilst this is part of the science national curriculum, it is currently not assessed and therefore remains under resourced within school science teaching. The underpinning concept in developing an ISL curriculum that examines big philosophical questions that bridge science and other disciplines is not to simply provide students with additional scientific content but to also engage them in the discussion through the support and scaffolding of research informed ISL curriculum. The divide between scholar-led and student-led activities enables students' engagement with the nature of science to explicit and reflective so that there is opportunity to discussion the nature, power, and limitations of the sciences.

As noted above in developing outreach activities that also fulfil an ISL agenda a further question is raised as to whether the activities should be focusing on knowledge application or knowledge generation. In an informal setting with students from multiple schools and ability range in each session the curriculum cannot be based on assumed prior scientific knowledge this can lead to a focus on knowledge generation over application. Where colleagues are working with students from individual schools, or groups of students that have previously engaged with ISL activities, it can be tempting to assume that students have a particular set of prior knowledge, but if students haven't retained knowledge from the previous session or where new students have come into a group this has the potential risk of leaving students feeling just as disenfranchised and unable to engage as they do in school. This provides a challenge for the development of "progressive" outreach activities—within the Inspiring Minds program the progression occurred within the multi-sessional intervention as students developed research skills and worked towards their award, however the development of multi-year progression models is still very under-researched and poses a unique set of challenges that starts with knowledge generation/application but moves far beyond that narrative.

The epistemic insight curriculum approach is innovative through the focus on the use of multidisciplinary Big Questions, enabling students to engage with both tasks. Students can access the STEM activities (including the CREST award) through application of their existing knowledge in science and (as importantly) other disciplines. The nature of the curriculum provides multiple access points to STEM engagement through a multidisciplinary and "Big Questions" framework. This aims to ensure that students aren't faced with a starting point of feeling unable to undertake STEM research because they have already disengaged from/had a poor experience with STEM at school. Therefore, in providing a vehicle to overcome misperceptions and barriers to STEM engagement students are presented with an opportunity to both apply their existing knowledge and engage with knowledge generation. For some students the generation is through the development of their STEM content knowledge whereas for others it is through developing their epistemic awareness of the links between and powers/limitations of different disciplines. In addition, the curriculum for Inspiring Minds were designed to offer an alternative to the close-ended epistemic processes modelled within formal science learning. Close-ended processes require students to find a single "right" answer to the question/project, this model can lead to students feeling under pressure with a fear of "getting it wrong" that can negatively impact their engagement (Allchin, 2013). The use of Big Questions, and student-led investigation enables students to contribute to the STEM debate and facilitates their entry at different levels by enabling them to develop their own smaller close-ended process/question (through a narrow focus CREST project for example) or to continue to engage at an open-process level where the output draws together approaches or responses from a range of disciplines.

In this sense the development of an epistemically insightful curriculum, as with the creation of the learning environment adopts a blend of formal and informal attributes (as noted in H. Colley et al., 2003) relating to the purpose and content of the sessions. Whilst the purpose of the student-led research was to progress towards a CREST Award, and it followed a designed curriculum (both more formal attributes) there was a conscious decision to have "high stakes" knowledge acquisition with the focus instead on students' developing or "uncovering" how they can apply their wider knowledge to STEM-related issues and in turn to adopt a "tinkering" or (informal) CDIO approach to the development of their projects, encouraged to capture and value the iterative development as part of the learning process rather than seeing setbacks as "failure" or arrival at the "wrong" response. This isn't a move to validate "anything goes" or that "all answers are equally valid" but rather to support students to recognise that the learning process, and indeed the progress of science, isn't a strictly linear process.

It is this combination of developing students' awareness of the boundaries and uniqueness of difference disciplinary perspectives alongside supporting and growing students' epistemic agency and understanding of learning as an iterative process. Epistemic insight levels the starting point by starting outside the curriculum, but it is the fostering of intellectual humility and curiosity that we argue the true gains are found within the ISL context. In the final section of this chapter, we explain how evaluation was a central part of the development of the ISL activity and look forward, making some recommendations for the next steps for widening participation program design.

CATCHING THE REVIEWS—WHY MONITORING IS NOT ENOUGH AND EVALUATION MATTERS (A RESEARCH-LED APPROACH TO ISL)

University outreach departments excel in monitoring student participation (engagement) in outreach activities, and, through data sharing agreements with services such as the Higher Education Access Tracker (HEAT) in the

UK, can monitor the number of engagements students have with HE institutions through to their final destinations post-18. Monitoring of activities allows institutions to report the number of interactions, but without rigorous evaluation, it is at best difficult to monitor the impact the activities are having on students' aspiration and attainment.

With increasing divergent pressures on educational finances, it is becoming even more important to understand the impact outreach activities are having so that stakeholders can be better equipped to make informed choices about high-reach low intensity versus lower reach higher intensity/more sustained activities. Low intensity activities allow teams to reach greater numbers but without evaluation it is difficult to ascertain if these activities are impacting the ability of the most underrepresented students to access higher education though shift in attitudes and attainment. The evaluation of the Inspiring Minds program was, through collaboration between outreach practitioners, educational researchers and evaluation professionals at KMPF and HEAT, designed into the program at inception this meant that the data collection journey was built into the student experience, supported by the student ambassadors and the sustained relationships with lead teachers enabled the collection of re-engagement data.[13]

As we, as an outreach community, continue to develop our understanding of the interaction of multiple barriers to accessing HE it is imperative that outreach programs recognize and seek to minimize the multiple barriers to the most under-represented groups engaging with outreach opportunities however, whilst multiple barriers are recognised further evaluation needs to be conducted across outreach events to understand which, on their removal, have the greatest impact. The requires a combination of robust self-reported data and longitudinal studies to support the evaluation of the impact on student attainment. This is echoed in the direction of travel of the OfS, who's new Director for Fair Access and Participation highlighted the importance of published, independent evaluations (OfS 2022).

Additionally in order for the impact of outreach programs/interactions to fully evaluated three key processes need to be further addressed (a) continued and developed practice of shared data across institutions (through HEAT) that allows students' engagement journey to be followed through to their destination. (b) programs need to be able to access funding that allows for future planning and development of experienced, research-engaged teams (c) to understand the impact, both for attainment and participation there needs to be funding for long-term evaluation enabling projects to span five to seven years to re-engage students and assess the long-term impact of sustained relationships and opportunities. As noted above the development and delivery of sustained activity comes at a greater (per student) cost—the development of relationships requires high ratios of staff (including ambassadors) to students and repeat engagement with the same students (potentially) reducing the opportunity to reach "new" students. These negotiations between reach and sustained engagement need to be fully evaluated to understand if the cost can be justified, and this requires commitment from funders and institutions to develop an evidence base for what works.

However, whilst the cost to gain ratio will inevitably frame the institutional conversation it is also relevant for those undertaking smaller STEAM outreach activities in their schools and communities—studies have shown that sustained and progressive interactions have the greatest impact, and we argue that at the heart of this lies the opportunity to develop young people's confidence and capacity to be their own agents of change, equipped as critical thinkers and provided with opportunities to see themselves achieving more than they thought they were capable. As a team we will continue to develop our understanding of how the spaces where disciplines interact provide rich opportunity to support young people to engage with STEM, and we hope that this chapter provides others with ideas on how they can apply what we have learnt to their contexts.

NOTES

1. For those interested in the more technical aspects of the research detailed evaluation and discussion reports by Lawson et. al (2019, 2021) can be found at 10.13140/RG.2.2.33624.93448 (2019) and 10.13140/RG.2.2.12854.16964 (2021) and the attainment impact evaluation report by Anthony (2022) is available at 10.13140/RG.2.2.32986.82882
2. For those interested in a very practical discussion of some of the sessional content for secondary students see (Lawson et al., 2020) and for the use of the same pedagogy with primary aged children see (Oh & Lawson, 2020)
3. POLAR4 is a measure used by the OfS to classify local areas in the UK based on the proportion of young people who participate in HE. The areas are grouped into five quintiles of which quintile one has the lowest rate of participation. Further details on how this is calculated can be found at https://www.officeforstudents.org.uk/data-and-analysis/young-participation-by-area/about-polar-and-adult-he/
4. Those who did not achieve either didn't complete enough hours on the program or withdrew from the program ahead of the showcase.
5. Big questions, in this context, are defined as questions that touch on the nature of reality or human personhood and where science and religion are usually both able to inform our understanding of the issue—these are often questions where there is no definite or agreed answer, however we are often able to answer "smaller" or more focused questions to inform our thinking.
6. Campus is being used as synonymous for the university site, rather than making a distinction between "campus" and "city" universities.

7. KMPF was originally established in 2011 when the government's national Aimhigher program came to an end. It was one of just a handful of remaining partnerships in the country to continue beyond the end of central government funding in 2011, thanks to the support and contributions of its member organizations.
8. The potential benefits are discussed in relation to H. Colley's attributes of learning below.
9. Since its inception, individual sessions from the Inspiring Minds have been adapted for delivery as in-school "Roadshow" sessions, to meet the need to fit into a single or double lesson (50–140 minutes) the breadth of context is reduced, and the sessions are more heavily weighted to structured activities with a reduction in the student-led exploration opportunities.
10. It is important to note that these sessions are supported by academic staff with STEAM outreach experience, able to ensure that students aren't exposed to misinformation and to manage the students' expectations of what can be achieved in the timescale of the project—students are often more ambitious than the timescale allows for what they would like to create.
11. Cohorts one to three were in sixth form study (year 12 or 13) at the point of the re-engagement survey which presented a significant difficulty in reaching students from these groups as many of the participating schools did not have connected sixth forms, or students went on to study at FE college and therefore could not be contacted.
12. This is not to imply that students were misled in to attending, the advertising was clear that the opportunity was for a STEM program leading to a science qualification, however because the marketing was framed in terms of "Big Questions" and opportunity to undertake their own research—this perceived disconnect with their experience of science in school meant that their picture of what was being offered and what science was didn't match.
13. To understand how the attainment gains have been evaluated see (Anthony, 2022), and to understand the development and evaluation of the project in relation to students' self-reported data see (Lawson, Colley, & Harvey, 2021; Lawson et al., 2019).

REFERENCES

Allchin, D. (2013). Problem- and Case-Based Learning in Science: An Introduction to Distinctions, Values, and Outcomes. *CBE—Life Sciences Education, 12* (3), 364–372.

Anthony, A. (2022). *Canterbury Christ Church University (CCCU) Inspiring minds impact evaluation: Examining the impact on Key Stage 4 (GCSE) exam result.* https://doi.org/10.13140/RG.2.2.32986.82882.

Archer, L., Moote J., Francis B., DeWitt J., & Yeomans L. (2017). Stratifying Science: A Bourdieusian Analysis of Student Views and Experiences of School Selective Practices in Relation to "Triple Science" at KS4 in England. *Research Papers in Education, 32* (3), 296–315.

Approaching STEAM via Inquiry-Based Responses to Big Questions • **47**

ASE (2018). *APPG Meeting 4: Social Mobility in STEM.* ASE. Retrieved from https://www.britishscienceassociation.org/appg-meeting-4-social-mobility-in-stem

ASE (2020). *Inquiry on equity in STEM education: Final report.* APPG on diversity and inclusion in STEM. Retrieved from https://diversityuk.org/wp-content/uploads/2020/06/Final_report_Inquiry_on_Equity_in_STEM_education.pdf

Barmby, P., Per M. Kind, & Jones, K. (2008). Examining changing attitudes in secondary school science. *International Journal of Science Education, 30*(8), 1075–1093.

Billingsley, B. (2017). Teaching and learning about epistemic insight. *School Science Review, 98*(365), 59–64.

Billingsley, B., & Hardman, M. (2018). Theme editorial: Epistemic insight and the power and limitations of science in multidisciplinary areas. *School Science Review, 99*(367), 16–18.

Billingsley, B., & Nassaji, M. (2019). Exploring secondary school students' stances on the predictive and explanatory power of science. *Science & Education, 28*(1), 87–107.

Billingsley, B., Nassaji, M., Fraser, S., & Lawson, F. (2018). A framework for teaching epistemic insight in schools. *Research in Science Education, 48*(6), 1115–1131.

Billingsley, B., & Ramos Arias, A. (2017). Epistemic insight and classrooms with permeable walls. *School Science Review, 99*(367), 44–53.

Colley, H., Hodkinson, P., & Malcolm, J. (2003). *Informality and formality in learning: A report for the learning and skills research centre.* Leeds: Learning and Skills Research Centre.

Craven, J. A., Hand B., & Prain, V. (2002). Assessing explicit and tacit conceptions of the nature of science among preservice elementary teachers. *International Journal of Science Education, 24*(8), 785–802.

Gartland, C. (2015a). Student ambassadors and STEM outreach: A study of practices in the USA. Retrieved from https://www.wcmt.org.uk/sites/default/files/report-documents/Gartland%20C%20Report%202015%20Final.pdf

Gartland, C. (2015b). Student ambassadors: "Role-models," learning practices and identities. *British Journal of Sociology of Education, 36*(8), 1192–1211.

Garland, C. (2016). *STEM strategies: Student ambassadors and equality in higher education.* Trentham Books.

KMPF. (2022). 'What we do'. Kent & Medway progression federation. Retrieved from https://kmpf.org/about/what-we-do

Lawson, F. I., Colley, S., & Harvey, D. (2021). *NEON Innovation Series Evaluation report inspiring minds through informal science learning: NEON Innovation Series Evaluation report. An evaluation of the impact when targeted outreach is delivered to increase science learning in schools.* https://doi.org/10.13140/RG.2.2.12854.16964

Lawson, F. I., Hunt, M., Goodwin, D., & Colley, S. (2019). *Inspiring Minds through Informal Science Learning: Interim Evaluation Report. Informing Research to Increase Science Learning in Schools.* Retrieved from https://doi.org/10.13140/RG.2.2.33624.93448

Lawson, F. I., Hunt, M., Goodwin, D., & Colley, S. (2020). Inspiring minds: How big questions can build students' epistemic insight and improve attitudes towards STEM. *School Science Review, 102*(378), 59–64.

Mevarech, Z., & Kramarski, B. (2014). *Critical maths for innovative societies: The role of metacognitive pedagogies* (Illustrated ed.). OECD Publishing.

Office for Students. (2022). *Next steps in access and participation.* Retrieved from https://www.officeforstudents.org.uk/news-blog-and-events/press-and -media/next-steps-in-access-and-participation

Oh, M., & Lawson, F. (2020). The Engineering Ed Project: Dealing with failure and the robotic future—Engaging students in multidisciplinary STEM learning. *School Science Review, 101*(376), 50–59.

Perry, J., Lundie, D., & Gill Golder, G. (2019). Metacognition in schools: What does the literature suggest about the effectiveness of teaching metacognition in schools?

CHAPTER 4

INVESTIGATORY APPROACHES TO THE TEACHING AND LEARNING OF HISTORY

Using a Constructivist Inquiry-Based Scientific Method

James Percival

In this chapter, a case is to be made that investigatory or enquiry approaches to history, often defined under the umbrella labels 'active' or 'experiential' forms of learning which can trace their roots back to Rousseau and the enlightenment (Gilead, 2005), can reconcile some of the key tensions and disagreements within the theory and practice of historical pedagogy and address both formal and informal approaches to teaching and learning; in short, a presentation of an intellectual 'third way' (Giddens, 1998). It is also necessary to briefly account for the principal philosophical and ideological divisions that emerged from the late 1960s onwards concerning the

Motivation and Engagement in Various Learning Environments, pages 49–64
Copyright © 2024 by Information Age Publishing
www.infoagepub.com
All rights of reproduction in any form reserved.

50 ▪ J. PERCIVAL

teaching and learning of history, in primary and secondary schools and in both state and private sectors, in terms of what is taught, the historical content, and how it is taught, the pedagogy of history. Hence, the focus of this chapter will address the history curriculum between the upper primary and the lower secondary years where history remains a compulsory subject in state-funded schools. As Phillips (1998a) argued, no other national curriculum (NC) subject, with the possible exception of the teaching of reading, has generated so much discussion and disagreement both educationally and politically, the latter evidenced by history becoming one of the most referenced school subject in Hansard (Phillips, 1998b, p.41), debates that were subsequently echoed by Gove's National Curriculum 2014 reforms, for example Boffey (2013) and Evans (2013). The significance of this observation is that history remains a contested and controversial curriculum subject, with points of agreement.

The chapter begins with an account of innovations and key debates from the 1960s onwards, the importance of disciplinary concepts, and the formation of the National Curriculum for England and Wales. A case is then presented in support of investigatory approaches, including the philosophical foundations and evidence for good practice. The final section examines some of the key evidence for the efficacy of investigatory approaches.

A SYNTHESIS BETWEEN THE "OLD"
AND "NEW" FORMS OF HISTORY

The principal argument presented within this chapter is that well-planned and skillfully directed investigatory approaches can reconcile some of the divisions that, according to Rogers (1980) emerged between what became known as the *new* approach to history pedagogy, which in turn can be interpreted as a battleground between formal and informal modes of teaching and learning, thus addressing the central theme of this text.

One statement that can be made with reasonable security is that the *'new'* forms of history pedagogy emerged by the late 1960s due to several significant educational movements. For example, disciplinary debates were certainly sparked by Bruner's (1960) influential work and his recommendation of adopting a conceptual approach to curriculum development. Similarly, many educationalist and policy makers were influenced by Piaget and Inhelder's (1969) work in Geneva, and their development of a constructivist, stage theory, model of learning which had a profound influence on English primary curriculum reforms via the Plowden report (CACE, 1967). Similarly, whilst retaining the focus on the English experience, reforms to the secondary curriculum were accelerated in the 1960s following the

Newsom Report (1963) which warned of the wastage of talent in the secondary school sector and recommended a more challenging and relevant curriculum.

One response to educational reform, which included history as a core subject, was the UK Government funded Schools Council Project (SCHP) (Shemilt, 1980) which pioneered new approaches in the lower secondary years with a particular focus on secondary moderns and the emerging comprehensive sector which were not well served by the existing 'O' level examination system.

According to Cannadine et al. (2011), in many respects the SCHP became the centre of the discussion that raged between the educational traditionalists, who defended the *old* history, who favoured historical knowledge and synthesis of key information, against the progressives who promoted the *new* history (Cannadine et al., 2011, pp. 165–166), which emphasised historical skills and understanding incorporated into teaching approaches based on enquiry and investigation, For the *new* historians, it was the *old* or traditional history's concentration on information and memorisation that was the problem. Sheldon (2011, pp. 12–3) argued that for the traditionalists, it was the emphasis of understanding at the expense of breadth and knowledge that was the critical weakness, and by the late 80s, some prominent historians, such as Robert Skidelsky, had started to campaign against the *new* history, notably the perception that there over emphasis on students' responses in secondary schools. The comparison between the two competing approaches can be summarized as in Table 4.1.

In several respects, this educational conflict reflected the long-standing debate in the philosophy of education surrounding the balance between

TABLE 4.1 Comparison Between Two Schools of History Pedagogy

"Old" History	"New" History
• Traditional and *formal* forms of pedagogy; teacher led.	• Often *informal* forms of pedagogy.
• *Knowledge* as the main outcome of historical study.	• *Understanding* as the main learning outcome.
• *Passive* forms of learning linked to discussion and written outcomes.	• Conceptual approach linked to *active* forms of learning (e.g., investigations and historical forms of enquiry).
• Teachers in position of *authority* as the principal source of historical knowledge.	• History sometimes combined with other subjects through *cross-curricular approaches*.
• Synthesis of ideas and *explanatory* accounts, based on a predominately fixed sense of the past	• Teachers as *Facilitators* working alongside and guiding children.
	• Questioning and *interpretive* approach to the past.
	• Historical knowledge considered *conditional* and *contested*.

Note: Content adapted from Percival (2020)

content and skills, often reflecting the distinction theorists such as Ryle (1949) have made between procedural (knowing how) and propositional (knowing what) knowledge, or Schwab's (1964) categorization of substantive and syntactic understanding.

However, from the vantage point of several decades of reflection and experience, it is arguable that neither position was truly reflective of what eventually emerged in schools, particularly in secondary schools, where history tended to be viewed more of a synthesis between skills, understanding and knowledge. Indeed, few theorists accepted the extreme version of the skills and understanding pedagogy over the transmission of knowledge; indeed, there were many powerful critiques of the former approach. For example, Rogers (1987), Counsell (2000), and Turner-Bissett (2005) from a primary perspective, separately argued for the importance of historical knowledge, essentially as a form of reference to help children scaffold their understanding, and the desirability of synthesizing skills and understanding with knowledge. Lee (1991, pp.43–8) was a particularly strong critic of the 'vicious relativism' that sometimes emerged from predominately skills-based approaches.

THE PLACE OF HISTORICAL CONCEPTS

Having cited the importance of Bruner's (1960) influence on the importance of identifying the conceptual underpinnings of disciplinary subjects, it is perhaps unsurprising that history educators began to think about history in a more conceptual way. One of the key theoretical distinctions was made between *'first order'* and *'second order concepts.'* These have often been included in key works on pedagogy and discussed in some length by theorists such as Guyver (1997) and Lee and Shemilt (2004, p.14), though rarely, if ever, have their origins and intellectual foundations been discussed. Further analysis suggests that their origin can be traced to Emmet's (1964) distinction between first-order, or factual questions, and second-order, or conceptual questions, which in turn were popularized by Ryan's (1970, p.4) highly successful and influential introductory text on the philosophy of the social sciences.

What is unquestionably true is that from the early 1970s onwards this distinction between first order forms of historical knowledge and second order concepts starts to appear in influential publications such as Coltham and Fines' Historical Association publication (1971) which challenged teachers in both primary and secondary sectors to think more analytically about their practice and included an embryonic list of suggested elements. As indicated, an important delineation that emerged from this period of exploration in the 1970s was the distinction between *first-order*, or *substantive*, concepts of history, linked to knowledge, such as "parliament,"

Investigatory Approaches to the Teaching and Learning of History • **53**

TABLE 4.2 **Definitions of Historical Concepts**	
First Order Historical Concepts	**Second Order Historical Concepts**
• Also termed as *substantive*; • Associated with important historical knowledge; • Central for the learner engagement with historical texts; • Examples include *parliament, democracy,* or *reform*.	• Also known as *procedural* or *'organizing'* concepts; • More directly linked to developing historical understanding and the learner's ability to assimilate historical knowledge; • Examples include *causality, significance, evidence, interpretation,* or *change*.

"democracy," or "reform," and *second-order*, sometimes termed *organizing* or *procedural*, concepts, such as "causality," "interpretation," or "change." Table 4.2 summarizes the key terminology and definitions.

INFLUENCE OF THE NEW HISTORY ON THE DEVELOPMENT OF THE NATIONAL CURRICULUM

It is difficult to fully assess the success of this more analytical and conceptual approach to the teaching and learning of history, although Shemilt's (1980) rigorous and fascinating evaluation study is discussed at the end of this chapter, but some statements can be made with a high level of confidence. The first is that these concepts shaped national projects such as the SCHP, which further developed and refined the key ideas into a form that could be assimilated by teachers; some of them not necessarily subject experts, in the form of projects such as Exploration Man (1972); and some which also were adopted by upper junior staff in primary schools. It is also the case the SCHP publications strongly emphasised the importance of children conducting historical investigation and enquiry-based forms of learning, which was influential, if far from universally adopted in either upper primary or the early years of secondary school settings.

The second evidence backed claim is that the work conducted by the History Working Group (HWG) (DES, 1989; DES, 1990) a team from a variety of backgrounds and forms of expertise, was created to design the first iteration of the National Curriculum for history. It was clearly influenced by the work of educators over the previous two decades. Indeed, reflecting the reality of the synthesis between *old* and *new* that often occurred within schools and history departments, the HWG's two reports recommended a clear synthesis between knowledge (content) and historical understanding via student engagement with important historical concepts and whilst developing key historical skills. Hence, the necessity of combining knowledge, skills and understanding into a recognisable and workable curriculum had

54 • J. PERCIVAL

clearly been assimilated by the educators, academics, and civil servants that formed the HWG.

The first NC for history (DES, 1991) specifically included Programs of Study (POS), which addressed key historical periods such as the Tudors or Victorians; and three Attainment Targets (ATs), which included key historical concepts to guide teacher assessment of children' progression in history, allied to key attitudes and skills. For example, accounting for historical change in AT1, *Knowledge and Understanding of History* clearly addressed this important second order concept; while active forms of learning such as engaging with historical evidence in AT3, *The Use of Historical Sources*, addressed the skills of enquiry alongside the key concept of interpretation. Admittedly some concepts that had emerged from the *new* history, such as bias and empathy, had clearly fallen out of favour, but most elements promoted by the Historical Association and the SCHP were recognisable in the first iteration of the National Curriculum.

The NC also covered children's learning from Key Stage 1 (5–7 years), Key Stage 2 (7–11 years), Key Stage 3 (11–14 years) and Key Stage 4 (14–16 years). This made the connection between primary and secondary phases in terms of curriculum and assessment official for the first time in maintained schools. As Sheldon (2012) noted, one of the biggest battles faced when determining the NC for history was whether to make history compulsory to 16. At the very last moment, and to his later regret, the new Secretary State for Education, Kenneth Clarke removed it from the list of compulsory subjects in Key Stage 4 (Sheldon, 2012, p.268). The political will had been there, not least because a curriculum that ended for many at 14 would necessarily be truncated and therefore less ambitious and complete, but there were too many organizational and practical obstacles. It only remains to note that despite subsequent iterations of the NC, specifically the Dearing Review (DFE, 1995) and the more values-based Curriculum 2000 (DfEE, 1999), the history curriculum largely remained in recognizable from as a clear synthesis between knowledge, skills and understanding.

CURRICULUM REFORM AND THE KNOWLEDGE DEBATE

The first main challenge to this new orthodoxy was the transatlantic "knowledge" debate which emerged from the work of ED Hirsch (1988) and his argument for something he termed "cultural literacy." There was also the burgeoning influence of the English conservative philosopher Michael Oakeshott (1972) and his argument for the importance of cultural inheritance, something he termed a 'transaction between the generations' (Oakeshott, 1972, p. 63). A third key figure in this debate has been the English sociologist Michael Young's (2008, 2013) whose rejection of his earlier position

Investigatory Approaches to the Teaching and Learning of History • 55

regarding active and investigatory forms of learning was replaced by something that he entitled "powerful knowledge" from a "social realist" position. Nor can the all-pervasive influence of Bourdieu's (1986) concept of "cultural capital" be ignored in this debate. All of these theorists and their key ideas and concepts can, of course, be critiqued and challenged; nor do they all share the same foundations or desired outcomes—for example, both Hirsch and Young similarly claimed that their arguments were founded upon arguments for social justice and a desire to increase social mobility, a position the conservative Michael Oakeshott would never have shared—but what they have in common was an influence on Michael Gove, Education Minister between 2010–2014, because he clearly cited the influence of Hirsch and Oakeshott on his developing ideas for educational reform and the importance of powerful and transformative form of knowledge, in which history would play a key role. Gove's (2009) speech to the Royal Society of Arts in 2009, when he was shadow minister, was arguably the clearest exposition of his burgeoning belief in the importance of cultural inheritance.

Hence, the NC 2014 presaged a return to substantive knowledge, and for history this took the form of a schema key historical knowledge to be covered by the end of each Key Stage. However, it is important to note that in the final version of the NC2014 for History, after considerable resistance and advice from academics and historians, refer for example to Richard Evans' (2019) strident and entertaining account of his role, historical concepts and skills were retained, albeit in a less detailed or prominent form. Nevertheless, the balance had clearly shifted in favour of historical knowledge over skills and understanding. The question that needs to be asked is this: does the distinction between knowledge and the processes of history, between the *old* and the *new* accurately and meaningfully represent the distinction between formal and informal forms of learning? Arguably, it does, but with certain qualifications.

If we refer to Table 4.3, traditional historical pedagogy, the *old* history, of the type advocated by Elton (2002), is typically presented as a predominately

TABLE 4.3 Formal and Informal Approaches to the Teaching and Learning of History

Formal Approach to Historical Learning	Informal Approach to Historical Learning
• Teacher led pedagogy; • Prioritising the acquisition and memorisation of knowledge; • Formal learning activities such as extended writing and examinations; • Individual work outcomes.	• Active learner/student-directed approaches; • Teacher as guide or facilitator; • Linked to investigation/enquiry; • Engagement with historical evidence; • Greater variety of work outcomes including presentations, etc.

Note: Student understanding of key disciplinary, second-order concepts. Adapted from Percival (2020)

56 ▪ J. PERCIVAL

teacher led, didactic activity, with an emphasis on the acquisition of knowledge and with extended writing outcomes as the main learning outcome, and certainly formal in style. It should therefore not be a surprise to learn that the National Curriculum 2014 (DfE, 2013) for both primary and secondary schools recommended opportunities for learners to write at length.

By contrast, informal approaches overlap considerably, but not completely, with the more conceptual *new* forms of history. The key elements are arguably the greater emphasis on active forms of student / learner-directed work; opportunities for collaborative approaches, often building upon student interests and previous study; and incorporating those elements adapted from constructivist psychology such as investigation and exposure to historical evidence. These ideas have often been described, for example Cunningham (1988), frequently pejoratively, as 'progressive' approaches within educational theory,

The main aspect of the *new* history that cannot be unequivocally identified as informal, is the emphasis on developing understanding through engagement with core disciplinary second-order concepts such as change, causality and chronology, etc. It would be foolish to claim that formal, traditional approaches ignore high levels of conceptual understanding, although their inclusion was often implicit. Indeed, the critique of progressivism made by Hirsch and Young included the claim that progressive and informal approaches had often failed learners, particularly those who most required teacher-led guidance and instruction.

AN ARGUMENT FOR THE 'THIRD WAY'

Indeed, having introduced the case for the primacy of historical knowledge, and subsequent curriculum reforms, it may be questioned why processes, skills and understanding should require reinstatement. The first point is, as this chapter has so far indicated, few educators or theorists argued for an uncritical investigatory approach for young learners, hence the balanced synthesis of elements in the original NC for history. But they argued strongly for a more thoughtful and conceptual approach which would result in deeper, more contextual forms of understanding. Hence, there is a danger that the pioneering work of Bruner, the Historical Association and SCHP, etc., will be lost due to the most recent iteration of the NC for history and the promotion of historical knowledge above engagement and understanding.

Second, as demonstrated by the first iteration of the NC for history (DES, 1991), the content of virtually any Key Stage 2 or 3 unit of work, including the most overview of British History contained in the most recent iteration, can be adapted for investigatory, active forms of learning. This is surely the most salient point: *that virtually all history study units can include some*

Investigatory Approaches to the Teaching and Learning of History • **57**

investigatory elements, thus uniting formal and informal elements. In the case of the NC, virtually all POS were designed to be taught through the lens of the ATs. Key variables, demonstrated by Shemilt (1980), include the availability of historical evidence for any given study unit, and the commitment and expertise of teaching staff.

However, arguably of far greater importance at a time when the status and professionalism of teachers is under review, it is important that the psychological and philosophical foundations of good practice are retained. In the case of investigatory, enquiry forms of historical learning, the intellectual foundations are very strong indeed, and help to maintain history's importance and distinctiveness as a mode of interpreting the world.

There are several synonyms, or near synonyms, for active forms of learning, including student-led, student initiated, discovery, experiential, etc., and as noted previously, include investigatory approaches. But what they all have in common are foundations that, as previously noted, can be traced to Rousseau and the enlightenment. Subsequent work by educational constructivists such as Dewey (1966), and his outline of 'problem-based learning', Piaget and Bruner have been supplemented by relatively recent translations of Vygotsky's (1978; 1986) pioneering work from the inter-war period. For most educators, the importance of active forms of learning for the development of student engagement and understanding scarcely requires making.

Constructivist psychology provides a general justification rather than directly relating to historical learning. More specific support can be identified from the philosophy of history and the methods of academic history. Indeed, it is surely significant that many historians have provided accounts support the idea of the investigatory nature of historical study. Two of the most important philosophers of history, RG Collingwood (1939; 1946) and Michael Oakeshott (1962), described history as a 'special form of research or enquiry' (Collingwood, 1946, p.9) which required historians to 'study problems not periods' (Collingwood, 1939, p.124).

There is also the question of the importance of historical evidence. Indeed, this consideration arguably acts as a bulwark against charges of relativism. For example, Bevir (1994) argued that rigorous forms of enquiry based on sound evidence have become a crucially important argument for demonstrating the objective truth of historical knowledge. Richard Evans (1997) extended this point in more detail, and further described how primary sources demand high levels of imagination from the historian in the form of conversations with the past, circumscribed by a complex set of rules that historians often adhere to implicitly (Evans, 1997).

For the academic historian, their professional aim is ultimately about creating new forms or interpretations of historical knowledge. This has sometimes been used as an objection against active, investigatory forms of learning in the classroom since the aim of school history is surely not to

58 ▪ J. PERCIVAL

produce a nation of historians. There are two important ripostes to this point. The first is the parallel with other disciplinary subjects, notably science, design technology or computing. Whilst no doubt politicians would be keener on higher numbers of school leavers becoming scientists, engineers, or software designers than historians, the fact remains that few will. Thus, the justification of conducting scientific experiments, or writing embryonic computer programs, is to gain some understanding of how this knowledge is created as well as the development of thinking skills. Indeed, this was exactly the point that the HWG (1990) made when they stated that the aim of school history is not about producing academic historians, but for children to understand something about the nature of historical knowledge and to train young minds in critical modes of thought.

Nor is this an insignificant point: at a time when official narratives are questioned, and conspiracy theories flourish online and in social media, it is arguably of ever greater importance that young people gain some understanding of the foundations of historical knowledge and can assess evidence for themselves. Whether we call this skill criticality, or something else, the term the 'post-truth' world has emerged from the shadows. As former U.S. President Barak Obama discussed in a 2020 BBC interview, it is essential that young people develop the skills to challenge what he has termed 'truth decay' (Sharma, 2020).

Indeed, one of the fears about political control of the history curriculum, from several ideological positions, is that there is always a political risk when politicians determine the history curriculum. Robert Phillips (2000, pp.15–17) summarized debates around the first NC as the 'battle for the big prize' of determining Britain's heritage and cultural legacy.

In conclusion, the case made in this chapter is that the most powerful, transformative knowledge of all is the personal knowledge gained through exposure to the methods of history and exposure to genuine forms of historical evidence, whilst engaging with key disciplinary concepts. Thus, investigatory approaches can arguably satisfy both formal and informal approaches to history and supplement the work of knowledge acquired by more passive forms of learning.

RECOMMENDED PRACTICE

The aim of this short section is not to provide a blue-print for professional practice, but simply to share general points of guidance taken from policy documents and research. An important and rather obvious point is that all effective historical investigations require a clear, relevant, and achievable question to guide enquiry. For academic historians, this might take the form of a hypothesis based on previous research. For example, Karl Popper

Investigatory Approaches to the Teaching and Learning of History ▪ **59**

employed the metaphor of a searchlight shining into the dark places of the past, guided by a hypothesis, and based firmly on previous research (Popper, 1966). For younger, less experienced, and skilled historians, the pedagogical implications include modelling the wording and formation of suitable questions, including guiding, and intervening when necessary, and also discussing feasibility based on an evaluation of available sources.

There is also the consideration, explored by Fines and Nichol's (1997) long term Nuffield primary history project between 1991–9, that enquiry questions should emerge roughly half-way through a unit of history. This is to allow children sufficient time to acquire historical knowledge related to the unit of study, provoke their curiosity, and support the identification of a suitable research question. The forms of historical evidence available and appropriate for young learners, and for the purposes of this chapter they have been defined as between 7–14 years old, also demand a brief discussion. Naturally, one would expect greater independence demonstrated by older learners, although the important caveat is that research into historical understanding, not to mention reading ages, demonstrated an unexpectedly wide range, and therefore overlap between different ages and stages, in unstreamed classrooms. For example, the extensive CHATA project (Lee and Shemilt, 2004), which was predominately conducted in secondary classrooms reported a seven-year differential in historical understanding in any average classroom.

Considerations of this sort have sometimes resulted in recommendations that younger children, perhaps all primary school children, should *not* engage with written sources, the staple of professional historians. The counter argument has been that they can be used, but even with young adolescents, careful selection is required and should include modelling of the process of interpretation. Research, such as the Nuffield Project, highlighted the crucial role of the teacher in terms of selection and preparation of sources and modelling their investigation and interpretation; any individual who has looked at even fairly modern documentation, whether it be local or family history, will recognize the challenges in trying to decode information from the past. There are more accessible forms of historical information, however:

- *Artefacts*—pioneering work began in the late 1960s. They hold obvious advantages for younger learners and can be brought into the classroom.
- *Buildings*—can provide several sources of historical information.
- *People*—oral history is now taken more seriously by academic historians. Research, such as Loader (1993) has indicated that careful preparation is needed before visitors or visits are arranged, including review and rehearsal.
- *Visual* (photographs and art)—schemes such as the National Gallery's 'Take One Picture' project have demonstrated how rewarded investi-

60 ▪ J. PERCIVAL

gatory approaches towards significant paintings and artwork can be. There are now many significant online photographic archives.

- *Maps*—contain many advantages, not least visual information rather than textual, and also the ability to compare maps to engage with concepts such as change.
- *Online databases*—these should be considered given the increasing availability of historical evidence in virtual form, including maps, documents, images, and recordings.

In addition to studying some units of history in depth, the local study has been a consistent feature with the NC for history, and geography, and naturally some schools pioneered its use long before the introduction of the National Curriculum. It remains in the NC, though as with other things now less emphasized, but it remains the single most researched, accessible, meaningful, and practical opportunity for young learners to engage with historical investigation linked to evidence (i.e., Percival, 2020). According to Douch (1970), the increasing use of local study units within schools arguably reflected the increasing seriousness with which it was taken by university departments of history, not least due to the pioneering work of Stephens (1977), and it is now a prominent feature in several prestigious universities including Oxford. Nevertheless, the previous point about posing questions to guide enquiry remains: the key consideration is what aspect of the locality would young learners wish to explore in depth?

A further consideration should be that investigations based on secondary sources, including online accounts, should always be considered. Recall, the aim has never been to produce academic historians. And the opportunity to critically evaluate competing and contrasting accounts, whilst addressing the disciplinary concept of interpretation, can be anticipated. Indeed, teachers can deliberately select the availability of contrasting texts and sources. As noted previously, investigatory forms of historical study allow opportunities for collaborative work, which more accurately replicate the tasks and challenges that will ultimately face them in the workplace, and similarly work outcomes may include things other than extended writing and include presentations, displays, artwork, exhibits, computer databases and posters.

EVIDENCE OF EFFECTIVENESS

Having made a case, albeit in truncated form, that historical investigations offer an opportunity to combine both formal and informal approaches to the teaching and learning of history, and an opportunity to develop deeper and more genuine forms of historical understanding based on engagement with historical evidence and important historical concepts. However,

Investigatory Approaches to the Teaching and Learning of History • **61**

these claims should not be accepted uncritically, hence this final section will briefly outline some of the evidence that predates the muted and synthesized approaches that followed the introduction of the NC. To begin with, it should be acknowledged that the traditionalists, those who favored more formal, teacher-directed approaches, increasingly received support from official reports conducted by Her Majesties Inspectorate (HMI) in the 1970s and '80s. Three reports will serve as examples. The 1978 HMI survey of English primary schools (DES, 1978), noted that history was mostly absent in infant classes, patchy in the mid-primary years, and inconsistently taught in the upper-juniors. It further noted that resources were often poor, with teachers often relying on an uncritical use of television and radio programs, while work outcomes often included great swathes of indiscriminate copying from reference books (DES, 1978, pp. 72–75). It further noted the need for improved planning at the whole school level, and specialist subject leadership; it also argued that a "framework is required to provide some ordering of the content being taught" (DES, 1978, p. 73), in order to provide greater coherence and consistency throughout the primary sector.

Evidence for the dangers of indiscriminate enquiry work in history, yet also its potential, can also be found in subsequent official reports: 'History in the Primary and Secondary Years' (HMI, 1985) was arguably something of a blue-print for pedagogy that influenced the later NC, but it did note that even in the best classrooms the new forms of history were often "historically weak" and "erratic" and "generally unsatisfactory" (HMI, 1985, p. 41). The 1989 HMI report, 'The Teaching Learning of History and Geography' (HMI, 1989), was generally equally critical of cross-curricular and enquiry-based work. The report noted the lack of consistent coverage, indiscriminate and highly individual content choices, and the work outcomes that often "consisted of little more than copying notes and illustrations" (HMI, 1989, p. 10). The report concluded that only one in five history lessons were satisfactory or better (HMI, 1989). The Inspectorate certainly had more independence than subsequent regulatory bodies, and so reports from this time cannot be dismissed easily. However, a careful scrutiny of the reports reveals that the weaknesses reported were often due to poor professional standards, including a lack of teacher subject knowledge allied to weak, or absent, planning and preparation, and low expectations for pupil outcomes; and that these weaknesses would have resulted in poor opportunities for learning whatever the pedagogical approach adopted.

The counter-evidence in support of active, investigatory approaches, in secondary school settings with skilled and resourceful specialist teachers, there is an opportunity to review Shemilt's (1980) SCHP evaluation project. Shemilt's report summarized one of the very few examples of a large scale research project that compared an experimental group directly with a control group whilst controlling for as many variables as possible. It researched several hundred students in 18 schools aged between 13–16 years over a three-year period (1976–79) who took history as an examination subject. The pupils were therefore older than the remit of this chapter, but the other conditions were satisfied: the schools who adopted the SCHP units of work aimed to increase pupil participation in their own learning and encouraged them to engage with higher levels of historical reasoning. The SCHP units were predominately based on investigatory approaches which included interpretation of historical evidence, but crucially covered the same content areas in preparation for external examinations (GCE O level and CSE) as the control groups taught through traditional, passive forms of pedagogy.

Students within the evaluation were controlled for age, gender, intelligence, and included some measures of social class and home background. The main aim was to assess historical understanding, "conceptual attainment," through a range of second-order, organizing concepts, such as causality. There was also an attempt to capture differences in attitudes towards history. Although judicious in the reporting of the findings, noting for example how important measures of intelligence and social class remain, the experimental group exceeded the control group in every respect, particularly an appreciation of the nature of historical enquiry. However, understanding did not translate as completely into work outcomes, particularly written examination responses, where Shemilt noted thinking often remained juvenile and inchoate.

Particularly stark, give the argument for the importance of developing criticality, 75% of learners in the experimental group rated history harder than mathematics compared to 12% from the control group, thus indicating that a comprehensive insight into the nature and intellectual challenge of historical understanding was gained. Genuine historical knowledge cannot be acquired easily, but it is arguably more likely to emerge from a synthesis of formal and informal pedagogical approaches, as suggested in this chapter, compared with traditional and formal teaching methods alone. And as Shemilt's study indicated, at the very least the acquisition of knowledge was not harmed by investigatory approaches. In conclusion, students and teachers have much to gain by synthesizing the formal and informal, namely enhancing traditional forms of knowledge acquisition with investigatory and participatory forms of pedagogy.

REFERENCES

Bevir, M. (1994). Objectivity in History. *History and Theory, 33*, 328–344.
Boffey, D. (2013). Historians attack Michael Gove over 'narrow' curriculum. *The Guardian.* The Guardian PLC.
Bourdieu, P. (1986). The forms of capital. In J. Richardson (Ed.), *Handbook of theory and research for the sociology of education* (pp. 241–258). Greenwood.
Bruner, J. (1960). *The process of education.* Harvard University Press.

Investigatory Approaches to the Teaching and Learning of History • **63**

CACE. (1967). Children and their primary schools: A report (Plowden report). In DES (Ed.). HMSO.

Cannadine, D., Keating, J., & Sheldon, N. (2011). *The right kind of history: Teaching the past in twentieth-century England.* Palgrave Macmillan.

Collingwood, R. G. (1939). *An autobiography.* Oxford University Press.

Collingwood, R. G. (1946). *The idea of history.* Oxford University Press.

Coltham, J. B., & Fines, J. (1971). *Educational objectives for the study of history (Historical Association pamphlet, 35).* The Historical Association.

Counsell, C. (2000). Historical knowledge and historical skills: A distracting dichotomy. In J. Arthur & R. Phillips (Eds.), *Issues in history teaching* (pp. 54–71). Routledge.

Cunningham, P. (1988). *Curriculum change in the primary school: Dissemination of the progressive ideal.* The Falmer Press.

DES. (1978). Primary education in England: A survey by HM Inspectors of Schools. HMSO, 224.

DES. (1989). *National curriculum: History working group.* Interim report. HMSO.

DES. (1990). *National curriculum: History working group.* Final report. HMSO.

DES.(1991a). *History in the national curriculum (England).* HMSO.

Dewey, J. (1966). *Democracy and education: An introduction to the philosophy of education.* Collier-Macmillan.

DFE. (1995). *History in the national curriculum* (England). HMSO.

DfE. (2013). *The national curriculum in England: Key Stages 1 and 2 Framework document.* HMSO.

DfEE. (1999). *The national curriculum: Handbook for primary teachers in England: Key stages 1 and 2.* HMSO.

Douch, R. (1970). Local history. In M. Ballard (Ed.), *New movements in the study and teaching of history* (pp. 105–115). Indiana University Press.

Elton, G. (2002). *The practice of history.* Blackwell.

Emmet, E. R. (1964). *Learning to philosophise,* Longmans.

Evans, R. J. (1997). *In defence of history.* Granta Books.

Evans, R. J. (2013). Michael Gove's history wars. *The Guardian.* The Guardian PLC.

Evans, R. J. (2019). The demented Dalek. *London Review of Books, 41,* 1–7.

Fines, J., & Nichol, J. (1997). *Teaching primary history—Nuffield primary history project.* Heinemann Educational Publishers.

Giddens, A. (1998). *The third way: The renewal of social democracy.* Polity Press.

Gilead, T. (2005). Reconsidering the roots of current perceptions: Saint Pierre, Helvetius and Rousseau on education and the individual. *History of Education, 34,* 427–439.

Gove, M. (2009). What is education for? Speech by Michael Gove MP to the RSA.

Guyver, R. (1997). National curriculum history: Key concepts and controversy. *Teaching History, 88,* 16–20.

Hirsch, E. D. (1988). *Cultural literacy: What every American needs to know.* Vintage Books.

HMI. (1985). *History in the primary and secondary years: An HMI view.* In DES (Ed.). HMSO, 65.

HMI. (1989). The teaching and learning of history and geography (Aspects of Primary Education). In DES (Ed.). HMSO, 41.

Lee, P. J. (1991). Historical knowledge and the national curriculum. In R. Aldridge (Ed.), *History in the national curriculum* (pp. 39–65). Bedford Way Series: Institute of Education, University of London.

Lee, P. J., & Shemilt, D. (2004). A scaffold, not a cage: Progression and progression models in history. *Teaching History, 113,* 13–23.

Loader, P. (1993). Historically speaking. *Teaching History, 71,* 20–22.

Newsom, J. (1963). *Half our future: A report of the Central Advisory Council for Education* (England). London: HMSO.

Oakeshott, M. (1962). The activity of being a historian. In T. Fuller (Ed.), *Rationalism in politics and other essays.* Liberty Press.

Oakeshott, M. (1972). Education: The enjoyment and the frustration. In T. Fuller (Ed.), *The voice of liberal learning: Michael Oakeshott on education* (pp. 89–109). Yale University Press.

Percival, J. W. (2020). *Understanding and teaching primary history.* Sage Publications.

Phillips, R. (1998a). *History teaching, nationhood, and the state: A study in educational politics.* Cassell.

Phillips, R. (1998b). Contesting the past, constructing the future: History, identity and politics in schools. *British Journal of Educational Studies, 46,* 40–53.

Phillips, R. (2000). Government policies, the state and the teaching of history. In J. Arthur & R. Phillips (Eds.), *Issues in the teaching of history* (pp. 10–23). Routledge.

Popper, K. R. (1966). *The open society and its enemies.* Routledge & Kegan Paul.

Rogers, P. J. (1980). *The new history: Theory into practice.* Historical Association.

Rogers P. J. (1987). History—The past as a frame of reference. In C. Portal (Ed.), *The history curriculum for teachers* (pp. 3–21). The Falmer Press.

Ryan, A. (1970). *The philosophy of the social sciences.* Macmillan.

Ryle, G. (1949). *The concept of mind.* Penguin Books Ltd.

SCG (1972). *Exploration man: An introduction to integrated subjects.* Schools Council Publications/Oxford University Press.

Schwab, J. J. (1964). The structure of the disciplines: Meanings and significances. In G. Ford & L. Purgo (Eds.), *The structure of knowledge and the curriculum.* Rand McNally.

Sharma, S. (2020). Obama says Biden victory won't be enough to stop US 'truth decay'. *The Independent.* Independent Digital News & Media Ltd.

Sheldon, N. (2011). *The national curriculum and the changing face of school history, 1988–2010.* History.ac.uk

Sheldon, N. (2012). Politicians and history: The national curriculum, national identity, and the revival of the national narrative. *History, 97,* 256–271.

Shemilt, D. (1980) *Evaluation study: Schools council history 13–16 project.* Holmes McDougall.

Stephens, W. B. (1977). *Teaching local history.* Manchester University Press.

Turner-Bissett, R. (2005). *Creative teaching: History in the primary curriculum.* David Fulton Publishers.

Vygotsky, L. S. (1978). *Mind in society (The development of higher psychological processes),* Harvard University Press.

Vygotsky, L. S., & Kozulin, A. (1986). *Thought and language.* MIT Press.

Young, M. (2008). From constructivism to realism in the sociology of the curriculum. *Review of Research in Education, 32,* 1–28.

Young, M., & Muller, J. (2013). On the powers of powerful knowledge. *Review of Education, 1,* 229–250.

CHAPTER 5

CREATIVITY AND DESIGN-BASED MARKERSPACES INFLUENCES ON STUDENT MOTIVATION IN ENGINEERING EDUCATION

Micaha Dean Hughes

STUDENT MOTIVATION AND CREATIVITY IN STEM

Engineering is part of a well-known integration of domain-specific learning in STEM, which is an acronym for science, technology, engineering, and mathematics [education]. Engineering is largely perceived as a hard science, with emphasis on high levels of math and science proficiency and little celebration for creative flexibility (Tolbert & Daly, 2013). Over the past decade, some researchers have called for the use of a new acronym— "STEAM"—which blends art education strategies into the otherwise no-frills world of STEM education. Engineering is consistently viewed as a top career field, with high earning potential and societal (and in the case of many students, parental) praise for a "good career" (McGee et al., 2016).

Motivation and Engagement in Various Learning Environments, pages 65–76
Copyright © 2024 by Information Age Publishing
www.infoagepub.com
All rights of reproduction in any form reserved.

These extrinsic motivators can drive students into engineering even when those students lack interest in the subject itself. In contrast, students with high levels of intrinsic motivation toward academic participation in engineering choose to engage with the content because they find enjoyment, challenge, or curiosity in it.Engineering content is commonly perceived as inflexible, difficult, and uncreative, typically due to its adherence to the "hard" topics of math and science, which leads to little room for student choice (Godwin, Potvin, Hazari, & Lock, 2016). However, this misconception overlooks one of the core concepts of engineering: the engineering design process. The engineering design process involves several steps, including defining the problem, imagining possible solutions, creating a prototype, testing the prototype (experimentation), and revising and improving the design. The engineering design process clearly involves creativity: students must use creative problem-solving strategies in order to develop novel solutions to problems, which is a primary definition of engineering.

Even though professional engineers are required to exercise creativity in design processes, there is currently very little support for engineering educators to incorporate creativity into the traditional engineering curriculum. This lack of support for creative integration is partially a result of the perception of engineering as a purely technical field. However, this dry attitude toward engineering has had consequences, including lower female participation, as women typically seek helping and creative professions due to stereotypical influences on interest in those areas (Calabrese Barton, Tan, & Rivet, 2008). An analysis of literature on the incorporation of creativity into the engineering curriculum will allow for examination of potential benefits to student motivation when we add the "A" to STEM, to create "STEAM." In light of design-based makerspaces popping up in colleges of engineering across the nation, this research is timely and relevant to the field of engineering education.

The purpose of the current study is to investigate the potential benefits of incorporating creativity into the engineering curriculum and its effect on student motivation. Research questions include:

1. Is creativity a malleable skill or an innate ability, and how does the research in this area affect its application to engineering education?
2. How does adding opportunities for creativity to engineering education classrooms influence student motivation?
3. How does the introduction of creative, design-based "makerspaces" impact these findings?

THEORETICAL FRAMEWORK: SELF-DETERMINATION THEORY

To explore the current research on this question, this study employs an integrative literature review. By framing this study using self-determination theory (Deci & Ryan, 2000), the current study summarizes and synthesizes the research on creativity in the engineering classroom and its effects on student motivation. Further, this chapter will highlight any potential gaps in the literature while providing direction for future research in the field. By synthesizing the current literature, engineering educators and researchers will be able to more easily identify functional integrations of creativity into engineering classrooms and understand the effects of creative activities on STEM student motivation. This literature review will examine potential benefits of incorporating creative thinking activities and strategies into engineering classrooms through the lens of self-determination theory.

Motivation is a widely-researched topic in education. A curious question on motivation in engineering education might be: What makes students more or less likely to engage with, give effort to, and persist in engineering? Self-determination theory (SDT, Deci & Ryan, 1985) is a useful theoretical framework for decoding what makes students take part—or not—in engineering as an academic subject and subsequently, as a career. SDT differentiates types of motivation based on the individual reasoning or goal behind the action or task (Deci & Ryan, 2000). Deci and Ryan made a two-pronged distinction between motivation types: *intrinsic* motivation and *extrinsic* motivation. Intrinsic motivation is internally driven by the individual, and refers to doing something because of personal interest or enjoyment (Schunk et al., 2013). On the other hand, extrinsic motivation is driven by an external reward or "separate outcome" that is a result of task participation (Deci & Ryan, 2000). Self-determination theory specifically examines three underlying psychological needs that drive human behavior: competence, autonomy, and relatedness. According to Deci (1985), "intrinsic motivation is the human need to be competent and self-determining in relation to the environment." The need for autonomy, or the ability to have choice and control over personal decisions, is evident in the classroom. By allowing students to have *choice* in activities that ultimately lead to competence, intrinsic motivation can be increased. Both intrinsic and extrinsic motivation are important to understand when considering what makes students engage with engineering, and neither is more important than the other.

Literature bridging the gap between self-determination theory, engineering education, and creativity is scant. Amabile (1983) developed the idea of the "intrinsic motivation hypothesis of creativity," hypothesizing that people are more creative when in situations that increase intrinsic motivation rather than decrease it (Ryan & Deci, 2017). This assumption opens the door to new research in engineering education: what constitutes and defines engineering creativity? And, how can K–20 engineering instructors develop classroom environments where creativity is infused and intrinsic motivation toward creativity is encouraged and supported?

CURRENT TRENDS IN THE LITERATURE

Perceptions of Engineering as "Non-Creative"

Engineering is generally perceived as a field of study and work that is low in creativity. Many of us are likely familiar with the image of a coder (computer programr, or computer scientist) alone in a dark room typing away behind a computer screen, or a man at a construction site wearing a hardhat and safety glasses. This is reflected by a simple web search of "engineer," where the first image in the results is the image seen in Figure 5.1. In these images are a hidden message: while engineering is a top-earning (and therefore societally worthy) profession, it is dull and repetitive, requires high math and science achievement, and does not value "soft skills" like communication and creativity (Valenti et al., 2016).

This is not fully accurate. Successful engineers need to develop communication skills to effectively engage with colleagues and project stakeholders, creativity skills to develop

and innovate new ideas and solutions for problems, and resiliency to overcome failure in design attempts (Hirudayaraj et al., 2021). In recent years, there has been a nationwide push from educators and STEM professionals to incorporate arts and creativity into STEM education in order to more comprehensively meet core curricular standards. The acronym STEM (science, technology, engineering, and mathematics) is widely known, and its child acronym, STEAM (science, technology, engineering, arts, and mathematics) has been a major source of debate in education circles since its inception (Mejias et al., 2021).

Figure 5.1   Image of an engineer (from *U.S News & World Report*, 2022).

Creativity and Design-Based Markerspaces Influences • **69**

Supporters of "STEAM" advocate for the integration of arts into the STEM curriculum for many reasons. One of the most salient rationales is acknowledging the value of incorporating arts education into STEM education as a way of engaging more students in STEM fields and increasing student curiosity about learning in general through creativity (Foley and Kazerounian, 2007). In order to fully grasp the importance of adding arts to STEM education for the purpose of increasing creativity into the engineering curriculum, we must first understand creativity as a concept and its potential applications.

What is Creativity?

Creativity is a complex concept that is not simple to define or assess, the challenges of which are reflected in existing scholarship. What makes someone "creative?" Creativity is an idea for which many researchers have developed definitions, and yet none are all-encompassing. Amabile (1983) described the difficulty in defining creativity as a problem of defining the root criterion. Existing definitions of creativity are historically defined "in terms of the creative process, the creative person, and the creative product" (Amabile, 1983, p. 358). In modern society, creativity is mostly defined in terms of the creative product: artists produce artwork, musicians produce music, and so on and so forth (Amabile, 1983). For the purposes of this review and its implications, we will utilize the definition of creativity as a creative process, as defined by Sternberg (2008): redefining problems to seek out solutions, taking sensible risks, accepting failure as part of the process, confronting obstacles when challenging the status quo, tolerating ambiguity, and continuing to grow intellectually (Menendez and Min, 2019).

In thinking about creativity as a *skill process* instead of an *individual trait*, it is easier to interpret that creativity is not just an innate ability: the creative process can be taught and refined through opportunities that allow students to experience it. According to Menendez and Min (2019), "to foster creativity, students must be provided with authentic opportunities to inspire motivation and reflection" (p. 143). If creativity is to be incorporated into the STEM curriculum, teachers must be willing and able to include opportunities for students to authentically engage in the creative process in the classroom.

Creativity in Engineering

The Next Generation Science Standards (NGSS) integrate engineering concepts into science curriculum. Part of these standards is the understanding of the *Engineering Design Process*, which is shown in Figure 5.2 in a

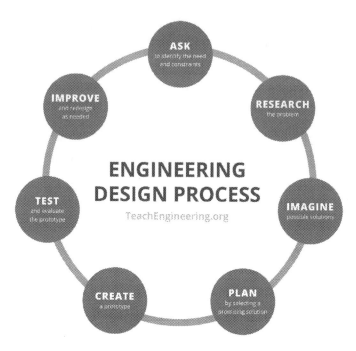

Figure 5.2 The engineering design process (*Source:* TeachEngineering.org)

graphic from the popular engineering education website teachengineering.org, which is hosted by the University of Colorado-Boulder and is funded by the National Science Foundation (NSF). Teachengineering.org states that the Engineering Design Process is "a series of steps that guides engineering teams as we solve problems. The design process is iterative, meaning that we repeat the steps as many times as needed, making improvements along the way as we learn from failure and uncover new design possibilities to arrive at great solutions" (TeachEngineering, 2022).

The addition of the Engineering Design Process as a grounding model in national science and engineering education standards illustrates that the creative process can be easily found in engineering. Through *inspiration* to "imagine possible solutions" to problems, in being *motivated* to innovatively create a prototype, and in *reflecting* on the effectiveness of the solution, I challenge the field to consider that engineering is, at its core, a creative field (Menendez and Min, 2019). In using the engineering design process, students can take those "hard" subjects of math and science and creatively apply what they have learned in the traditional classroom to real-world applications. Using this discussion as a framework, how can educators create learning environments that enable and encourage authentic experiences for infusing creativity into engineering?

Teacher Self-Efficacy in Teaching Engineering and Impacts on Creative Integration

Despite the addition of the Engineering Design Process into NGSS, there remains a dearth of engineering in K–12 schools. Notably, most teacher education programs in the United States. do not offer engineering education as a pathway, which has led to low teacher self-efficacy, or the "belief that their actions as a teacher can have a positive impact on student learning" in engineering education (Coppola, 2019, p. 162). Largely due to the lack of opportunities for preservice teachers to engage with engineering concepts during teacher training, compounded by the notion that teachers avoid teaching "content they are not comfortable teaching," K–12 students have limited opportunities to engage with engineering at all, let alone with enough time and intention to meaningfully participate in the creative process (Wendt et al., 2015; Brophy et al., 2008; Hammack & Ivey, 2017; Kang, Donovan, & McCarthy, 2018). These findings are not a secret; the literature regarding the lack of teacher preparation in engineering education is well-defined. Meanwhile, the national push to increase the number of postsecondary students who enter the engineering field continues (Handelsman and Smith, 2016). Pressure to increase the number of STEM-seeking high school graduates without adequate support for K–12 educators to teach the full integration of STEM subjects does not lend to adding another concept—the arts—to the core curriculum. Without teacher support to teach the engineering design process in its entirety, *including allowance for student exploration in engineering and ample time for reflective practices*, it is no surprise that students, and society, will fail to see engineering as a creative field.

Makerspaces as a STEAM Integration Compromise

The gap between teacher self-efficacy and the ability to engage students creatively in engineering can be diminished by intermediary experts and spaces where students can exercise their design skills. In an effort to better equip students to complete project-based learning assignments in engineering, K–12 schools, colleges, and universities have implemented student "makerspaces," or interactive spaces with equipment for students to engage with engineering learning hands-on, such as power tools, 3D printers, laser cutters, prototyping tools, and more (Nadelson et al., 2020). These makerspaces are usually community-style lab spaces where students can congregate and work on projects, either together or independently. While the literature on makerspaces heavily skews toward postsecondary education, makerspaces already have a significant existence in K–12 education. During the coronavirus pandemic, K–12 schools with access to prototyping tools were reporting student-led initiatives to develop items for healthcare workers. For example, students at a STEM-focused high school in Chattanooga, Tennessee worked together to address the personal protective equipment (PPE) shortage by using 3D printers to create more than 4,000 headbands to secure face shields for doctors and nurses (Stone, 2020). This is an excellent example of the engineering design process at work: students identified a problem, researched to find a solution, tried and tested their solution, and then reflected on how well it worked to solve the issue. In using makerspaces to enact the engineering design process, students reflexively engage in creative problem solving, while potentially filling gaps that are left from traditional science and mathematics coursework (Nadelson et al., 2020).

Another middle school in Cleveland County, North Carolina, utilized "MakerBot" printers to develop additional PPE and ear guards for healthcare workers (Stone, 2020). When asked how the initiative was developed, the science teacher stated: "My mom is a nurse, and she was telling me how they have to wear the same masks day in and day out because they don't have enough materials... then I started seeing the same thing in pictures from all over the country, and I realized just how big a problem this was" (Stone, 2020). In that excerpt, the science teacher expressed heightened self-efficacy in teaching engineering, as a response to strong identity alignment with a problem that could be solved by using the engineering design process. Because of her close personal connection with a nurse (her mother), the teacher was *self-motivated* to engage her classroom in producing a solution. And because the coronavirus pandemic affected all of society, the students in her class were likely just as motivated to assist in contributing to a positive solution.

Competence, Autonomy, and Relatedness (Self-Determination Theory)

Self-determination theory tells us that motivation is driven by three psychological needs: competence, autonomy and relatedness. These three psychological needs drive motivation—a student's motivation to engage in engineering or not is directly affected by the student's feelings of competence, autonomy and relatedness (Schunk et al., 2013). The use of makerspaces in engineering education is an extension or application of project-based learning (PBL) in STEM education. By assigning a real-world application problem for which students are expected to develop a solution, they engage in more authentic learning experiences, which leads to a more positive connection with all three of the psychological needs of self-determination theory.

Further, community-style, "come-as-you-please" makerspaces allow for student-directed projects. While teachers may assign students activities to work on in makerspaces, the inclination of makerspaces as open and free-range academic spaces indicate that students have more control over their own academic interests and the personal development therein. As Nadelson et al. (2020) found in their study, "there is an expectation that if students are supported to be in control of their learning and learning activities, they are more likely to be motivated and therefore persist in their learning" (p. 5).

DISCUSSION AND IMPLICATIONS

Underneath the debate between "STEM" and "STEAM" acronyms, there is a real problem that is affecting the perception of and participation in engineering education. The "art," the *creativity*, is missing from K–12 engineering education, at the very least in communication. The lack of calling engineering what it is and what it could be—creative—has had significant consequences on the identity alignment and motivation of students in relation to engineering as a potential field of study. K–12 teacher training and administrative support in developing engineering self-efficacy for educators has led to a shortage of opportunities for students to engage with the engineering design process, despite its incorporation into the Next Generation Science Standards (NGSS). However, the addition of makerspaces has opened a gap of opportunity for educators with less training in engineering education to help students engage with the engineering design process through student-led, teacher-supported, and possibly community-engaged, project-based learning activities. By allowing students the flexibility to participate in solving real-world problems with creative, self-driven applications, K–12 teachers can create classroom spaces that help students build creative processing skills through the engineering design process. Over time, these skills allow for activation of the three psychological needs of self-determination theory—competence, autonomy, and relatedness—in engineering design, and in turn, can increase motivation for pursuing engineering as a career.

There were several limitations in the development of this chapter. First, the lack of a singular definition of creativity is a hindrance to effectively sorting and understanding existing literature on the topic of creativity in engineering education. Second, this chapter assumes several notions: (a) that most K–12 teachers have little to no formal training in *engineering* education, (b) that most educational makerspaces are open, community-style spaces, and (c) that all K–12 students have equal access to quality math and science instruction and technology to fill instructional gaps. Despite these liberties, it is to be understood that these assumptions are not fully accurate or even all-inclusive of what is happening in K–12 STEM classrooms. Some teachers do have formal training in engineering education, not all schools have makerspaces, and if they do, they may be closed to only students enrolled in certain courses, and it is a certainty that not all students have equal access to quality math and science instruction. It is imperative to emphasize that despite the fact that it was not comprehensively addressed in this chapter, the field must address inequitable access to integrative STEM content, activities, and spaces for K–12 students, in order to truly broaden participation in postsecondary engineering.

Future research could take several different directions. First, researchers should examine how K–12 teachers use makerspaces, including what types of activities occur in the spaces, how much freedom students have or do not have to develop and follow their own projects, and how reflection occurs at the end of the engineering design process. Second, there is a sufficient amount of literature on the language surrounding engineering as a field of study—words like "hard," "non-creative," and "boring"—and the impacts of this dialogue on engineering participation (especially for minoritized students), but there is room for scholarship in investigating creativity as a mitigation tool for negative dominant discourse. Third, Harron and Hughes (2018) developed the title of "spacemakers" for these educators who work in makerspaces—future research should build upon this concept to evaluate how spacemakers influence student motivation in engineering. Fourth, researchers should investigate how much support inservice teachers have to gain knowledge in engineering concepts as well as experience in engineering education teaching strategies, and what programs are being developed to reduce this issue at the preservice teacher level. Finally, and perhaps most importantly, more research is needed on who has access to these spaces and how more students can obtain access to learning environments like engineering makerspaces for creative engagement. Not all students have the ability to access prototyping machines or power tools in the middle of their school day in order to deepen their understanding of math and science concepts (which they may or may not be learning in their classroom spaces). Identifying gaps and improving student access to makerspaces, these academic areas that can boost student motivation toward engineering as a vehicle for creative problem solving, is crucial to the continued increase of students who have interest in pursuing the field.

REFERENCES

Allina, B. (2018). The development of STEAM educational policy to promote student creativity and social empowerment. *Arts Education Policy Review, 119* (2), 77–87.

Amabile, T. M. (1983). The social psychology of creativity: A componential conceptualization. *Journal of Personality and Social Psychology, 45*(2), 357.

Creativity and Design-Based Markerspaces Influences • 75

Brophy, S., Klein S., Portsmore M., & Rogers, C. (2008). Advancing engineering education in P–12 classrooms. *Journal of Engineering Education 97*(3), 369–387.

Calabrese B., & Tan A. (2010). "We Be Burnin! Agency, Identity and Science Learning." *Journal of the Learning Sciences, 19*(2), 187–229.

Conradty, C., Sotiriou, S. A., & Bogner, F. X. (2020). How creativity in STEAM modules intervenes with self-efficacy and motivation. *Education Sciences, 10*(3), 70.

Deci, E. L., & Ryan, R. M. (2002). *Handbook of self-determination research.* University of Rochester Press.

Foley, S., & Kazerounian, K. (2007). Barriers to creativity in engineering education: A study of instructors and students' perceptions. In *International Design Engineering Technical Conferences and Computers and Information in Engineering Conference* (Vol. 48051, pp. 539–555).

Engineering Design Process. TeachEngineering.org. (n.d.). Retrieved from https://www.teachengineering.org/populartopics/designprocess

Handlesman, J., & Smith, M. (n.d.). *STEM for all.* National Archives and Records Administration. Retrieved from https://obamawhitehouse.archives.gov/blog/2016/02/11/stem-all

Harron, J. R., & Hughes, J. E. (2018). Spacemakers: A leadership perspective on curriculum and the purpose of K–12 educational makerspaces. *Journal of Research on Technology in Education, 50*(3), 253–270.

Hennessey, B. A. (2000). Self-determination theory and the social psychology of creativity. *Psychological Inquiry, 11*(4), 293–298.

Hirudayaraj, M., Baker, R., Baker, F., & Eastman, M. (2021). Soft skills for entry-level engineers: What employers want. *Education Sciences, 11*(10), 641.

Kim, Nam Ju (2017). Enhancing students' higher order thinking skills through computer-based scaffolding in problem-based learning. All Graduate Theses and Dissertations. 5488. https://digitalcommons.usu.edu/etd/5488

Margot, K. C., & Kettler, T. (2019). Teachers' perception of STEM integration and education: a systematic literature review. *IJ STEM Ed 6*, 2 https://doi.org/10.1186/s40594-018-0151-2

Mativo, J. M., & Park, J. (2012). Innovative and creative K–12 engineering strategies: implications of pre-service teacher survey. *Journal of STEM Education: Innovations and Research, 13*(5).

McGee, E. O., White, D. T., Jenkins, A. T., Houston, S., Bentley, L. C., Smith, W. J., & Robinson, W. H. (2016). Black engineering students' motivation for PhD attainment: Passion plus purpose. *Journal for Multicultural Education, 10*, 167–193.

Mejias, S., Thompson, N., Sedas, R. M., Rosin, M., Soep, E., Peppler, K., . . . & Bevan, B. (2021). The trouble with STEAM and why we use it anyway. *Science Education, 105*(2), 209–231.

Menéndez, A. F., & Min, H. (2019). Embracing Creativity in K–12 Engineering Pedagogy. In *Promoting language and STEAM as human rights in education* (pp. 141–149). Springer.

Nadelson, L. S., Villanueva, I., Bouwma-Gearhart, J., Soto, E., Lenhart, C., Youmans, K., & Choi, Y. H. (2020). Student perceptions of and learning in makerspaces embedded in their undergraduate engineering preparation programs. In *Zone 1 Conference of the American Society for Engineering Education* (Vol. 30699).

Nazzal, L. J., & Kaufman, J. C. (2020). The relationship of the quality of creative problem solving stages to overall creativity in engineering students. *Thinking Skills and Creativity, 38*, 100–734.

NGSS Lead States. (2013). *Next generation science standards: For states, by states.* The National Academies Press.

Perkins Coppola, M. (2019). Preparing preservice elementary teachers to teach engineering: Impact on self-efficacy and outcome expectancy. *School Science and Mathematics, 119*(3), 161–170.

Ryan, R. M., & Deci, E. L. (2000). Intrinsic and extrinsic motivations: Classic definitions and new directions. *Contemporary Educational Psychology, 25*, 54–67.

Schunk, D. H., Meece, J. R., & Pintrich, P. R. (2013). *Motivation in education* (4th ed.). Pearson Education.

Smith, H. M. (2018). *Exploring students' internal motivation for engineering creativity: Creative confidence and the arts* (Order No. 10999550). Available from ProQuest Dissertations & Theses Global. (2125432315).

Smith, S., Talley, K., Ortiz, A., & Sriraman, V. (2021). You want me to teach Engineering? Impacts of recurring experiences on K–12 teachers' engineering design self-efficacy, familiarity with engineering, and confidence to teach with design-based learning pedagogy. *Journal of Pre-College Engineering Education Research, 11*(1), 2.

Saorín, J. L., Melian-Díaz, D., Bonnet, A., Carrera, C. C., Meier, C., & De La Torre-Cantero, J. (2017). Makerspace teaching–learning environment to enhance creative competence in engineering students. *Thinking Skills and Creativity, 23*, 188–198.

Sternberg, R. J. (2008). The WICS approach to leadership: Stories of leadership and the structures and processes that support them. *The Leadership Quarterly, 19*(3), 360–371.

Stone, A. (2022, April 18). *K–12 schools leverage 3D printers to make a difference.* Technology Solutions That Drive Education. Retrieved from https://edtechmagazine.com/k12/article/2020/05/k-12-schools-leverage-3d-printers-make -difference

US News & World Report. (2022). *Civil engineer ranks among best jobs of 2022.* Retrieved from https://money.usnews.com/careers/best-jobs/civil-engineer

Valenti, S. S., Masnick, A. M., Cox, B. D., & Osman, C. J. (2016). Adolescents' and emerging adults' implicit attitudes about STEM careers: "Science is not creative." *Science Education International, 27*(1), 40–58.

Webb, D. L., & LoFaro, K. P. (2020). Sources of engineering teaching self-efficacy in a STEAM methods course for elementary preservice teachers. *School Science and Mathematics, 120*(4), 209–219.

Wendt, S., Isbell, J. K., Fidan, P., & Pittman, C. (2015). Female teacher candidates' attitudes and self-efficacy for teaching engineering concepts. *International Journal of Science in Society, 7*(3).

CHAPTER 6

TEACHING SCIENCE IN CHARTER SCHOOLS

Facilities, Equipment, and Teacher Preparation

Pamela M. Huff and M. Gail Jones

Although there has been a significant expansion in the types of public and private pre-college schools around the world, little is known about the science education programs in these schools. This perspective is essential due to teachers' critical role in orchestrating science instruction to achieve effective science teaching, which has a great impact on student science learning. This study explored secondary charter school science teachers' perceptions of their school's science programs. With the use of the *Science Laboratory Classroom Facility and Science Instructional Materials Survey* and a semi-structured interview protocol, secondary charter school science teachers' access to laboratory equipment, safety equipment, facilities, use of science standards, and instructional autonomy were examined. One hundred and six science teachers were surveyed about their experiences, and a sub-sample of 21 teachers was interviewed. Results showed that many teachers

Motivation and Engagement in Various Learning Environments, pages 77–95
Copyright © 2024 by Information Age Publishing
www.infoagepub.com
All rights of reproduction in any form reserved.

reported lacking laboratory equipment, safety equipment, and facilities for optimal science teaching. While teachers conveyed that autonomy was a significant positive aspect of teaching science in charter schools, teachers also said that isolation and a lack of professional development were negative aspects. All teachers reported using either state or national science standards to develop their science curricula. These findings suggest that effective science teaching in charter schools could be strengthened by adequately funding science laboratories, equipment, and safety equipment and engaging science teachers in program and facilities planning. Many countries have laws and regulations allowing publicly funded and privately managed pre-college schools. In different parts of the world, these schools are given different names; for example, in Sweden, Chile, the Netherlands, and New Zealand, these schools are called partnership schools; in England, they are called free schools; and in the United States, they are called charter schools (Jha & Buckingham, 2015).

In the United States, charter schools are independent, public schools of choice, funded from both tax dollars and private donations (Bankston et al., 2013) and run by private administrations either as for-profit or non-profit entities with mostly non-unionized teachers (De Luca, 2018). The charter school movement has rapidly exploded in the United States, yet very little is known about the nature of charter school science programs. Charter schools do not receive funding to cover the cost of facilities but instead receive a per-student allotment that is expressly prohibited from being used for the cost of the facility (Rebarber, 2014). As a result, charter schools are often housed in non-traditional school buildings where space is at a premium (Hassel, 2001), which limits dedicated space for science classes, potentially impacting specialized laboratory space that has a central and distinctive role in science education (Hofstein & Kind, 2012). Charter schools have opened in shopping malls, business office spaces, and churches, among other venues (Hassel, 2001). The rapid development of the charter school movement has required these new schools to adapt quickly without the benefit of traditional school infrastructure to support laboratories and materials for science instruction (Arsen, 2012).

One of the most fundamental ways students experience science education is through learning in science laboratory classrooms. The laboratory is seen as having a central and distinctive role in science education (Hofstein & Lunetta, 2004; Hofstein & Mamlok-Naaman, 2007), and, as a learning environment, the laboratory is unique to science disciplines (White, 1988). Given the critical need for future citizens who can participate in societal science decisions, providing high-quality instruction to all students is essential (DeBoer, 2000).

Greenwald, et al., 1996, using meta-analytic methodology, found that a broad range of resources were positively related to student outcomes

(Greenwald, et al., 1996). More specifically, it has been reported that adequately equipped science laboratories with traditional laboratory and safety equipment, as well as adequate science teaching facilities, are related to effective science teaching and student outcomes (Godomsky, 1971; Hellman et al., 1986; Tanner, 2000; Cheryan et al., 2014). Moreover, students who had access to a wide range of science resources, including textbooks, technology, and hands-on materials, had higher levels of achievement and engagement in science compared to students who had limited resources (Stohr-Hunt, 1996; Freedman, 1997; Geleta, 2018). On the other hand, a lack of science resources can have a negative impact on student learning and performance. Students who had limited access to science resources, such as textbooks and laboratory equipment, or who had science resources which were not optimally utilized, had lower levels of achievement in science compared to their peers who had access to a wider range of optimized resources (Dahar & Faize 2011; Musah & Umar, 2017; Galeta, 2018).

Teacher autonomy and flexibility are key features of charter schools. The ability of teachers to make independent decisions in their classrooms has been a significant part of the definition of teacher autonomy (Feldmann, 2011). The merits of teacher autonomy have been well documented in the literature, including job satisfaction, teacher professionalism, and teacher motivation (Gurganious, 2017). Although some studies have addressed the laboratory equipment, facilities, teacher autonomy, and teaching standards in public schools (Banilower et al., 2013), little is known about these in charter schools. This study addressed this need by exploring the types of materials, resources, laboratories, facilities, and autonomy available to science teachers in charter schools. Furthermore, this investigation examined science instruction and the advantages, and constraints teachers report while teaching science in a charter school.

RESEARCH QUESTIONS

This study focused on critical elements of science instruction within the context of the steadily growing presence of charter schools. These critical elements include adequately-equipped science laboratories that increase students' problem-solving abilities (Godomsky, 1971) and increase student science achievement (Boghai,1979); essential laboratory safety equipment that is critical to decreasing high rates of accidents and student and staff injury (Hellman et al.,1986); adequate science teaching facilities that impact teacher and student outcomes as well as teacher recruitment and retention (Tanner, 2000); science teaching standards that enhance student science skills and understanding (Bybee, 2014); and teacher autonomy that supports teachers' capacity to address students' needs, teacher satisfaction, recruitment and retention (Gurganious, 2017).This research sought to examine charter school science programs and to answer the following questions:

1. What laboratory equipment is available to science teachers in charter school classrooms?
2. What laboratory safety equipment is available to teachers in charter school science classrooms?
3. What types of facilities are used by charter schools for science instruction?
4. What are the guiding science standards for charter school curricula? and 5) What are charter school science teachers' perceptions of autonomy for science instruction?

THEORETICAL FRAMEWORK

Science education programs in charter schools are highly variable and are influenced by financial, resource, and facility constraints that operate as a complex social process involving many stakeholders. This study is situated within two theoretical frameworks to address this complexity. The first, Bourdieu's theory of cultural capital, focuses on how people use cultural knowledge to undergird their place in the societal hierarchy (Bourdieu, 1987). Archer et al. (2015) extended this theory to include "science capital" as science-related forms of cultural and social capital. Here science laboratories and resources are examined as a form of science capital. The second theoretical perspective applied in this study is that of Vygotsky's activity theory and extended by Engeström (Vygotsky, 1978; Holt & Morris, 1993), which provides a lens with which to examine human activity (Hasan, 2014), specifically science education programs directed by science teachers (Figure 6.1). This study is focused on the perceptions of science teachers, given their critical role in shaping instruction within charter schools.

METHODS

This descriptive case study utilized a mixed method, explanatory sequential design (Creswell & Creswell, 2017), examining charter school secondary science teachers' perceptions of science capital resources and affordances and constraints of science education programs in charter schools. Secondary charter school science teachers were recruited from charter schools located in a state in the Southeast region of the United States. The study began with a quantitative online survey of 105 participants, followed by interviews of 21 of these science teachers. A mixed methodology was used

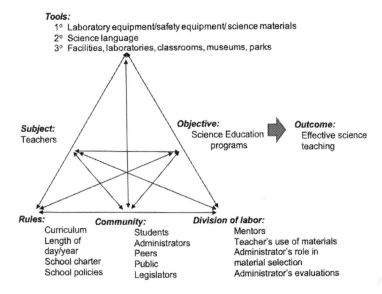

Figure 6.1 Activity theory science capital model applied to charter school science instruction. *Note:* Tools are designated as primary, secondary, and tertiary (adapted from Vygotsky, 1978).

with a two-phase structure that included collecting quantitative data first, followed by qualitative data as described below (Creswell & Creswell, 2017). The study was designed so the qualitative interview data could provide details and context for the quantitative results. As such, the results of the two phases are tied together to clarify any confusion, contradictory, or unusual survey responses (as suggested by Creswell & Creswell, 2017). The human ethics Institutional Review Board (IRB) approved the survey in 2020.

Quantitative Phase

Survey Participants

Science teachers were recruited through various means to participate in the study. First, a list of available 6th–12th grade charter school science teachers' email addresses was compiled using information published on the state's website. Second, during a charter school yearly conference, science teachers were given the link to the online survey and invited to participate in this study. Third, science teachers associated with the university's graduate school program were contacted and asked to take the online survey if they taught in a charter school. Finally, an email to all charter school principals in the state was sent with a request for science teachers to participate

82 ▪ P. M. HUFF and M. GAIL JONES

TABLE 6.1 Teacher Demographics

Characteristic	Survey		Interview	
	n	%	*n*	%
Gender				
Female	70	72	15	71
Male	27	28	6	29
Race				
White	86	91	18	85
Black	6	6	1	5
Asian	2	2	1	5
Mixed	1	1	1	5
Ethnicity				
Non-Hispanic	90	93	20	95
Hispanic	7	7	1	5
School locations				
Suburban	50	51	9	43
Rural	32	32	5	24
Urban	17	17	7	33

in the study. A sample of 140 teachers agreed to participate in the survey via email. Initially, 132 participants responded to the survey. After cleaning the data as described below, 105 survey participant responses were analyzed. Table 6.1 lists the demographics of the participants. These data are consistent with the findings from the 2012 National Survey of Science and Mathematics Education (Banilower et al., 2013), in which 70% of traditional public school middle school science teachers and 54% of high science teachers were female, and 90% were white with the majority of teachers being between 26 and 47 years old. The schools for the survey participants were 51% suburban, 32% rural, and 17% urban; for the interview participants, 43% were suburban, 24% rural, and 33% urban.

The survey participants had a wide range of teaching experience, as 25% of teachers had 1–5 years of teaching, followed by 24% with 6–10 years of teaching experience, 21% with 11–15 years of teaching experience, 19% with 16–20 years of teaching experience, and 10% with 21 plus years of teaching experience. These participants taught various middle and high school courses and had different education levels (Table 6.2).

The survey participants were also certified in many areas within science and non-science disciplines, as shown in Table 6.3.

Teaching Science in Charter Schools · **83**

TABLE 6.2   Survey Participants' Courses Taught and Educational Background

Characteristic	Middle school only		High school only		Total	
	n	%	*n*	%	*n*	%
Courses Taught						
General Science	45	94	5	10	50	48
Life Science/Biology	9	19	19	39	28	19
Physical Science/Chemistry	10	21	33	67	43	41
Earth/Environmental Science	9	19	28	57	37	35
College Degree Education General	42	69	35	56	62	59
Natural Sciences	28	46	41	66	39	37
Other	5	8	5	8	4	4

Note: The last column, "Total," for courses taught is not always additive to the prior groups as it indicates all courses, including those who teach classes in both middle and high school.

TABLE 6.3   Survey Participant Certification Areas

Certification area	*n*	%
General Science	79	75
Biology/life science	31	30
Chemistry	18	17
Earth Science	15	14
Environmental Science	15	14
Physics	15	14
Other	38	36
Elementary Ed	1	1
Mathematics	7	6
Special Education	1	1
School administration	1	1
Pharmacology	1	1
Agriculture education	1	1
Social studies	1	1
National Board	1	1
Lateral entry	10	10

Note: Some teachers were certified in multiple areas.

Survey Questionnaire Development

The Science Laboratory survey used was developed specifically for this study. The survey items were designed to measure teachers': access to laboratory and safety equipment; types of school facilities; use of science standards; status of licensure; extra-curricular science programs (e.g., Science Olympiad, science clubs); instructional spaces; and teacher autonomy, including the amount of control over course goals, selecting curriculum materials, selecting content, topics, the timeline of topics, and skills to be taught. Initially, a pool of 80 items was developed based on existing instruments in the literature (Banilower et al., 2018). The initial 80-item draft survey underwent multiple iterations of review for clarity and validity. Pilot testing of the survey was conducted with four teachers to establish the face validity of scores on the instrument, to provide an initial evaluation of the targeted constructs of the items, and to improve questions, format, and instructions (Creswell & Creswell, 2017). The final survey consisted of 35 multiple choice questions and three open-ended questions asking teachers to comment on the advantages and disadvantages of teaching science in a charter school and their perception of the quality of science education in their charter school.

Data Collection

Survey data were collected online using a Qualtrics platform (Qualtrics, LLC, Provo, Utah). The data included responses to 35 multiple choice questions and three open-ended questions. Survey responses were removed if data were incomplete ($N = 26$). The final data set included responses from 105 participants.

Data Analysis

Frequencies, means, and standard deviations for age, gender, ethnicity, years of experience, science course types, school location (rural, urban, or suburban), and years of experience in a charter school on the survey were determined. Other analyses included frequencies of available laboratory equipment; safety equipment; types of school facilities; science standards used; status of licensure; extra-curricular science programs (e.g., Science Olympiad, science clubs); instructional spaces; and the amount of autonomy. The open-ended question responses were coded for themes identified in the research questions (Elliott, 2018), and the frequencies of those themes were tabulated.

Qualitative Phase

Interview Participants

Twenty-one of the 105 survey participants volunteered to be interviewed, as discussed below (Table 6.1 lists their demographics). The mean teacher age of the interview participants was 45 years (*SD* 11). The interviewees' mean number of years teaching was 15 (*SD* 11). All the interview participants held bachelor's degrees, 19% held a master's degree in teaching, 10% held a master's degree in science, and 5% held a non-education master's degree. Of the 21 teachers, 34% were not licensed to teach science, while the remaining 66% held a teaching license. Forty-three percent of the schools were suburban, 33% urban, and 24% rural.

Interview participants taught in a variety of school types that included college preparatory (53%), whole child (43%), and arts (4%). Title 1 schools, defined as a school receiving federal money to assist economically and educationally disadvantaged children, were uncommon (24%). The student populations at each school ranged from 200 to 2,000, with 67% of the teachers teaching in schools with 500–1000 students. The class size ranged from 10 to 30, with 62% of teachers having 21to 25 students per class. Most (71%) of teachers taught in schools with 1 to 5 science teachers. Finally, the number of teachers in the school who taught the same content as the participants ranged from 1 to 8, with 71% of the participants being the only teacher teaching a specific subject. The interview participants taught a wide range of courses (Table 6.4).

Interview Protocol Development

The interview protocol was designed for this study based on the research questions. The protocol was reviewed by a panel of science educators and scientists for clarity and validity and revised (Franklin & Ballan, 2001). It was then piloted for further clarity of language and meaning, and additional items were modified or removed based on feedback. The final protocol consisted of 65 open-ended questions related to classroom laboratory equipment, laboratory safety equipment, laboratory spaces, instructional materials, teaching credentials, professional development opportunities, and extra-curricular science opportunities for students in charter schools.

Data Collection and Data Analysis

Individual interviews lasting from 45 to 60 minutes were conducted and recorded using the Zoom video conferencing platform. The interviews were transcribed for analysis. The interview transcripts and open-ended survey responses were then reviewed for consistency and analyzed using a two-step

TABLE 6.4   Courses Taught by Interview Participants

Course type	Middle school		High school		Total	
	n	%	*n*	%	*n*	%
General science	5	24	0	0	5	24
Life science/Biology	3	14	5	24	8	38
Physical science/Physics	0	0	7	33	7	33
Earth/Environmental science	1	5	5	24	6	29

86 ▪ P. M. HUFF and M. GAIL JONES

deductive analysis approach (Hayes & Sliwa, 2003). First, an extensive literature review of science programs in traditional public schools to identify elements within those programs that promote effective science teaching within
the scope of study research questions was conducted, and then the use of
study constructs defined by the research questions were used to identify the
effective teaching elements in charter schools (Canary, 2019). A second coder
coded 30% of the interview data using the predetermined codes as described
below, and subsequently, the inter-rater reliability score was calculated as described by Miles and Huberman (2014). The interrater reliability score for
the survey's open-ended questions was 95% and for the interviews was 90%.

RESULTS

Charter School Science Classrooms Laboratory Equipment

While high school and middle school teachers reported having access to
a wide range of laboratory equipment, many teachers lacked basic laboratory equipment such as lab tables, sinks, and balances (Table 6.5). High

TABLE 6.5 Non-Accessible Laboratory Equipment

Items	Middle school (N = 47)		High school (N = 45)		All (N = 105)	
	n	%	n	%	n	%
Laboratory tables	16	34	4	9	20	28
Electric outlets	1	2	0	0	1	2
Sink	5	11	1	2	6	13
Gas	47	100	23	49	59	53
Fume hood	47	100	18	38	57	55
Balances	7	15	18	38	8	17
Probes (Temp., pH, etc.)	16	34	16	34	47	46
Thermometers	3	6	0	0	8	17
Microscopes	1	2	0	0	44	43
Glassware	4	9	0	0	4	4
Chemicals	9	19	1	2	12	12
Disposable materials	2	2	1	2	4	4
Meter stick	0	0	0	0	2	2
Stopwatch	0	0	1	2	4	4

Note: Non-accessible means the items are not in the classroom or the building. "All" includes
the responses of teachers who teach K–12 who were excluded from the middle and high
school only calculations.

Teaching Science in Charter Schools • **87**

school teachers tended to have greater access to equipment such as fume hoods and gas than middle school teachers.

In response to the open-ended question on the survey, "Do you have any challenges teaching science in a charter school," 45 of 96 (47%) teachers specifically raised the lack of resources and equipment compared to traditional public school science laboratory resources as an issue. Specifically, these charter school science teachers reported having to find free lesson plans using readily available materials for their laboratory experiments from multiple sources. When planning laboratory experiments for their students, teachers had to often borrow equipment from other departments in the school, which created another level of complexity. Also, they often had to purchase laboratory materials out of "their own pocket," which led many teachers to scour stores for inexpensive materials. Finally, they stated that the lack of resources in science laboratories required "developing creative approaches" for laboratory experiments, but it came as a possible cost to the students because "students get less exposure to more traditional laboratory practices."

Charter School Science Classrooms Laboratory Safety Equipment

Many teachers reported that they did not have access to basic safety equipment (Table 6.6). Remarkably, 19% of high school teachers did not have safety showers, 13% did not have spill control materials, and 13% of middle school teachers did not have access to fire extinguishers. High

TABLE 6.6 Non-Accessible Laboratory Safety Equipment						
	Middle school (*N* = 47)		High school (*N* = 45)		All (*N* = 105)	
Items	*n*	%	*n*	%	*n*	%
Safety Goggles	4	9	0	0	4	4
Gloves	8	17	2	4	12	11
Apron/coats	23	49	5	11	32	31
Eye Wash station	18	38	0	0	20	19
Shower	24	51	9	19	37	35
Spill Control	29	62	6	13	39	37
First Aid kit	3	6	0	0	3	3
Fire Extinguisher	6	13	0	0	6	6

Note: Non-accessible refers to items not available in the classroom or in the building. "All" includes the responses of teachers who teach in grades K–12 who were excluded from the middle and high school only calculations

school teachers reported having more safety equipment than middle school teachers.

In response to the open-ended question on the survey and the interviews, "Do you have any challenges teaching science in a charter school?" many teachers stated that there was a lack of basic science safety equipment in their laboratories as compared to traditional public schools where funding for safety is more available. However, due to the lack of adequate safety equipment, many teachers identified with the statement of one teacher, "we have to be creative inside the classroom [meaning that not all experiments are doable]."

Charter School Facilities

The responses to the open-ended questions from the survey revealed that most science teachers taught in buildings designed for charter school purposes. However, 16% reported teaching in repurposed buildings. These included facilities that were initially designed for a shopping mall, a bank, business offices, a car dealership, a cotton mill, a rehabilitation center, a warehouse, and a church. In response to the open-ended question, "Do you face challenges teaching science in charter schools?" 15 of 96 (16%) of the participating teachers specifically raised inadequate facilities, including limited laboratory space, no dedicated laboratory space, and sharing laboratory space, as issues.

Similarly, during the interviews, teachers emphasized these inadequate space issues and reiterated their frustrations at not being consulted about the laboratory spaces as they were being designed and constructed in new and repurposed buildings. For example, when asked about science spaces used outside the classroom due to lack of adequate space, some teachers stated that external spaces such as parks, hiking trails, streams, and other natural areas near the schools are utilized. Finally, all teachers reported using state or national science standards to inform lesson plans.

Teacher Autonomy

Teachers rated their level of control as complete, moderate, or none for a series of survey questions about instructional autonomy. Specifically, teachers were asked, "How much control do you have over each of the following for science instruction in your classes?" for determining course goals and objectives; selecting curriculum materials such as textbooks/modules; selecting content, topics; and skills to be taught; selecting the sequence in which topics are covered; determining the amount of instructional time to spend on each topic, and selecting teaching techniques.

The majority (83%) reported complete control over the instruction sequence, and 79% noted they had complete control over instructional time and techniques. These results were further supported by 80 of 93 respondents (83%) who emphasized instructional flexibility, control, and autonomy in the survey's open-ended question, "Do you think as a science teacher working in a charter school that you have unique instruction opportunities that traditional science teachers do not have? If yes, what?" As one teacher succinctly stated, "[I have] control over what I teach, when I teach, and how I teach. I am treated as the professional expert that I am!"

Instructional autonomy was also a significant finding in the open-ended interview items. Teachers emphasized that in public schools they were overwhelmed by constant demands on their time from their administrators. In contrast, one charter school science teacher reported, "I feel like they [the charter school administrators] trust me. They will say, 'you are the chemistry expert here. You do what you think is going to prepare our students well for college and what you think will prepare them well for science down the road.'"

DISCUSSION

In summary, this study showed that secondary science teachers in charter schools face challenges related to lack of science equipment, safety equipment, and inadequate school facilities. Although charter schools offer pedagogical flexibility to teachers, it became clear that there were additional constraints on science teachers that had negative influences on them. The survey and interview data revealed the shared and different aspects of perceptions and experiences with teaching science in a secondary charter school. These results should be interpreted within the context of the unique structures and framework of charter schools, and the following sections discuss these issues in more detail.

Laboratory Equipment

While the premise for establishing charter schools was to enhance educational innovation and pedagogical flexibility (Lubienski, 2003), their unique structure, which often lacks extensive funding for equipment, may harm science programs. Because of the limited resources, many science teachers in this study indicated that they are teaching with sub-optimal laboratory equipment, but are attempting to "make science work" with their equipment. However, the results showed that many teachers needed more equipment to implement their science programs fully. In most cases, these deficiencies were more significant than those seen in traditional public schools. For example, a recent study of traditional United States public school science resources by the National Survey of Science and Mathematics Education NSSME+ (Banilower et al., 2018) showed that middle science teachers had greater access to balances and probes compared to charter middle school science teachers as discovered in this study (96% vs. 85%, 68% vs. 66%, respectively). Similar findings were found in high schools where science teachers had greater access to balances, fume hoods, and gas burners (97% vs. 62%, 82% vs. 62%, and 82% vs. 51%). These deficiencies significantly limit the type of experiments available to students and burden teachers to design assignments that can be performed with the available equipment.

This lack of adequate equipment requires alternative workarounds, such as using online and other teaching tools and doing wet labs without a sink. These deficiencies also limit the students' capacities to learn how to do experiments and their exposure to the complete science experience. The concern for students includes the potential to enter post-secondary education without meaningful experiences in science laboratories. This study shows that many charter school students do not have the opportunity to experience one of the most fundamental ways traditional secondary school students learn science: learning and exploring in science laboratory classrooms (Hofstein & Lunetta, 2004).

Laboratory Safety Equipment

As described above, a surprisingly large number of teachers reported the absence of safety items, including spill control (37%), showers (35%), eyewash stations (19%), and fire extinguishers (6%). Most of these items are considered essential to conducting safe laboratory experiments (Richmond, 2000). Conducting science experiments without proper safety equipment puts everyone at risk and is a medical and legal liability. Because of the lack of safety equipment, science teachers described their lesson preparation and implementation as "creative" as they struggled to teach the content while maintaining a safe environment. The negative consequences from a student's perspective are that they do not gain the science safety skills to handle caustic or flammable materials safely. Again, this presents a problem for students who have not been exposed to proper safety precautions when they enter a science field in college, as they will have to learn the safety procedures and the course content.

Facilities

While minimum facility standards have been defined for public schools (Safe schools facility planner–NC, 2013), 16% of the teachers reported using repurposed and other buildings that resulted in what they thought were inadequate spaces for science teaching. Other researchers have noted that teachers' access to good facilities is key to fostering inquiry (Ainley, 1981). To adapt to these limitations, teachers reported often holding classes outside or in other facilities. The full range of implications of outdoor science instruction are unknown but could have both advantages and disadvantages, depending on the topic being taught (Glackin & Jones, 2012). Having the flexibility as a science teacher to take students outside and allow them to experience the outdoors, using their sense of wonder and curiosity where lab space is limited, could be advantageous as it allows for exploration of science alfresco.

Science Standards for Curriculum Development

The combined survey and interview data revealed that all science programs within the study used state or national science standards for their curriculum development. This was surprising because charter schools are not mandated to use science standards (Wixom, 2018). Next Generation Science Standards (NGSS) and state science standards stress skills such as communication, collaboration, inquiry, problem-solving, and flexibility, which work together to give students a comprehensive understanding of science and support best practices in science education (North Carolina Department of Public Instruction, 2018; National Research Council, 2012).

Autonomy

One of the significant themes that emerged from the survey and the interviews was teachers' autonomy in the charter school environment. For example, an overwhelming majority of the teachers reported being able to tailor their approaches to students as a major area of importance and as the primary advantage of teaching in a charter school. This autonomy gave teachers control over what, when, and how they taught, and a sense of being respected as professionals. Regarding implications, teacher autonomy has been reported to be important for job satisfaction, teacher retention, and quality of life, and may impact the quality of student learning (Malloy & Wohlsetter, 2003).

CONCLUSIONS AND IMPLICATIONS

Limitations

This study had several limitations. These include a relatively small number of participants from a single state that limited sampling and statistical power, as well as possible non-representative perspectives of the self-selected sample. It is important to note that these data were collected at a single period in time during the COVID-19 pandemic. Furthermore, the survey and interviews elicited teachers' reported experiences with teaching science in a charter school and have the typical limitations of phenomenological data.

Implications

This study highlights the unique challenges that secondary charter school science teachers face regarding laboratory equipment, laboratory safety equipment, and school facilities. The study also documented the important role of autonomy as reported by science teachers in charter schools. Overall, charter school science teachers reported that they enjoyed their work, felt appreciated, and could be flexible in completing their missions. However, many reported needing more equipment, better facilities, and more consultation during the planning stages of facility and laboratory design and science equipment budgets to meet their unique needs. The results indicate that charter school stakeholders could better support high-quality science instruction by adequately funding science laboratory equipment and safety equipment and engaging science teachers in program and facilities planning. Given today's technologies, collaborations among charter schools could allow for more accessible partnerships and the development of mutual support systems that would improve their science teachers' experiences. These proposals, taken together, should enhance current and future investments in charter schools. Therefore, it is imperative that teachers, who are the mainstay of our science programs, are supported with appropriate safety equipment, laboratories, and materials. More research into how charter schools' administrators and other stakeholders make financial decisions for science programs is needed to inform school planning and administration better.

Access to high-quality resources and technology, as well as the opportunity to engage in hands-on learning, can enhance student engagement, motivation, and achievement in science. Moreover, a lack of resources can hinder a student's ability to fully participate in the science curriculum and may lead to lower levels of achievement. Thus, the implications of charter school science programs lacking adequate laboratory equipment, safety equipment, and facilities are becoming greater as the number of students affected increases. As stated earlier, the global school choice movement, which includes charter schools in the United States, is growing. In an era when science is increasingly under fire, science education is vitally important as it allows students to participate in the scientific method, learn critical thinking skills, and practice these skills in a classroom environment with peers and mentors. Every effort must be made to ensure that all students have the opportunity to experience effective, well-equipped science programs so that future citizens may have the skills available to make decisions on societal issues based on sound scientific reasoning.

REFERENCES

Ainley, J. (1981). The importance of facilities in science education. *European Journal of Science Education, 3*(2), 127–138.

Archer, L., Dawson, E., DeWitt, J., Seakins, A., & Wong, B. (2015). "Science capital": A conceptual, methodological, and empirical argument for extending bourdieusian notions of capital beyond the arts. *Journal of research in science teaching, 52*(7), 922–948.

Arsen, D., & Ni, Y. (2012). Is administration leaner in charter schools? Resource allocation in charter and traditional public schools. *education policy analysis archives, 20*, 31.

Banilower, E., Smith, P., Malzahn, K., Plumley, C., Gordon, E., & Hayes, M. (2018). Report of the 2018 NSSME+. *Horizon Research, Inc.*

Bankston III, C. L., & Caldas, S. J. (2015). *Controls and choices: The educational marketplace and the failure of school desegregation.* Rowman & Littlefield.

Boghai, D. M. (1979). A comparison of the effects of laboratory and discussion sequences on learning college chemistry.

Bourdieu, P. (1987). What makes a social class? On the theoretical and practical existence of groups. *Berkeley journal of sociology, 32*, 1–17.

Bybee, R. W. (2014). NGSS and the next generation of science teachers. *Journal of science teacher education, 25*(2), 211–221.

Canary, A. (2019, January 19). *How to analyze interview transcripts in qualitative research.* https://www.rev.com/blog/analyze-interview transcripts-in-qualitative-research

Cheryan, S., Ziegler, S. A., Plaut, V. C., & Meltzoff, A. N. (2014). Designing classrooms to maximize student achievement. *Policy Insights from the Behavioral and Brain Sciences, 1*(1), 4–12.

Creswell, J. W., & Clark, V. L. P. (2017). *Designing and conducting mixed methods research.* Sage Publications.

Creswell, J. W., & Creswell, J. D. (2017). *Research design: Qualitative, quantitative, and mixed methods approaches.* Sage Publications.

Dahar, M. A., & Faize, F. A. (2011). Effect of the availability and the use of science laboratories on academic achievement of students in Punjab (Pakistan). *European Journal of Scientific Research, 51*(2), 193–202.

DeBoer, G. E. (2000). Scientific literacy: Another look at its historical and contemporary meanings and its relationship to science education reform. *Journal of Research in Science Teaching: The Official Journal of the National Association for Research in Science Teaching, 37*(6), 582–601.

De Luca, B. M., & Wood, R. C. (2016). The charter school movement in the United States: Financial and achievement evidence from Ohio. *Journal of Education Finance, 41*(4), 438–450.

Elliott, V. F. (2018). Thinking about the coding process in qualitative data analysis. *The Qualitative Report, 23*(11).

Franklin, C., & Ballan, M. (2001). Reliability and validity in qualitative research. *The handbook of social work research methods, 4*(273–292).

Freedman, M. P. (1997). Relationship among laboratory instruction, attitude toward science, and achievement in science knowledge. *Journal of Research in Science Teaching: The Official Journal of the National Association for Research in Science Teaching, 34*(4), 343–357.

Feldmann, D. (2011). The Maintenance of Teacher Autonomy in a Policy-Driven Era. *Mid-Western Educational Researcher, 24*(1), 2–4.

Geleta, K. (2018). The Upshot of availability and utilization of Science laboratory inputs on students' academic achievement in high school Biology, Chemistry and Physics in Ilu Abba Bora Zone, Southwestern Ethiopia. *International Journal of Scientific and Research Publications, 8*(9), 298–307.

Glackin, M., & Jones, B. (2012). Park and learn: improving opportunities for learning in local open spaces. *School Science Review, 93*(344), 105–113.

Godomsky, Stephen F., Jr. (1971). Programmed instruction, computer-assisted performance problems, open ended experiments and student attitude and problem solving ability in physical chemistry laboratory. *Dissertation Abstracts, 31*(11), 5873A.

Greenwald, R., Hedges, L. V., & Laine, R. D. (1996). The effect of school resources on student achievement. *Review of educational research, 66*(3), 361–396.

Gurganious, N. (2017). *The relationship between teacher autonomy and middle school students' achievement in science* (Doctoral dissertation, Walden University).

Hasan, H., & Kazlauskas, A., (2014). "Activity Theory: who is doing what, why and how." *Faculty of Business–Papers* (Archive). 403. https://ro.uow.edu.au/buspapers/403

Hassel, B., & Page, B. (2001). Charter School Facilities: Report from a National Survey of Charter Schools.

Hayes, K. R., & Sliwa, C. (2003). Identifying potential marine pests—a deductive approach applied to Australia. *Marine Pollution Bulletin, 46*(1), 91–98.

Hellman, M. A., Savage, E. P., & Keefe, T. J. (1986). Epidemiology of accidents in academic chemistry laboratories. Part 1. Accident data survey. *Journal of Chemical Education, 63*(11), A267.

Hofstein, A., & Kind, P. M. (2012). Learning in and from science laboratories. In *Second international handbook of science education* (pp. 189–207). Springer.

Hofstein, A., & Lunetta, V. N. (2004). The laboratory in science education: Foundations for the twenty-first century. *Science Education, 88*(1), 28–54.

Hofstein, A., & Mamlok-Naaman, R. (2007). The laboratory in science education: the state of the art. *Chemistry Education Research and Practice, 8*(2), 105–107.

Holt, G., & Morris, A. (1993). Activity theory and the analysis of organizations. *Human Organization, 52*(1), 97–109.

Jha, T., & Buckingham, J. (2015). Charter schools, free schools, and school autonomy. *Policy: A Journal of Public Policy and Ideas, 31*(2), 52–58.

Lubienski, C. (2003). Innovation in education markets: Theory and evidence on the impact of competition and choice in charter schools. *American Educational Research Journal, 40*(2), 395–443.

Malloy, C. L., & Wohlstetter, P. (2003). Working conditions in charter schools: What's the appeal for teachers? *Education and Urban Society, 35*(2), 219–241.

Miles, M. B., Huberman, A. M., & Saldaña, J. (2014). *Qualitative data analysis: A methods sourcebook.*

Musah, A., & Umar, A. A. (2017). Effects of availability and utilization of biology laboratory facilities and students' academic achievements in secondary schools in Yobe State, Nigeria. *International Journal of Innovative Social & Science Education Research, 5*(2), 1–8.

National Research Council. (2012). *A framework for K–12 science education: Practices, crosscutting concepts, and core ideas.* National Academies Press.

North Carolina Department of Public Instruction. (2018). *North Carolina charter school report.* https://www.dpi.nc.gov/students-families/alternative-choices/charter-schools

Qualtrics, I. (2013). *Qualtrics.* Provo, UT.

Rebarber, T., & Zgainer, A. C. (2014). *Survey of America's charter schools.* The Center for Education Reform. https://www. edreform. com/wp-content/uploads/201, 4(02).

Richmond, V. (2000). *Safety in science teaching.* Retrieved January 22, 2022, from https://www.doe.virginia.gov/instruction/science/middle/safety_science_teaching.pdf

Safe Schools Facility Planner–NC. (2013). Retrieved January 16, 2022, from https://files.nc.gov/dpi/documents/schoolplanning/safe-schools-facility-planner.pdf

Stohr-Hunt, P. M. (1996). An analysis of frequency of hands-on experience and science achievement. *Journal of Research in Science Teaching: The Official Journal of the National Association for Research in Science Teaching, 33*(1), 101–109.

Tanner, C. K. (2000). The influence of school architecture on academic achievement. *Journal of Educational Administration.*

Vygotsky, L. S. (1978). *Mind in society: The development of higher psychological processes.* Harvard University.

White, R. T. (1988). *Learning science.* Basil Blackwell.

Wixom, A. (2018) *Charter schools: What rules are waived for charter schools? 50 State Comparison.* Education Commission of the States. Retrieved January 22, 2022, from https://www.ecs.org/charter-school-policies/

CHAPTER 7

MOTIVATIONS FOR TECHNOLOGY USE AMONG MOTHERS OF YOUNG CHILDREN

Tech as a Tool for Self-Determination

Catherine Noonan

MOTHERHOOD, TECHNOLOGY, AND SOCIAL SUPPORT

The current study aims at investigating mothers of young children (MOYC) and their motivations for technology use. Specifically, this literature review will explore how and why mothers engage in technology use and how it relates to their perceptions of social support and their ability to balance their multiple roles. Motivations for technology use will be viewed through the lens of Self-Determination Theory (SDT). A secondary aim of the research study is to better understand the motivations for technology use of mothers of young children of children with special needs (MOYC-SN). The primary research questions are as follows:

Motivation and Engagement in Various Learning Environments, pages 97–118
Copyright © 2024 by Information Age Publishing
www.infoagepub.com
All rights of reproduction in any form reserved.

98 • C. NOONAN

1. What motivates MOYC to engage with technology?
2. How do MOYC perceive that technology either enhances or detracts from their systems of social support?
3. Do motivations surrounding technology use differ between MOYC and MOYC-SN?

In the current study, *technology* is defined as: "the use of science in industry, engineering, etc., to invent useful things or to solve problems" (Merriam-Webster, 2022). *Development* refers to both aspects child development (motor development, cognitive development, academic growth, etc.) as well as personal development or self-actualization for mothers (i.e., making progress toward one's perceived life purpose). Finally, *motivation* is defined as: "the process whereby goal-directed activities are instigated and sustained" (Schunk, Meece, & Pintrich, 2019, p. 43).

Maternal Health and Support Systems

Across diverse categories (mothers, fathers, single, or married) parents experience a lack of social support, however mothers (57%) are more likely to say they have inadequate support than fathers (39%) (Zero to Three, 2018). According to the American Psychological Society (APA) social support is defined as:

> The provision of assistance or comfort to others, typically to help them cope with biological, psychological, and social stressors. Support may arise from any interpersonal relationship in an individual's social network, involving family members, friends, neighbors, religious institutions, colleagues, caregivers, or support groups. It may take the form of practical help (e.g., doing chores, offering advice), tangible support that involves giving money or other direct material assistance, and emotional support that allows the individual to feel valued, accepted, and understood (APA Dictionary of Psychology, 2022).

Thus, social support can be received on an individual or familial level (such as from a partner), on a workplace level, a community level, or even a national or global level. Social support can be delivered in any of the following forms: emotional, instrumental, informational, or appraisal. Emotional social support includes expressions of "empathy, love, trust, and caring," while instrumental support refers to "tangible aid and service" (Glanz, Rimer, & Viswanath, 2008). Informational social support includes "advice, suggestions, and information" and appraisal social support refers to "information that is useful for self-evaluation" (Glanz, Rimer, & Viswanath, 2008). Expectant mothers value social support, and its presence in their lives relieves anxiety about childbirth and contributes to greater comfort with and

Motivations for Technology Use Among Mothers of Young Children ▪ **99**

knowledge about parenting (Backstrom et al., 2017). Greater social support can also reduce rates of post-partum depression (Leahy-Warren, McCarthy, & Corcoran, 2012; Negron et al., 2012). Negron et al. (2012) found that mothers in the post-partum period regarded instrumental social support as critical to their physical and emotional recovery. In contrast, however, cortisol levels (indicating stress) in low-income, minority mothers were not mediated by social support (Hollenbach, 2019).

Linking Maternal Wellbeing to Child Wellbeing

Prior research has identified links between support systems, maternal health, and child developmental outcomes. Hether et al. (2016), for example, notes that pregnant women who receive limited social support face higher risks of negative health consequences, including preterm birth of their child, a condition which has potentially serious and lifelong health implications for the child. Prior work has also demonstrated that women who face stressful conditions show decreased engagement with their children, which in turn, has negative developmental consequences for those children (Atif et al., 2015; Baudry et al., 2017; Bennett et al., 2016; Clowtis, 2016; Costa et al., 2021; Hether, 2016; Litzelman, 2011; USDHHS 2006; Vaz et al., 2021). Bennett et al. (2016) found that risk of maternal mental health disorders was associated with child psychosocial and cognitive development delays as well as growth delays in first year of life (lasting up to 8 years old). Atif et al. (2015) noted that maternal depression was associated with a host of poor developmental outcomes for children, including preterm birth, low birth weight, poor infant growth and cognitive development, higher rates of health concerns such as increased diarrheal illnesses, lower rates of immunization, and earlier cessation of breastfeeding, which has implications for long-term health.

Maternal Health—Vulnerable Groups

Mothers from vulnerable groups experience even higher levels of stress that impact their health and the development of their children. Children of teen mothers often experience a negative developmental ecology due to unstable parental relationships, financial hardship, and lower levels of maternal education, and demonstrate lower levels of cognitive development as infants, greater difficulty with school entry, and lower academic achievement (Baudry et al., 2017). Hollenbach and colleagues (2019) found that low-income, minority mothers' hair cortisol levels and their children's hair cortisol levels were linked. Clowtis and colleagues (2016) found that higher

100 • C. NOONAN

levels of maternal stress predicted poorer child health outcomes and lower levels of maternal-child engagement. Lower levels of maternal–child engagement, in turn, predicted higher biological markers of stress in children (Clowtis et al., 2016). Hispanic children represent the largest percentage of children who are considered obese in the United States, which may be partially related to societal stressors (financial hardship, limited health literacy, language barrier) that impact their mothers (Bender, 2014).

Mothers of Children With Disabilities

Extensive research has found that stress is higher and quality of life lower among parents of children with disabilities, including autism and intellectual disability (Vaz et al., 2021; Litzelman et al., 2011) and children with chronic illnesses (Litzelman et al., 2014). Parents of children with autism and those of parents with intellectual disability both experience higher levels of stress and lower quality of life, and compromised leisure and productivity (Vaz et al., 2021). Parents of children with co-occurring autism and intellectual disability spend significantly less time preparing meals or socializing with friends and require higher need for respite care (Vaz et al., 2021). Litzelman et al. (2011) found that increased caregiving burden among parents caring for children with cancer or brain tumors resulted in greater stress and poorer mental quality of life, and suggested that future interventions be directed at improving parental quality of life through reduction of caregiver burden and stress. In a separate study, Litzelman and colleagues (2014) found that informal (unpaid) caregivers of children or adults with disabilities or chronic illness experienced worse mental Health Related Quality of Life (HRQoL) than non-caregivers. Those with higher levels of caregiving strain, as measured by Caregiver Strain Index, reported worse mental and physical HRQoL (Litzelman et al., 2014). Among Mongolian families of children with disabilities, Kim and colleagues (2020) found that, "the burden of care was highest when the monthly family income was low, when the perceived health status of the caregiver was unhealthy, when the degree of disability of the children with intellectual disabilities was severe, and when there was no alternative caregiver"—indicating that financial and logistical supports, as well as caregiver health, have direct impact on family functioning. Kim et al. (2020) noted that, as in many other countries, most primary caregivers (74.1%) were women.

Mothers of children with disabilities who perceive their children as having a high level of disability are also likely to receive less social support, and suffer higher rates of anxiety and depression (Carlson & Miller, 2017). Social support may also shift in response to having a child with a disability: Brandon (2007) found that working mothers of children with disabilities lost personal time but increased time spent engaging socially in response to their new parenting responsibilities. In the same study, fathers' personal time was unchanged after the birth of their children, suggesting that working mothers of children with disabilities seek social support outside of their spousal relationship in response to their increased caregiving demands (Brandon, 2007). Higher levels of social support were found to mediate stresses associated with caregiving for mothers of preschool-aged children with developmental disabilities (Plant & Sanders, 2007).

Working Mothers

Working mothers, especially first-time parents and parents of younger children, experience significant stress, including role stress due to the competing demands of parenting and professional life (Costa et al., 2021). The additional demands of "wife" or "partner" may, somewhat counterintuitively, create additional role stress. Married or cohabiting women (in heterosexual relationships) are more likely to do more housework and sleep less, with no differences in time spent engaging in childcare, than divorced or never-married mothers (Pepin, 2018). Psychological stress due to role stress can in turn impact mental and physical health (Costa, 2021). Internationally, mothers sacrifice physical activity (as well as sleep and leisure activities) to meet the dual demands of parenting and work, suggesting that mothers of young children can experience chronic physical and emotional stress that may endure for years (Craig & Brown, 2017; Craig & Mullan, 2011). Costa et al. (2021) note that "a full-time non-flexible work schedule reduces mother's time with her child, whereas low levels of social support by either her co-workers or partner can result in conflict between work and childcare responsibilities" (p. 4).

Both fathers and mothers suffer time burden and feel stresses because of their multiple roles, which frequently present with conflicting demands (Young, Schieman & Milke, 2013). However, evidence also suggests that working mothers feel this stress most acutely (Pepin et al., 2018; Offer & Schneider, 2011). Mothers who work outside the home face exorbitant childcare costs, the "motherhood penalty" (lower earnings and advancement compared to childless women) in their careers, around-the-clock work schedules, and physical and emotional toll from post-partum recovery, nursing, and separation from their children (Costa et al., 2021; Kahn, García-Manglano, & Bianchi, 2014; Chatterji, 2013; Craig & Mullen, 2011). The motherhood penalty is most extreme when women are raising young children (Kahn, García-Manglano, & Bianchi, 2014), when children's needs for caregiving are most intense. Gender differences exist in both the type of work mothers and fathers provide outside the home and in expectations

102 ▪ C. NOONAN

within the home (Craig & Brown, 2017). Mothers are more likely to fulfill routine and time-bound child and home-related tasks, such as making dinner or school pick-up, while fathers are more apt to provide less regular, time-restricted forms of caregiving and domestic support (for example, taking out the garbage) (Schieman, Ruppanner, Milkie, 2017). Mothers sacrifice sleep, leisure time, and exercise in order to balance the demands of working motherhood (Craig & Mullen, 2011; Pepin et al., 2018). When they can afford it, dual-earner families often rely upon paid support to shift caregiving and domestic workload off parents, particularly mothers (Craig & Mullen, 2011). However, such resources—particularly childcare—have been limited since the onset of the COVID-19 pandemic in the United States (Gordon & Wagner, 2020; Granados, 2020), suggesting that working mothers' burdens may have grown, rather than lessened, in recent years. Not coincidentally, there has also been a simultaneous exodus of women from the paid workforce (Fry, 2022; Cassella, 2021; Cerulo, 2021).

The workplace—including its organizational culture and specific policies—can serve as a facilitator to role reconciliation or a barrier. National policies surrounding work and parenthood also contribute to the developmental ecology of mothers and children (Costa et al., 2021). Male-dominated workplaces may be less amenable to shifting schedules or workloads for working parents (Craig & Brown, 2017) and expectations for working men may be different and less responsive to familial needs, placing additional childcare responsibility on mothers (Craig & Powell, 2011). Changes brought on by the mixture of the virtual office (for some), pre-pandemic work expectations, and loss of childcare may disproportionately impact women (Ammerman & Groysberg, 2020; Cerulo, 2021; Ellengrud & Siegel, 2021; Hsu, 2021). Additionally, some research indicates that mothers and fathers often parent differently, with mothers more likely to feel both internal and external pressure to perform "intensive mothering" that leaves less time and energy for paid work or self-care (Musick, Meier, & Flood, 2016; Rizzo et al., 2012). A lingering pay gap in the United States also causes some families to prioritize the work of the higher paid, typically male, working parent, thereby increasing the burden of other responsibilities on mothers and limiting their professional advancement (Ellengrud & Siegel, 2021; Bateman, 2020; Miller, 2017). Working MOYC, thus, present with significant need for instrumental social support.

Technology, Support, and Working Mothers

The last decade in the United States (U.S.), and particularly the last two years of the COVID-19 pandemic, have been characterized by an infiltration of technology into everyday life (NAEYC & Fred Rogers Center, 2012).

Motivations for Technology Use Among Mothers of Young Children · **103**

Yet mothers' relationship to technology is ambiguous. Despite increased emphasis on supporting women and girls to enter STEM fields, the technology sector of the U.S. economy is still heavily dominated by men—this sector is predominantly male (Richter, 2021) and may represent a source of wage inequality and a culture unfavorable to working mothers (Gonzalez, 2021; Maynard, 2021). According to the Pew Research Center, "women make up a quarter or fewer of workers in computing and engineering, are overrepresented in health-related jobs" (Fry, Kennedy & Funk, 2021). With the transition to online learning during the pandemic, mothers disproportionately took responsibility for facilitating their children's learning and school participation—often at the expense of their own career advancement (Cassella, 2021; Cerulo, 2021). Still other research has suggested that technology—specifically the use of mobile technology—can interfere with maternal engagement during childcare (Beamish, 2019).

Conversely, the shift to work-from-home or telework policies since the pandemic may represent a work-life balance that better supports mothers (Cassella, 2021). Group interventions—including those delivered online—have been shown to be successful at alleviating stress and improving mental health among new mothers, possibly due to creating a new support system and reducing isolation (Baudry et al., 2017; Costa et al., 2021). Some evidence suggests that mothers show a preference to give and receive such support online, which may suggest an avenue for providing caregiver support to mothers (Duggan, 2019). Following the Zika virus outbreak in Latin America, researchers analyzed mothers' use of social media and found that mothers use social media to seek information, celebrate milestones, and find support (Motti, 2020). Hether et al. (2016) examined social support through social network analysis and content analysis of posts via social media platforms for pregnant women and found that women receive primarily informational and emotional support through these platforms. More research is needed to understand why and how MOYC and MOYC-SN experience and use technology in their daily lives, and how interaction with technology either offers or limits social support.

THEORETICAL CONSIDERATIONS AND METHODOLOGY

Significance of Research Topic

Healthcare providers, educators, counselors, and social workers all provide education to families, including MOYC and MOYC-SN. Understanding effective ways to enhance social support systems for children and families can improve delivery of services and outcomes for families, and technology may offer avenues for improving social support. MOYC experience significant demands on their time and energy, and may experience limited social support (Craig & Brown, 2017; Craig & Mullan, 2011; Costa et al., 2021; Young, Schieman & Milke, 2013). These conditions can negatively impact MOYC's health, their career advancement, and the development of their children (Baudry et al., 2017; Clowtis et al., 2016; Costa et al., 2021; Musick, Meier, & Flood, 2016; Rizzo et al., 2012. These conditions are often intensified for mothers caring for children with special needs (Vaz et al., 2021; Litzelman et al., 2011). The role of technology in mother's lives has not been thoroughly explored, and more research is needed to understand MOYC's motivations to engage with technology and how they perceive that technology acts either as a means of, or a barrier to, obtaining social support.

Theoretical Framework

MOYC's motivations for engaging (or not) with technology will be viewed through the lens of self-determination theory, developed by Ryan and Deci. Self-determination theory views motivation as varying in both quantity (magnitude) and quality (type and orientation) (Cook & Artino, 2016; Ryan & Deci, 2000). Because of human beings' innate desire to be autonomous, intrinsic motivation is at its highest when people are engaged in activities they freely choose and inherently enjoy (Cook & Artino, 2016). As people reach maturity, a variety of external factors (work obligations, academic expectations, social norms) tend to dampen intrinsic motivation which can, in turn, decrease motivation (Cook & Artino, 2016). Cook and Artino write:

> Cognitive evaluation theory, a sub-theory of self-determination theory, proposes that fulfillment of three basic psychosocial needs will foster intrinsic motivation: autonomy (the opportunity to control one's actions), competence (self-efficacy) and relatedness (a sense of affiliation with or belonging to others to whom one feels [or would like to feel] connected). (Cook & Artino, 2016, p. 1009)

According to Ryan and Deci (2000) extrinsic motivation operates on a continuum, from external regulation to integrated regulation. Although integrated regulation is closest to intrinsic motivation in the conceptual model below, Ryan and Deci take pains to note that extrinsic motivation never becomes intrinsic, because intrinsic motivation stems from inherent enjoyment of a task (Ryan & Deci, 2000). However, aspects and qualities of extrinsic motivation can increase or decrease motivation. Those external conditions which limit autonomy, do not appropriately challenge competence, or interfere with relatedness tend to decrease motivation (Ryan

& Deci, 2000). Examples of external motivators that decrease motivation include: threats, deadlines, directives, and competition pressure (Ryan & Deci, 2000). In contrast, external motivation that offers choices, appropriately challenges competence, and fosters relatedness can increase motivation and move participants toward integrated regulation (i.e., farther right on the conceptual model below) (Ryan & Deci, 2000). Intrinsic motivation results in: mastery learning, creativity, curiosity, and desire for growth of knowledge and skills (Ryan & Deci, 2000). Greater integration of external motivation results in "greater persistence, more positive self-perceptions, and better quality of engagement" (Ryan & Deci, 2000, p. 61).

The transition to parenthood, and especially the transition to motherhood, can be viewed as a sudden and drastic imposition of external factors that limit autonomy (due to the overwhelming needs of another). The new role may also challenge competence (either in the caregiving role or other contexts, such as one's career), and can strain relatedness through increased isolation or stress to existing relationships (for example, a romantic partnership). Such a transition creates conflict between the basic needs of autonomy, competence, and relatedness, and such conflicts can result in diminished wellbeing and psychopathology (Cook & Artino, 2016). Appropriate social support, however, may act as a buffer to these new demands. More specifically, I propose that elements of social support can impact the basic needs of autonomy, competence, and relatedness (see Table 7.1).

I hypothesize that MOYC will engage in use of technology that supports relatedness, autonomy, and competence. Furthermore, I hypothesize that MOYC will engage with technology to enhance informational, emotional, and to a lesser degree, appraisal and instrumental support, but that this support will largely correspond to their roles as mothers (versus workers, partners, athletes, etc.). I hypothesize that MOYC-SN will use technology for informational and emotional support to a greater extent than MOYC. Finally, I hypothesize that technologies, or uses of technology, that detract from relatedness, autonomy, and/or competence will likely be avoided by MOYC.

TABLE 7.1 The Influence of Social Support on Basic Needs	
Type of Social Support	Associated Type of Basic Need (Self-Determination Theory)
Emotional	Relatedness
Instrumental	Autonomy, Competence
Informational	Autonomy, Competence
Appraisal	Autonomy, Competence, Relatedness

106 ▪ C. NOONAN

Methods

A search was conducted via the NC State Library Summon search for peer-reviewed papers with full text available in English that addressed mothers' motivations to use technology to address social support. Search terms included: mother, social media, motivation, social support; working mother, technology, motivation, social support; and mother, motivation, social support, self-determination theory. After reviewing the returned list of articles, 27 were determined to be germane to the topic of this review. Careful reading of the abstracts reduced the data set further to 19 articles that met the inclusion criteria (i.e., MOYC or MOYC-SN, some role played by technology, etc.). Articles were read through and coded for self-determination concepts (autonomy, competence, relatedness) and for the four types of social support (emotional, instrumental, appraisal, informational).

FINDINGS

Overall results of the literature review are shown in Table 7.2. A majority of articles centered around the period of time immediately before or after giving birth, with topics such as breastfeeding and preparing for labor being popular topics. Mothers of children with healthcare needs was another represented group but was a relatively small subset of the literature. Most studies focused on applications of social media or other communication technology, such as texting. Few studies investigated mothers' use of technology to support them in arenas separate from parenting (such as career). Mothers' primary use of technology seemed to be to gather information and connect with other people for emotional support. Thus, the SDT concepts of relatedness and competence were most strongly represented, with autonomy being less prevalent.

Self-Determination

Chatwin and colleagues (2021) investigated expectant mothers' use of a National Health Service social media site to receive antenatal support during the early part of the COVID-19 pandemic in the United Kingdom. SDT concepts of relatedness and competence were the primary ones represented: Women used the site to reduce isolation and to seek out and verify information. Rouhi, Stirling, and Crisp (2021) studied MOYC's use of online forums to address post-partum problems, finding that women sought emotional support and information. Archer and Kao (2018) investigated the use of social media as a form of social support for mothers of

TABLE 7.2 Summary Evidence Table

First Author	Year of Publication	Self-determination concepts • R—relatedness • A—autonomy • C—competence	Social Support concepts • E—emotional • IS—instrumental • IF—informational • A—appraisal
Archer	2018	R, A, C	E, IF
Chatwin	2021	R, C	E, IF
Drentea	2005	R, C	E, IF, A
Dunham	1998	R, C	E, IS, IF
Frizzo	2017	R, A	E
Guillory	2014	C	IF
Ho	2021	R, A, C	E, IS, IF
Holtz	2015	R, A, C	E, IS, IF
Jolly	2017	R, A, C	E, IS, IF
Lebron	2020	R, C	E, IF
Morse	2021	R, C	E, IF
Nicholl	2017	R, C	E, IF
Nikken	2018	R, C	E, IF
Nolan	2017	R, C	E, IF
Pettigrew	2015	R, A	E, IS
Price	2018	R, C	E, IF
Regan	2019	R, C	E, IF
Rouhi	2021	R, C	E, IF
Thoren	2013	R, C	E, IF

children aged birth to four years old. Their findings suggest that mothers used social media to support relatedness through gaining contact with the outside word, competence through reading news and gathering information, and autonomy through following an influencer or business of interest (i.e., a personal interest aside from their mothering role). The authors noted that social media use was associated with both positive and negative effects for these Australian MOYC. Negative effects included finding social media addictive and superficial, relating it to feelings of depression, and concern over the behavior they were modeling to their children. Drentea and Moren-Cross (2005) also investigated mothers' use of a social media site, but in the U.S. over a decade previously, with similar findings: mothers used the site to garner emotional support and build and protect community, and to gather information. A unique finding was that one type of information gathered related to comparison (aligning with appraisal support in the social support paradigm) to other mothers ("Am I the only one?"). Not all effects were positive: Women gained a variety of forms of support but also experience disagreement and anger. In an older study, Dunham (1998) investigated the use of a social network for single mothers supported through technologies including public messaging, private e-mail, and text-based communication. Analysis of the messages, as well as pre- and post-test data and mothers' self-report information, showed that women primarily used the site for emotional support (relatedness). Information, followed by tangible aid, were other benefits of participation in the network, and mothers who participated reported significantly less stress on post-test measures when compared to controls. Holtz, Smock, and Reyes-Gastelum (2015) investigated the use of a mothering-focused Facebook page on expectant mothers or MOYC of children aged four or younger. As with other studies, the desire for social connection and information (relatedness and competence) were driving forces for engagement with technology. This study also found themes associated with the SDT concept of autonomy, which will be discussed further below. Nolan and colelagues (2017) performed a literature review investigating the effect of participation in online groups among adolescent mothers. These MOYC primarily used the groups for information-seeking (competence) but also increased their social support and social capital through participation in these groups. Price et al. (2018) investigated how first-time mothers used online support in the first six months of the postpartum period. These MOYC primarily used online support for information-seeking and social connection. These Canadian mothers particularly valued support from peers and frequently met in person with fellow MOYC after connecting online, suggesting one avenue for obtaining instrumental support (playdate arrangements, shared childcare responsibility) via technology.

Breastfeeding Support

Breastfeeding support was a popular topic in the data set. Lebron et al. (2020) performed content analysis of a breastfeeding support forum on Babycenter.com and found that MOYC sought out encouragement and information, and participated in knowledge-sharing. These findings were echoed by Morse and Brown (2021), who found that MOYC used breastfeeding support Facebook pages to promote connection, competence, and self-efficacy. Regan and Brown (2019) also looked at breastfeeding support online. Similar to previous studies, they found the MOYC sought information and social connection. However, these authors also addressed the challenge of misinformation online and advocated for greater healthcare provider participation to moderate discussions and correct misinformation.

Morbidity and Mortality

Several studies investigated use of technology among MOYC experiencing illness or death of their child or children. Frizzo et al. (2017) studied blogs written by mothers who had experienced the death of a child. The authors found that the primary motivation for blogging centered around relatedness, including building a relationship network and sharing their feelings of loss and difficulty moving forward. Self-expression was also an important motivator, which relates to the concept of selfhood or, in the SDT paradigm, autonomy. Nicholl and colleagues (2017) examined of Irish parents of children with rare health conditions and found that parents primarily used the Internet to seek out information and garner interpersonal support. Peer interactions were most common and were valued, but parents noted limited engagement with experts or healthcare providers. Thoren and colleagues (2013) studied parents of pre-term infants, with similar findings: Parents sought (and shared) information and interpersonal support online.

Autonomy

A small set of studies in the data set evoked the SDT concept of autonomy, largely through the practice of self-expression. Jolly and Matthews (2017) studied blogs written by homeschooling mothers. In addition to the prevalent themes of relatedness (social interaction and maintaining community) and competence (information exchange), these mothers also blogged as a form of self-expression. Holtz et al.'s 2015 study of mothers and mothers-to-be using a Facebook page ("Ask the Chicks") also revealed the MOYC used the communication platform as a means of self-expression and entertainment. Pettigrew et al. (2015) studied "mommy blogs" and found that mothers blogged as a form of self-validation. They also blogged for mental stimulation and to gain and hone skills. Ho and Cho (2021) found that MOYC in Taiwan used social media to have personal leisure time and for work achievement purposes, in addition to finding social connection. These MOYC also used social media to find information about family or child-friendly activities.

Other Findings

Guillory et al. (2014) approached social support and technology use from a novel perspective, compared to the rest of this data set, investigating the impact of level of social support on mothers' online information-seeking behaviors. They found that married women and women who reported better social support were more likely to seek information online, suggesting that—at least in this population and study—competence may be self-reinforcing. In other words, those mothers who feel well supported may also feel more competent to get information and solve problems by seeking information online, thus increasing their competence further. Nikken

(2018) explored how parents use technology in childrearing and how family characteristics relate to these practices. Parents used technology to give themselves a break from parenting duties, modify children's behavior, or to act as a "babysitter" when the parent was not available. Families where social support was lower, those who reported behavioral problems with their children, were less confident about their parenting, or who expected positive effects from the media were more likely to use technology as a part of childrearing.

Social Support and Other Themes

MOYC's use of technology to garner social support was heavily weighted toward informational and emotional support. Themes of instrumental and appraisal support were present but were far less common. For example, MOYC sought appraisal support to compare themselves to other mothers, for example regarding their parenting processes (Drentea & Moren-Cross, 2005). MOYC also used technology for instrumental support, for example using media as a babysitter (Nikken, 2018) or using it to procure personal leisure (Ho & Cho, 2021)—a theme of "control over time."

"Giving support" was another theme that emerged. MOYC not only sought out information and support online but also shared it with other MOYC. In some cases, this occurred after moving through a similar experience (breastfeeding, losing a child), while in other case this was manifested as development into an expert through the creation of a blog. Some negative effects of using technology reported in these studies included the addictive nature of social media and modeling associated behaviors in front of children (Archer & Kao, 2018), receiving misinformation (Regan & Brown, 2019), and becoming involved in conflict and disagreement (Drentea & Moren-Cross, 2005).

DISCUSSION AND IMPLICATIONS

Family-centered care posits that the primary patient and their family members are active and equal members of the healthcare team (IPFCC, 2022). Practices of family-centered care include: open exchange of information and resources, shared power in decision making, and honoring families' individual cultural differences (IPFCC, 2022). Family-centered care views family members as interconnected and as having influence upon one another (IPFCC, 2022). Part of the role of the healthcare provider (or other support professional—teacher, counselor, social worker) is to educate the individual and his or her family. In the context of FCC, the educator is not the "sage on the

Motivations for Technology Use Among Mothers of Young Children • **111**

stage" banking information into the receptive minds of the learner. Rather, the educator is a facilitator, one who empowers the family through the sharing of information and the provision of support. Thus educators, counselors, social workers, and healthcare providers have a potential role to play in online communities such as Facebook pages, online forums, and blogs and Websites. Yet this literature review shows that these professionals in fact play a limited role in supporting MOYC online (Nicholl et al., 2017). Peer to peer support is more common and is highly valued by MOYC; however, it can also be a source of misinformation (Regan & Brown, 2019). Healthcare providers and other professionals should consider the ways in which they could use technology to enhance their support of families and MOYC and support the publication of accurate information online.

Technology imbues modern life. The fields of healthcare and education are no exception. Therefore, it is imperative to discover the ways in which technology and its application in daily life are either supporting or failing to support families. Mothers typically fulfill the role of the primary caregiver in their children's lives. Yet the same gendered cultural expectations that equate caregiving with mothering may also equate technological know-how with masculinity (Wacjman, 2009). It is therefore critical to understand how and why mothers interact with technology, as it has implications both for their own health and wellbeing and that of their children. This literature review shows that MOYC use technology to foster relatedness and competence in their mothering role. This body of literature shows that, to a lesser extent, they also use technology to foster autonomy. However, it is unclear whether MOYC do not use technology to support autonomy as often or whether this use of technology has simply been researched less. The few articles in this data set that discussed MOYC's use of technology to support autonomy suggest that it is a means of self-expression, a way to be intellectually stimulated and gain skills, a means of achieving work success, and a way to protect time for themselves (Ho & Cho, 2021; Holtz, 2015; Nikken, 2018; Pettigrew, 2015).

MOYC-SN appear to use technology in similar ways to mothers of young children without special needs, however there is limited research on this topic suggesting a possible research gap. One of the few articles on this topic in the data set suggested that healthcare providers could play a bigger role online for this population (Nicholl et al., 2017).

An unexpected finding of this literature review was that MOYC use technology not only to receive social support but also to give it. The articles included in this review seem to suggest one trajectory in which mothers experience some aspect of motherhood—breastfeeding, parenting a child with a rare disorder, etc.—and then obtain a level of expertise or comfort with the experience such that they are able to provide support to others. This is suggested, for example, in those articles addressing mothers who have become bloggers. However, other trajectories may also exist, wherein parents "in the trenches" of an experience at the same time may support one another, as shown in Dunham's study of single mothers.

The experience of mothering young children is often intensive with a sudden and drastic imposition of new and intense demands on a mother's time, physical, and emotional resources (Craig & Brown, 2017; Craig & Mullan, 2011; Costa et al., 2021; Young, Schieman & Milke, 2013). MOYC can experience isolation and challenges addressing the basic needs of their children (for example, breastfeeding) (Archer & Kao, 2018). These conditions are opposite to those which, according to SDT, are conducive to intrinsic motivation (Cook & Artino, 2016; Ryan & Deci, 2000). This literature review suggests that MOYC may use technology as a coping strategy to gather social support in a variety of forms—but particularly in the realm of emotional and informational support. These articles suggest that they may enhance competence by seeking out information and they may build relatedness by finding alternate social networks and emotional connection. To a lesser extent, they may use technology to protect aspects of their autonomy including their time, self-expression, and professional pursuits. As they do so, they may moderate the intense extrinsic demands of mothering young children to intrinsic ones propelled by new expertise or the desire for self-expression.

Finally, a concern for others was an unexpected finding of this review. This suggests that, according to the SDT paradigm, MOYC may increase relatedness not only by seeking emotional connection and support but by giving it, but mediated through technology. The use of technology to create and manage relationships may also relate to MOYC's need for autonomy. Internet relationships can be scheduled, turned off, ignored, or put to sleep, in controllable ways that the real world demands of young children cannot.

Limitations

This literature review examined a relatively small set of articles (n = 19). Most articles focused on a narrow time and scope of women's experiences and roles during the time they are mothering young children.

CONCLUSION

This literature review sought to explore the motivations of MOYC for either engaging with or avoiding technology. In particular, it used the theoretical perspective of self-determination theory as a lens to view the ways in which women engage with technology to enhance their social support or, conversely, the ways in which women perceive that technology acts as a barrier to social support. Findings suggest that technology supports competence and relatedness in MOYC and, to a lesser extent, autonomy. MOYC use technology for emotional and informational support and, less often, for appraisal and instrumental support. Technology may also offer a way to give social support for others but with manageable boundaries.

REFERENCES

American Psychological Society (2022). Social support. *APA dictionary of psychology.* Retrieved from: https://dictionary.apa.org/social-support.

Ammerman, C., & Groysberg, B. (2020). Why the crisis is putting companies at risk of losing female talent. *Harvard Business Review.* Retrieved from https://hbr.org/2020/05/why-the-crisis-is-putting-companies-at-risk-of-losing-female-talent

Archer, C., & Kao, K.-T. (2018a). Mother, baby and Facebook makes three: Does social media provide social support for new mothers? *Media International Australia Incorporating Culture & Policy, 168*(1), 122–139. https://doi.org/10.1177/1329878X18783016

Atif, N., Lovell, K., & Rahman, A. (2015). Maternal mental health: The missing "m" in the global maternal and child health agenda. *Seminars in Perinatology, 39*(5), 345–352.

Bateman, N. (2020). *Working parents are key to COVID-19 recovery.* Brookings. https://www.brookings.edu/research/working-parents-are-key-to-covid-19-recovery/

Baudry, C., Tarabulsy, G. M., Atkinson, L., Pearson, J., & St-Pierre, A. (2017). Intervention with adolescent mother–child dyads and cognitive development in early childhood: A meta-analysis. *Prevention Science, 18*(1), 116–130.

Beamish, N., Fisher, J., & Rowe, H. (2019). Parents' use of mobile computing devices, caregiving and the social and emotional development of children: A systematic review of the evidence. *Australasian Psychiatry: Bulletin of the Royal Australian and New Zealand College of Psychiatrists, 27*(2), 132–143.

Bender, M. S., Clark, M. J., & Gahagan, S. (2014). Community engagement approach: Developing a culturally appropriate intervention for Hispanic mother–child dyads. *Journal of Transcultural Nursing, 25*(4), 373–382.

Bennett, I. M., Schott, W., Krutikova, S., & Behrman, J. R. (2016). Maternal mental health, and child growth and development, in four low-income and middle-income countries. *Journal of Epidemiology and Community Health (1979), 70*(2), 168–173.

Brandon, P. (2007). Time away from "smelling the roses": Where do mothers raising children with disabilities find the time to work? *Social Science & Medicine (1982), 65*(4), 667–679.

Carlson, J. M., & Miller, P. A. (2017). Family burden, child disability, and the adjustment of mothers caring for children with epilepsy: Role of social support and coping. *Epilepsy & Behavior, 68*, 168–173.

114 • C. NOONAN

Cassella, M. (2021). *The pandemic drove women out of the workforce. Will they come back?* Politico.com. https://www.politico.com/news/2021/07/22/coronavirus-pandemic-women-workforce-500329

Cerulo, M. (2021). Nearly 3 million U.S. women have dropped out of the labor force in the past year. Retrieved from https://www.cbsnews.com/news/covid-crisis-3-million-women-labor-force/

Chatterji, P., Markowitz, S., & Brooks-Gunn, J. (2013). Effects of early maternal employment on maternal health and well-being. *Journal of Population Economics, 26*(1), 285–301.

Chatwin, J., Butler, D., Jones, J., James, L., Choucri, L., & McCarthy, R. (2021). Experiences of pregnant mothers using a social media based antenatal support service during the COVID-19 lockdown in the UK: Findings from a user survey. *BMJ Open, 11*(1), e040649–e040649.

Clowtis, L. M., Kang, D.-H., Padhye, N. S., Rozmus, C., & Barratt, M. S. (2016). Biobehavioral factors in child health outcomes: The roles of maternal stress, maternal-child engagement, salivary cortisol, and salivary testosterone. *Nursing Research (New York), 65*(5), 340.

Cook D., Artino, A. (2016). Motivation to learn: An overview of contemporary theories. *Medical Education, 50*, 997–1014. https://doi.org/10.1111/medu.13074

Costa, J., Santos, O., Virgolino, A., Pereira, M. E., Stefanovska-Petkovska, M., Silva, H., Navarro-Costa, P., Barbosa, M., das Neves, R. C., Duarte E Silva, I., Alarcão, V., Vargas, R., & Heitor, M. J. (2021). Maternal Mental Health in the Workplace (MAMH@WORK): A protocol for promoting perinatal maternal mental health and wellbeing. *International Journal of Environmental Research and Public Health, 18*(5), 2558.

Craig, L., & Brown, J. E. (2017). Feeling rushed: Gendered time quality, work hours, nonstandard work schedules, and spousal crossover. *Journal of Marriage and Family, 79*(1), 225–242.

Craig L., & Mullan, K. (2011). How mothers and fathers share childcare: A cross-national time-use comparison. *American Sociological Review, 76*(6), 834–861.

Craig, L., & Powell, A. (2011). Non-standard work schedules, work–family balance and the gendered division of childcare. *Work, Employment and Society, 25*(2), 274–291.

Drentea, P., & Moren-Cross, J. L. (2005). Social capital and social support on the web: The case of an internet mother site. *Sociology of Health & Illness, 27*(7), 920–943.

Duggan, M., Lenhart, A., Lampe, C., & Ellison, N. (2019). *Parents and social media: Mothers are especially likely to give and receive support on social media.* Pew Research. Retrieved from https://www.pewinternet.org/2015/07/16/parents-and-social-media/.

Dunham, P. J., Hurshman, A., Litwin, E., Gusella, J., Ellsworth, C., & Dodd, P. W. D. (1998). Computer-mediated social support: Single young mothers as a model system. *American Journal of Community Psychology, 26*(2), 281–306.

Ellengrud, K., & Segel, L.H. (2021). *COVID-19 has driven millions of women out of the workforce. Here's how to help them come back.* Fortune.com. Retrieved from https://fortune.com/2021/02/13/covid-19-women-workforce-unemployment-gender-gap-recovery/

Frizzo, H.C.F., Bousso, R. S., Rossi de Faria Ichikawa, c., & Nigro de Sá, n. (2017). Grieving mothers: Design of thematic blogs about loss of a child. *Acta Paulista De Enfermagem, 30*(2), 116.

Fry, R. (2022). *Some gender disparities widened in the U.S. workforce during the pandemic.* Pew Research Center. https://www.pewresearch.org/fact-tank/2022/01/14/some-gender-disparities-widened-in-the-u-s-workforce-during-the-pandemic/

Fry, R., Kennedy B., Funk C. (2021). *STEM jobs see uneven progress in increasing gender, racial and ethnic diversity.* Pew Research Center. https://www.pewresearch.org/science/2021/04/01/stem-jobs-see-uneven-progress-in-increasing-gender-racial-and-ethnic-diversity/

Glanz, K., Rimer, B., & Viswanath, K.V. (Eds.). (2008). Social support. *Health behavior and health education: Theory, research, and practice (4th ed.).* https://www.med.upenn.edu/hbhe4/part3-ch9-key-constructs-social-support.shtml

Gonzalez, C. (2021). *Men got higher pay than women 59% of the time for same tech jobs.* Bloomberg.com. https://www.bloomberg.com/news/articles/2021-05-19/gender-pay-gap-in-tech-male-job-candidates-paid-3-higher-than-women.

Gordon, B., & Wagner, A. (2020). 'COVID-19 is killing enrollment.' As school begins, child care centers struggle to stay open. *News & Observer.* Retrieved from https://www.newsobserver.com/news/coronavirus/article244246542.html

Granados, A. (2020). Testing and virtual learning: How the state board is addressing COVID-19 for schools this fall. *Education NC.* https://www.ednc.org/how-the-state-board-is-addressing-covid-19-for-schools-this-fall/

Guillory, J., Niederdeppe, J., Kim, H., Pollak, J. P., Graham, M., Olson, C., & Gay, G. (2014). Does Social Support Predict Pregnant Mothers' Information Seeking Behaviors on an Educational Website? *Maternal and Child Health Journal, 18*(9), 2218–2225.

Hether, H.J., Murphy, S.T., & Valente, T.W. (2016). A social network analysis of supportive interactions on prenatal sites. *Digital Health,* 2, 2055207616628700-2055207616628700. https://doi.org/10.1177/2055207616628700

Ho, C.-H., & Cho, Y.-H. (2021). Social media as a pathway to leisure: Digital leisure culture among new mothers with young children in Taiwan. *Leisure Sciences,* 1–19.

Hollenbach, J. P., Kuo, C., Mu, J., Gerrard, M., Gherlone, N., Sylvester, F., Ojukwu, M., & Cloutier, M. M. (2019). Hair cortisol, perceived stress, and social support in mother-child dyads living in an urban neighborhood. *Stress* (Amsterdam, Netherlands), *22*(6), 632–639.

Holtz, B., Smock, A., & Reyes-Gastelum, D. (2015). Connected Motherhood: Social Support for Moms and Moms-to-Be on Facebook. *Telemedicine Journal and E-Health, 21*(5), 415–421.

Hsu, J., Pitt, C., Greco, G., Berman, P., & Mills, A. (2012). Countdown to 2015: Changes in official development assistance to maternal, newborn, and child health in 2009–10, and assessment of progress since 2003. *The Lancet (British Edition), 380*(9848), 1157–1168.

Institute for Patient and Family-centered Care. (2022). *Project background: Patient and family-centered care defined.* https://www.ipfcc.org/bestpractices/sustainable-partnerships/background/pfcc-defined.html

116 ▪ C. NOONAN

Jolly, J. L., & Matthews, M. S. (2017). Why we blog: Homeschooling mothers of gifted children. *Roeper Review, 39*(2), 112–120.

Kahn, J. R., García-Manglano, J., & Bianchi, S. M. (2014). The motherhood penalty at midlife: Long-term effects of children on women's careers. *Journal of Marriage and Family, 76*(1), 56–72.

Kim, J., Kim, H., Park, S., Yoo, J., & Gelegjamts, D. (2021). Mediating effects of family functioning on the relationship between care burden and family quality of life of caregivers of children with intellectual disabilities in Mongolia. *Journal of Applied Research in Intellectual Disabilities, 34*(2), 507–515.

Leahy-Warren, P., McCarthy, G., & Corcoran, P. (2012). First-time mothers: Social support, maternal parental self-efficacy and postnatal depression. *Journal of Clinical Nursing, 21*(3–4), 388–397.

Lebron, C. N., St. George, S. M., Eckembrecher, D. G., & Alvarez, L. M. (2020;2019;). "Am I doing this wrong?" breastfeeding mothers' use of an online forum. *Maternal and Child Nutrition, 16*(1), e12890-n/a. https://doi.org/10.1111/mcn.12890

Litzelman, K., Catrine, K., Gangnon, R., & Witt, W. P. (2011). Quality of life among parents of children with cancer or brain tumors: The impact of child characteristics and parental psychosocial factors. *Quality of Life Research, 20*(8), 1261–1269.

Litzelman, K., Skinner, H. G., Gangnon, R. E., Nieto, F. J., Malecki, K., & Witt, W. P. (2014). Role of global stress in the health-related quality of life of caregivers: Evidence from the Survey of the Health of Wisconsin. *Quality of Life Research, 23*(5), 1569–1578.

Maynard, P. (March 3, 2021). *Are we really closing the gender gap in tech?* Forbes. com. Retrieved from https://www.forbes.com/sites/forbesbusinesscouncil/2021/03/03/are-we-really-closing-the-gender-gap-in-tech/?sh = 5c5a7fc15d71

Merriam-Webster Dictionary. (February 13, 2022). Technology. https://www.merriam-webster.com/dictionary/technology.

Miller, C. C. (May 13, 2017). The gender pay gap is largely because of motherhood. *The New York Times.* https://www.nytimes.com/2017/05/13/upshot/the-gender-pay-gap-is-largely-because-of-motherhood.html

Morse, H., & Brown, A. (2021). Accessing local support online: Mothers' experiences of local Breastfeeding Support Facebook groups. *Maternal and Child Nutrition, 17*(4), e13227-n/a. https://doi.org/10.1111/mcn.13227

Motti, V. G., Kalantari, N., & Neris, V. (2020;2021;). Understanding how social media imagery empowers caregivers: An analysis of microcephaly in Latin America. *Personal and Ubiquitous Computing, 25*(2), 321–336.

Musick, K., Meier, A., & Flood, S. (2016). How parents fare: Mothers' and fathers' subjective well-being in time with children. *American Sociological Review, 81*(5), 1069–1095.

National Association for the Education of Young Children (NAEYC) & Fred Rogers Center for Early Learning and Children's Media at Saint Vincent College. (2012). *Position statement: Technology and interactive media as tools in early childhood programs serving children from birth through age 8.* Retrieved from https://www.naeyc.org/sites/default/files/globally-shared/downloads/PDFs/resources/position-statements/ps_technology.pdf

Negron, R., Martin, A., Almog, M., Balbierz, A., & Howell, E. A. (2012). Social support during the postpartum period: Mothers' views on needs, expectations, and mobilization of support. *Maternal and Child Health Journal, 17*(4), 616–623.

Nicholl, H., Tracey, C., Begley, T., King, C., & Lynch, A. M. (2017). Internet use by parents of children with rare conditions: Findings from a study on parents' web information needs. *Journal of Medical Internet Research, 19*(2), e51–e51. https://doi.org/10.2196/jmir.5834

Nikken, P. (2018). Parents' Instrumental use of media in childrearing: Relationships with confidence in parenting, and health and conduct problems in children. *Journal of Child and Family Studies, 28*(2), 531–546.

Nolan, S., Hendricks, J., Ferguson, S., & Towell, A. (2017). Social networking site (SNS) use by adolescent mothers: Can social support and social capital be enhanced by online social networks? A structured review of the literature. *Midwifery, 48*, 24–31.

Offer, S., & Schneider, B. (2011). Revisiting the gender gap in time-use patterns: Multitasking and well-being among mothers and fathers in dual-earner families. *American Sociological Review, 76*(6), 809–833.

Pepin, J.R., Sayer, L.C., & Casper, L.M. (2018). Marital status and mothers' time use: Childcare, housework, leisure, and sleep. *Demography, 55*, 107–133.

Pettigrew, S., Archer, C., & Harrigan, P. (2015). A thematic analysis of mothers' motivations for blogging. *Maternal and Child Health Journal, 20*(5), 1025–1031.

Plant, K. M., & Sanders, M. R. (2007). Predictors of care-giver stress in families of preschool-aged children with developmental disabilities. *Journal of Intellectual Disability Research, 51*(2), 109–124.

Price, S. L., Aston, M., Monaghan, J., Sim, M., Tomblin Murphy, G., Etowa, J., Pickles, M., Hunter, A., & Little, V. (2018). Maternal knowing and social networks: Understanding first-time mothers' search for information and support through online and offline social networks. *Qualitative Health Research, 28*(10), 1552–1563.

Richter, F. (2021). *Women's representation in big tech.* Statistica.com. Retrieved from https://www.statista.com/chart/4467/female-employees-at-tech-companies/

Regan, S., & Brown, A. (2019). Experiences of online breastfeeding support: Support and reassurance versus judgement and misinformation. *Maternal and Child Nutrition, 15*(4), e12874-n/a. https://doi.org/10.1111/mcn.12874

Rizzo, K. M., Schiffrin, H. H., & Liss, M. (2012). Insight into the parenthood paradox: Mental health outcomes of intensive mothering. *Journal of Child and Family Studies, 22*(5), 614–620.

Rouhi, M., Stirling, C., & Crisp, E. P. (2021). The 'fallacy of normalcy': A content analysis of women's online post-childbirth health-related support. *Women and Birth: Journal of the Australian College of Midwives, 34*(3), e262–e270. https://doi.org/10.1016/j.wombi.2020.04.007

Ryan, R., & Deci E. (2000). Intrinsic and extrinsic motivations: Classic definitions and new directions. *Contemporary Educational Psychology, 25*, 54–67 (2000). https://doi.org/10.1006/ceps.1999.1020

Schieman, S., Ruppanner, L., & Milkie, M. A. (2017). Who helps with homework? Parenting inequality and relationship quality among employed mothers and fathers. *Journal of Family and Economic Issues, 39*(1), 49–65.

Schunk, D. H., Meece, J. R., & Pintrich, P. R. (2019). *Motivation in education: Theory, research, and applications (4th ed.)*. Pearson.

Thoren, E. M., Metze, B., Bührer, C., & Garten, L. (2013). Online support for parents of preterm infants: A qualitative and content analysis of Facebook 'preemie' groups. Archives of Disease in Childhood. *Fetal and Neonatal Edition, 98*(6), F534–F538. https://doi.org/10.1136/archdischild-2012-303572

United States Department of Health and Human Services. (2006). *The NICHD study of youth and child development—findings for children up to age 4½ years*. USDHHS, National Institute of Health, National Institute of Child Health and Development. Retrieved from https://www.nichd.nih.gov/sites/default/files/publications/pubs/documents/seccyd_06.pdf

Vaz, S., Thomson, A., Cuomo, B., Falkmer, T., Chamberlain, A., & Black, M. H. (2021). Co-occurring intellectual disability and autism: Associations with stress, coping, time use, and quality of life in caregivers. *Research in Autism Spectrum Disorders, 84*, 101765.

Wajcman, J. (2009). Feminist theories of technology. *Cambridge Journal of Economics. 34*, 143–152. https://doi.org/10.1093/cje/ben057

Young, M., Schieman, S., & Milkie, M.A. (2014). Spouse's work-to-family conflict, family stressors, and mental health among dual-earner mothers and fathers. *Society and Mental Health, 4*(1).

Zero to Three. (2016). *Tuning in: Parents of young children speak up about what they think, know and need. Tuning in: National parent survey report.* Retrieved from https://www.zerotothree.org/resources/2517-home-visitors-parent-educators-and-family-services-professionals-critical-resources-for-parents-and-families

CHAPTER 8

STUDENTS' PERCEPTION OF SCIENTISTS AND THEIR WORK

Stereotypes and Misconceptions

Margareta M. Thomson and Zarifa Zakaria

Students' understanding of science, as well as their perceptions of the scientists are deeply grounded in their learning experiences and exposure to science. Research shows that such exposures are strongly influencing and shaping students' perceptions of science and scientists, and their understanding of who scientists are and what is the work that they do (Griffith, 2010; Nix, Perez-Felkner, & Thomas, 2015). Identifying students' understanding of science and their perceptions of scientists is a first step in capturing the stereotypes they have about "who is a scientist," "who can go into science" and if they themselves "belong to a science career." Drawing is a very powerful way of measuring young children's understanding of the world around them as it reveals their cognitive schemas about how things work, the meaning of relationships, cultural norms or behaviors. In studies investigating children's representations of scientists, drawings revealed their beliefs and stereotypes about scientists. Such beliefs can play a central

---

Motivation and Engagement in Various Learning Environments, pages 119–146
Copyright © 2024 by Information Age Publishing
www.infoagepub.com
All rights of reproduction in any form reserved.

role in shaping students' science interests and their identification with science careers (Miller, Nolla, Eagly, & Uttal, 2018; Losh, Wilke, & Pop, 2008).

The current study describes a research project in which elementary students' depictions of scientists were investigated. Students from public schools in rural and urban areas in Romania participated in the study. Contributions from this study can help understand how students understand science and the work of scientists, but also help identify some of the sociocultural factors that may influence students' perceptions of scientists and their understanding of science.

PERCEPTIONS OF SCIENTISTS AND THEIR WORK

Recent studies emphasize the importance of investigating how students' perception of science and scientists has developed over the time (Miller, Nolla, Eagly, & Uttal, 2018). Students' perception of scientists may play an important role in developing their science interest and attitudes to science (Kahle, 1988; Mead & Metraux, 1957). This topic has been investigated for five decades, starting with Mead and Metraux's (1957) study, in which 35,000 high school students were asked to write essays about scientists. Their findings reported several stereotypical characteristics which were supported by other studies later (i.e., Beardslee & O'Dowd, 1961; Etzioni & Nunn, 1974; Krajkovich & Smith, 1982). From the time frame of 50s' to 80s', most studies found stereotypical characteristics in the visual and descriptive images of scientists, such as scientists wearing lab-coats and eyeglasses, working with tubes/bottles full of chemicals, and sometimes having a sinister or eccentric expression on their faces.

Chambers (1983) developed and introduced the Draw-a-Scientist-Test (DAST) to collect information more elaborately about students' perceptions of scientists. In Chambers' study, students were given a blank paper and asked to draw a scientist. Afterwards, the drawings were coded per seven specific attributes. These attributes were: lab coat, eyeglasses, facial growth of hair, symbols of research, symbols of knowledge, technology, and relevant captions. Studying data from 4,807 elementary students, Chambers found a standard image of the scientist which was in line with Mead and Metraux's (1957) findings. Chamber's study (1983) also found an alternative image of scientists where magical portrayals, fictional characters like Frankenstein were represented as scientists.

Studies examining students' drawings using the DAST instrument investigated how students perceived of scientists in different countries and cultures (i.e., Christidou, Bonoti, & Kontopoulou, 2016; Monhardt, 2003; Rodari, 2007; Ruiz-Mallen & Escalas, 2012; Thomas, Henley, & Snell, 2006; Türkmen, 2008). Almost all studies confirmed that students have a stereotypical view of scientists where, scientists are mainly represented as white males wearing lab-coats, eyeglasses, facial hair and with an eccentric appearance (Buldu, 2006; Chambers, 1983; Christidou et al., 2016; Finson, 2002; Losh et al., 2008; Samaras et al., 2012).

Common Stereotypes

Research shows that students and public alike, hold stereotypes about scientists' images (how they look like), the nature of their work, and what do they do (Finson, 2002; Karaçam, 2016; Minogue, 2010; Ruiz-Mallen & Escalas, 2012). Findings from U.S. studies for instance, where most of the DAST research has been conducted, have shown that scientists were depicted as individuals serving greedy corporations, playing God, tempering with nature and misusing technology (Funk, 2003; Losh et al., 2008). Other stereotypes were related to scientists' gender and ethnicity. Most scientist were depicted by students in their drawings as White males; other representations show a that Hispanic and Asian scientists were underrepresented. Female scientists were occasionally represented in students' drawings, and most of the time, females were presented as "superwomen" (Flicker, 2003).

White male scientists have dominated students' depictions of scientists for almost five decades (Chambers, 1983; Finson, 2002; Fort & Varney, 1989; Jones et al., 2000; Steinke et al., 2007). Male scientists were depicted by both male and female students; the few female scientists were mostly represented by female students (Bodzin & Gehringer, 2001; Buldu, 2006; Cheryan et al., 2013; Maoldomhnaigh & Hunt, 1988). Many studies, including a meta-analysis on 78 studies (Miller et al., 2018) found that only about half or even fewer female students draw female scientists (Bodzin & Gehringer, 2001; Barman, 1999; Chambers, 1983; Fort &Varney, 1989). Miller et al. (2018) in their meta-analysis study showed that children's representations of scientists have changed over time; they drew male scientists less often in recent years compared to earlier decades. Findings show that children drew 99.4 % scientists as males in Chambers' study (1983) compared to 72% in studies conducted later (e.g., from 1985–2016).

In addition to gender stereotypes in students' drawings, most DAST studies show that stereotyping scientists as professionals is present. Most scientists are depicted as chemists, working in chemistry laboratories (Finson, 2002; Rodari, 2007).

Influences in Stereotyping

Most common factors influencing students' perceptions are media, children's literature, or students' lack of exposure to scientists' work. Several studies found that media represents a major influential source in reinforced the gender roles and gender stereotypes in professions (Barman, 1999; Buldu, 2006; Long et. al., 2001). In order to change this stereotypic trend, several experimental interventions have been implemented, such as media literacy programs (Steinke et al., 2007), teacher intervention programs (Huber& Burton, 1995; Mason, Kahle & Gardner, 1991), teaching strategy reform initiatives (Akerson et al., 2008), visiting scientists' programs (Hopwood, 2012), and science camps (Farland-Smith, 2012). These were a few initiatives and interventions that showed a positive effect in changing students' perceptions about scientists.

CURRENT STUDY

The current study aimed at investigating young students' representations of scientists. Participants ($N = 210$) were students in grades 3rd, 4th and 5th from rural and urban public schools in Romania and ranged in age (mean of 10 years old). Participants were recruited from six different public schools. Among them, four schools were rural, and two schools were urban. Most atudies on this topic have been conducted in the United States and Western European countries (i.e., UK, Italy), however there is a lack of research in this field in Eastern Europe, especially in Romania.

Participants were from schools located in regions that are diverse ethnically (i.e., Romanian, Hungarian, Ukrainian, Roma), thus capturing a cultural diversity, besides cultural diversity specific to certain settings (e.g., urban and rural). Results from international assessments, such as the Progress of International Student Assessment (PISA, 2016) show that Romania has the *highest low-achieving rate in science literacy* compared to other EU countries; about 37% of students were classified as low-achievers in science. Additionally, Romania is second to last on low achievers in reading literacy (37%) and mathematics (41%) compared to other EU countries. While these statistics are alarming, they also speak about *the need to improve* students' academic experiences, especially in the STEM fields which are vital in an increasingly worldwide competitive culture.

The main research questions addressed by the current study were:

1. What do students' drawings reveal with respect to scientists' appearance, specialty, and gender?
2. In what ways do student characteristics, such as ethnic membership, religion, school location (i.e., rural versus urban), gender, grade level and age, influence their perceptions of scientists?
3. In what ways does access to scientific and educational places, such as science laboratories, and science museums, influence students' perceptions of scientists?

METHODOLOGY

Participants

Participants ($N = 210$) in the current study were students from Romania aged between 9–12 years old (average age was 10 years old). Demographic data showed that 108 (47.6%) students were female, and 100 (51.4%) students were male. Among them, 143 (68.1%) participants were from 4th grade, 42 (20%) were from 3rd grade, and 25 (11.9%) were from 5th grade.

With respect to their ethnic membership, the majority of students were Romanians ($n = 156$; 74.3%), followed by students from another ethnic groups, such as Roma ($n = 15$; 7.1%), Hungarian ($n = 7$; 3.3%), and Ukrainian ($n = 11$; 5.2%). With respect to religion, students indicated in their survey that a total of 158 (75.2%) identify themselves as Romanian-Orthodox, 11 (5.2%) as Greek-Catholics, 7 (3.3%) as Romano-Catholics, and 34 (16.2%) students indicated their religion as "Other." Participants' demographic data is displayed in Table 8.1.

Data Collection

The primary data for the current study were students' depictions of scientists using the DAST (Draw-a-Scientist-Test). Additionally, a survey (post-drawing) collected demographic data such as students' age, gender, ethnic membership, rural or urban setting, and if they visited science labs or science museums before. Two researchers involved in the current study collected data spanning across one academic year (during 2016). Both researchers are native Romanians, thus speak the language. All students received materials in Romanian and instructions to complete the study in Romanian. Study materials were collected in Romanian and later translated into English.

The DAST activity lasted for about 30 min, followed by a 10-min survey; students completed these activities in their own classrooms. One researcher collected data from a set of classrooms, while the other researcher collected data from another set of classrooms. All students in the study received the same instructions for completing the activity and a standardized procedure was put in place for data collection. The students completed first the DAST activity, and then completed the demographic survey (paper-and-pencil).

On their drawings students were instructed to: (a) provide a title for their drawing, (b) draw a person who works in science, and (c) provide a short description (in one or two sentences) of what the person is doing in their representations. Because Romanian is part of the Romance languages, similarly to Spanish and French, the word "scientist" has already a gender connotation (i.e., "un om de stiinta" means literally "a male scientist"). In order to avoid gender bias, and thus avoid influencing students'

124 • M. M. THOMSON and Z. ZAKARIA

TABLE 8.1 Participants' Characteristics

Characteristics	n	%
Age		
9–10	159	77.56
11–12	46	12.6
Total	205	97.6
Missing	5	2.4
Grade		
3rd grade	42	20.0
4th grade	143	68.1
5th grade	25	11.9
Gender		
Female	108	51.4
Male	100	47.6
Total	208	99.0
Missing	2	1.0
Religion		
Orthodox	158	75.2
Greek-Catholic	7	3.3
Romano-Catholic	34	16.2
Others	52	24.7
Location		
Urban	166	79.0
Rural	44	21.0
Visits to a science laboratory	39	18.7
Visits to a science museum	126	60.6

Note: Total number of study participants, $N = 210$

depictions, we worded the instructions on the activity as gender neutral, asking children to draw "a person who works in science."

Data Analysis

Students' drawings of scientists were the primary data in our study. Quantitative data analyzed in the current study consisted in students' scores on their drawings, and survey data (i.e., demographic information, visits to science labs and science museum).

The first step in data analysis consisted in data coding. A numerical code was assigned to each drawing. The coding rubric (see Appendix A) was adapted from Mason, Kahle, and Gardner (1991) and included coding categories for stereotype indicators on six areas, as follows: personal characteristics (i.e., lab coats, eye glasses), symbols of research (i.e., test tubes, experimental animals), symbols of knowledge (i.e., equations on board), signs of technology (i.e., machines, solutions in glassware), and, specialty of the scientist (i.e., chemist, biologist, physicist). Each category also had a "Others" section where we coded any significant items identified in the students' drawings (e.g., representations of rockets, computers, syringes). Each drawing thus, received a stereotype indicator score based on the total number of stereotypical items identified in the drawing. The total stereotype indicator score can range from 0 to 17. A score of 0 indicates a drawing without specific stereotypes in depicting the scientists (e.g., having both a male and female scientist working in an outdoor science project with a neutral physical appearance). A score of 17 indicates a drawing with the highest stereotype indicator score (e.g., a male scientist working in a chemistry laboratory with a specific physical appearance, such as unkempt, sinister, or eccentric).

Additionally, each drawing was labeled as "positive," "neutral," "sinister," or "eccentric" (see coding rubric in Appendix A). The scientists' depictions were labeled as "positive" when they were portrayed in a non-traditional setting, using uncommon or outdoor lab equipment, such as working in an outdoor environment or in a setting other than a typical laboratory. Scientists were labelled "eccentric" when students portrayed them with unkempt appearances, bloodshot eyes, antisocial (nerdy) characters, and "sinister" if images had violent explosions, evil facial expressions, or displayed violent behavior. Also, part of the coding, we included characteristics related to whether the students' drawings appeared to be some kind of nonhuman rendering, such as a "fantasy" figure or a "monster." Additionally, coding included the presence or absence of occupational details (e.g., animals, syringes, lab coats, head lamps, chalkboards, books).

The coding procedure followed the guidelines of qualitative research (Creswell, 2013) and consisted in two phases, as follows:

Phase 1: Testing and Reliability. Two coders read all drawings and tested the existing coding scheme to establish reliability. To test the coding scheme, both coders selected randomly 15 drawings, a portion of the existing data. These 15 drawings were then coded independently by each coder. Once the independent coding was done, the two coders met to compare their codes, discuss their coding procedures, and adjust the coding scheme as needed.

Phase 2: Data Coding. In the second phase of the coding, all drawings were coded by one coder only, after both coders made sure they tested the coding scheme and they reached 100% agreement on coding procedures (Creswell, 2013). One researcher coded thus the rest of the drawings using the same coding scheme which was tested and proved reliable.

126 • M. M. THOMSON and Z. ZAKARIA

Further, to answer each research question, comparative analyses (i.e., one-way analysis of variance, ANOVA and t-tests), chi-square tests and regression analysis were conducted. Results from these analyses are presented below.

FINDINGS AND DISCUSSION

Scientist's Appearance, Specialty, and Gender

Appearance

Findings answering our first research question reveal that students hold stereotypes with respect to scientists' appearance, specialty, and gender. In the current study, the obtained average stereotype indicator score for students' drawings was 3 ($SD = 2.3$, $min = 0$, $max = 9$). The overall stereotype indicator score can range from 0 –17. Scores for scientists' representations, including appearance, specialty and gender are summarized in Table 8.2.

TABLE 8.2 Students' Overall Representation of Scientists					
	All Students $N = 210$ **(%)**		**Female** $n = 108$ **(%)**		**Male** $n = 100$ **(%)**
Personal Characteristics					
Lab coats[a]	66	(31.4)	37	(34)	29	(29)
Eyeglasses	57	(07.1)	30	(27.7)	27	(27)
Facial hair	8	(04.3)	4	(3.7)	4	(4)
Unkempt appearance	58	(28.1)	27	(25)	31	(31)
Symbols of Research					
Test-tubes[a]	107	(51.0)	58	(53)	49	(49)
Flasks[a]	103	(49.0)	59	(54)	44	(44)
Microscopes	22	(10.5)	7	(6)	15	(15)
Bunsen-burner[a]	35	(16.7)	21	(19.4)	14	(14)
Experimental Animals	18	(8.6)	13	(12)	5	(5)
Symbols of Knowledge					
Books	8	(03.8)	5	(4.6)	3	(3)
Filing cabinets	12	(05.7)	7	(6.4)	5	(5)
Symbols of Technology					
Solutions in Glassware[a]	113	(53.8)	60	(55.5)	53	(53)
Machines	15	(7.6)	7	(6.4)	8	(8)
Gender of scientists					
Female	49	(23.3)	48	(44)	1	(1)
Male	142	(68)	53	(49)	89	(91.7)

[a] representations of chemistry

Data was analyzed based on frequencies of stereotypic indicators represented in students' drawings. The majority of drawings, 164 (78.1%) portrayed the scientists with a *neutral overall appearance*- neither positive, sinister, or eccentric attributes were present. However, the rest of drawings, 51 (28.1%) represented scientists with an unkempt appearance (i.e., wild hair, blood shot eyes, antisocial, unusual expression). Additionally, in terms of depicting scientists' *personal characteristics*, 66 (31.4%) of the drawings presented scientists wearing a lab coat and 57 (27.1%) of the drawings depicted scientists wearing eyeglasses. See Figure 8.1 in Appendix B for an illustration [Drawing ref. RO204]

Specialty

Relative to the entire sample size, a large number of students, 129 (61.4%) used at least one indicator of a chemistry laboratory. Specifically, 107 (51%) drawings included test tube(s) and 103 (49%) had flasks. Solutions in glassware were present in 113 (53.8%) of the drawings. Additionally, 35 (16.7%) of the drawings had Bunsen-burners in their depictions of scientists. Students not only have drawn elements of a chemistry related lab, many of them 14 (6.7%), even wrote the words 'chemist', 'chemistry', and 'chemical scientist' in their drawings. In the coding rubric, five categories were identified as stereotype indicators of a laboratory in chemistry or related area (i.e., biochemistry, chemical engineering). These five categories were: lab-coats, test-tubes, flasks, Bunsen-burner, and solution in glasses. Figure 8.2 and 8.3 (in Appendix B) illustrate students' representations of chemists.

However, a few other specialties ($n = 15$; 7.1%) were also represented in students' drawings. Among them, microbiologists and physicists are notable, but also archaeologists and astronauts were included. Interestingly, doctors have been represented as scientists on 23 (11%) of the drawings. Among them, 7 (3.3%) drawings included medical masks, 7 (3.3 %) included syringes, and 3 (1.4%) included stethoscopes. A small number of students ($n = 4$; 1.9%) used the term "medical scientist" in their title and other ($n = 19$; 9%) used the term "doctor" either in their title or in the short description provided alongside their drawings (to describe what the person working in science is actually doing). Figure 8.4 in Appendix B illustrate a representation of scientists as doctors.

Gender

A prominence of male scientists was observed among students' drawings (see Table 8.2). The scientist's gender was recognized by the body shape, facial structure, length of hair, and presence or absence of make-up. The majority of drawings, 142 (67.6%) represented drawings of male scientists. Only about a quarter, 50 (23.8%) of the drawings represented a female scientist.

128 • M. M. THOMSON and Z. ZAKARIA

Student Characteristics and Stereotyping Scientists

To explore how students' characteristics can predict stereotyping, we conducted a multiple hierarchical regression using factors in the following three stages: (a) Stage 1, primary characteristics (age and gender), (b) Stage 2, secondary characteristics (school location, grade, religion, ethnicity), and (c) Stage 3, probable characteristics (visit to a science laboratory and visit to a science museum). At stage one, age and gender accounted for a significant 6% of the variance in the stereotype indicator scores, F $(2,200) = 7.446$, $p < .001$. Introducing grade, location (urban or rural), religion and ethnicity explained an additional 9.7% of the variance, F $(6,196) = 4.601$, $p < .001$. Finally, the addition of "visit to a science lab" and "visit to a science museum" to the regression model explained an additional 12.7% of the variance in stereotype indicator score, F $(8, 194) = 4.585$, $p < .001$. Together, all independent variables accounted for 12.4% of the variance in stereotyping, $Adj. R^2 = .124$, F $(7, 194) = 4.585$, $p < .001$. Table 8.3 summarizes the results.

TABLE 8.3   Multiple Hierarchical Regression Analysis Predicting Scientists' Representations

Model	Independent Variables	Standardized Coefficient (β)	t	F	Adj. R^2
1	Age	−0.257	−3.761[***]	7.446[***]	0.060
	Gender	−0.043	−0.625		
2	Age	−0.007	−0.070	4.601[***]	0.097
	Gender	−0.059	−0.861		
	Grade	−0.347	−3.347[**]		
	Religion	−0.078	−1.058		
	Ethnicity	0.075	0.905		
	Location (urban/rural)	−0.039	−0.487		
3	Age	0.004	0.037	4.585[***]	0.124
	Gender	−0.061	−0.908		
	Grade	−0.338	−3.294[***]		
	Religion	−0.072	−.996		
	Ethnicity	0.100	1.223		
	Location (urban/rural)	−0.049	−0.618		
	Visit to a science lab	0.038	0.560		
	Visit to the science museum	−0.196	−2.816[**]		

[*] $p < .05$, [**] $p < .005$, [***] $p < .001$

Students' Perception of Scientists and Their Work • **129**

Ethnicity, Religion and School Location

Our findings revealed no significant differences with respect to students' ethnic membership ($\beta = 0.100$, $t = 1.22$, $p = .430$), students' religion ($\beta = -.072$, $t = -.996$, $p = .755$), or school location, such as urban or rural ($\beta = .463$, $t = -.618$, $p = .320$), and the score for indicators of stereotyping scientists. Additionally, one-way analysis of variance (ANOVA) results showed no significant differences in stereotyping between students from different religions, $F(3, 206) = .399$, $p = .755$. No significant differences were found with respect to students' ethnicity, $F(3, 206) = 2.63$, $p = .051$, or school location (rural versus urban), $F(1, 208) = .995$, $p = .320$.

Student Gender and Indicators of Stereotyping

The majority of students' drawings, 142 (67.6%) presented drawings of male scientists, and only 50 (23.8%) drawings represented a female scientist. Among the 108 female students, 48 (44%) drew female scientists and 53 (49%) drew male scientists. In contrast, among the 100 male students, 91 (91%) drew a male scientist and only 1 (1%) drew a female scientist. In the other 8 (8%) drawings, the scientists' gender could not be identified. Figure 8.5 in Appendix B illustrates a female scientist.

A chi-square test of interdependence was calculated to compare the frequency of scientists' gender between boys and girls. A significant interaction was found ($\chi^2(3) = 54.33$, $p < .001$) which suggests that there are significant differences in frequencies ($p < .001$) between boys' and girls' depictions of scientists with respect to scientists' gender. However, further results from an independent *t*-test found no statistically significant differences between female ($M = 3.1$, $SD = 2.4$) and male students ($M = 2.8$, $SD = 2.1$), $t(206) = 0.809$, $p = 0.419$ with respect to their *obtained score on stereotypic indicators.*

Student Grade Level and Age

Students' grade level statistically significantly and negatively correlated with students' stereotype indicator scores ($r = -.341$, $p < .001$). In the multiple hierarchical regression model, controlling for other demographics and "visit to a science lab" and "visit to a science museum," grade level can statistically significantly predict the stereotype indicator score ($\beta = -.338$, $t = -3.29$, $p = .001$). To further analyze how grade level was associated with stereotype indicators, ANOVA was used. The grouping variable in the ANOVA were the three grade levels, namely, 3rd, 4th and 5th grade (see Table 8.4).

As group sizes largely differed and the Levene's test revealed, the homogeneity of variance was not met ($p < .001$). Thus, the *Welch's F* test was used. The *Welch's* ANOVA between students' grade level and stereotype indicator was statistically significant, *Welch' F*(2, 75.6) = 36, $p < .001$. Additionally, as

130 ▪ M. M. THOMSON and Z. ZAKARIA

TABLE 8.4 Means and Standard Deviations of Social Stereotype Score by Grade Level

Grade level	Age (years)	n	M	SD
Grade 3 ($n = 42$)	8–9	35	4.04	2.24
	10–11	7		
	12–13	0		
Grade 4 ($n = 143$)	8–9	13	3.01	2.28
	10–11	126		
	12–13	0		
	Not indicated	4		
Grade 5 ($n = 25$)	8–9	0	1.08	1.03
	10–11	17		
	12–13	7		
	Not indicated	1		

Note: Total number of study participants, $N = 210$

there was a slight skewness in two of the groups, a non-parametric *Kruskal–Wallis H* test was also used and the results confirmed that there was statistically significant difference in stereotype indicator scores between the grade levels, $H(2) = 26.9$, $p < .001$, with a mean rank of 133.2 for grade 3, 106.3 for grade 4, and 54.5 for grade 5. Games-Howell post hoc revealed that grade 3 ($M = 4.04$, $SD = 2.24$) had a significantly higher average score than grade 4 ($M = 3.01$, $SD = 2.28$) and grade 5 ($M = 1.08$, $SD = 1.03$). See Table 8.5 for a summary of results.

Students' age level statistically significantly and negatively correlated with students' stereotype indicator scores ($r = -.258$, $p < .001$). However, in the multiple hierarchical regression, controlling for the other demographics and "visit to a science lab" and "visit to a science museum," the model showed that students' age cannot statistically significantly predict the stereotype indicator score ($\beta = .004$, $t = .037$, $p = .971$). Although, in the first stage (block 1), age can significantly predict stereotyping ($\beta = -.257$,

TABLE 8.5 Post-Hoc Results for Stereotype Indicator Scores by Grade Level

Grade Level	Mean (SD)	Mean Differences ($\bar{X}_i - \bar{X}_j$)		
		1	2	3
Grade 3	4.04 (2.42)	—		
Grade 4	3.01 (2.28)	1.03*	—	
Grade 5	1.08 (1.03)	-2.96***	-1.93***	—

* $p < .05$, ** $p < .005$, *** $p < .001$

$t = -3.76$, $p < .001$) on the second and third stage (block 2 and (c) when, grade, location, religion, ethnicity and visits to science labs and museums were introduced, age did not significantly predict stereotyping.

Visits to Science Laboratory and Stereotyping

For our third research question, study findings show that only 39 (18.6%) students indicated in their survey responses that they visited a science laboratory. The regression model shows that vising a science laboratory did not significantly predict students' stereotyping ($\beta = .038$, $t = .560$, $p = .576$). Independent t-test results showed no significant differences in the stereotype indicator scores between students who visited a science laboratory and students who did not, $t(207) = .216$, $p = .829$.

Visits to Museums and Stereotyping

The multiple hierarchical regression model suggests that controlling for students' age, gender, grade and location, students' visit to science museums can statistically significantly predict students' stereotype indicator scores ($\beta = -.187$, $t = -2.8$, $p < .01$). For further analysis independent sample t-tests were performed comparing the score of stereotypic indicators and students' visit to museums. Table 8.6 presents the results.

Results show that students who indicated in their survey responses that they *visited science museums* ($n = 126$; $M = 3.4$, $SD = 2.4$) *scored significantly*

TABLE 8.6 Students' Visit to Science Museums and Scores on Stereotype Indicators

Indicators	Visits to museums		t
	Yes (n = 126) Mean (SD)	No (n = 82) Mean (SD)	
Indicators of a chemistry laboratory (5 components in total)	2.3 (1.7)	1.6 (1.6)	3***
Total indicators of stereotyping	3.4 (2.4)	2.4 (2.0)	3***
Personal Appearances (5 components)	1 (1.0)	0.7 (0.9)	1.9*
Symbol of Research (5 components)	1.5 (1.2)	1.1 (1.1)	2.4*
Symbols of knowledge (2 components)	0.1 (0.4)	0.04 (0.2)	1.6
Symbol of Technology (2 components)	0.7 (0.6)	0.5 (0.6)	2.4*

higher in stereotyping indicators than students who indicated in their survey that they have not visited science museums ($n = 82$; $M = 2.4$, $SD = 2.0$, t (206) = 3, $p < .05$). With respect to scientists' specialty, students' who visited science museums ($M = 2.3$, $SD = 1.7$) represented more often a chemistry laboratory than students who have not visited a science museum, t (206) = 3, $p < .05$.

CONCLUSION

Overall, study findings showed that most students *represented male scientists* in their drawings; the common image of a scientist was that of a white male wearing a lab-coat with a facial appearance resembling images of popular scientists (i.e., Einstein). In terms of specialty, most students represented *scientists as chemists*; a few drawings represented scientists as medical doctors.

Further, our results indicated a statistically significant difference in students' score of stereotyping indicators with respect to student *grade level*. In the current study students from grades 3rd, 4th and 5th were included. Students in lower grade levels tended to have higher stereotyping indicator scores. Moreover, an interesting finding revealed that students who indicated in their survey responses that they *visited science museums scored significantly higher in stereotyping indicators* than students who indicated in their survey answers that they have not visited science museums. However, there were no significant differences between students who indicated in their survey responses that they *visited a science laboratory* compared to students who indicated in their survey answers that they have. The main key points from our findings, along with a brief discussion, are summarized below.

Perceptions of Scientists' Gender and Specialty

Gender

Most drawings represented male scientists, and only about a quarter represented a female scientist. Male students drew predominantly male scientists; only one male student drew a female scientist. Among the female students, about half of them drew female scientists, and the other half, drew male scientists. Reflecting on previous studies (i.e., Buldu, 2006; Finson, 2002; Losh et al., 2008; Miller et al., 2018) an overall dominance of male scientists is present in both female and male students' drawings. Although students tend to draw images of the same sex people (Bodzin & Gehringer, 2001; Dickson et al., 1990; Halim et al., 2017), this factor seem to be less influential in our study. However, as Miller et al. (2018) pointed out, young children possibly draw images of their own sex because they have limited knowledge of scientists. Studies conducted with K–12 students and teachers in which they were asked to depict engineers (i.e., Carreño, Palou, & López-Malo, 2010; Cruz López et al., 2011; Lyons & Thomson, 2006), showed similar results in terms on gender stereotypes. Cruz López et al. (2011) point out that even though the female participants in their study were almost 60% of the participants, the majority (63%) of the drawings depicted a male engineer at work, while 24% of K–12 students included a male and a female or a neutral figure in their drawing.

Specialty

Findings revealed that chemistry reins in stereotyping scientists among our study population, which is in line with previous findings (Finson, 2002; Rodari, 2007). Relative to the entire sample size, a large number of students used at least one indicator of a chemistry laboratory. Interestingly, in the current study, doctors have been represented as scientists in about a quarter of drawings. However, all representations of scientists as doctors were found in students' drawings from rural schools. This could indicate that their most closely encounter with a science like lab was that of a doctor's office.

Differences in Students' Grade Level and Age

In our study, we found statistically significant differences between student grade level and indicators of stereotyping scientists. A hierarchical multiple regression model revealed that students' grade level statistically significantly predicted their stereotyping score. Students in grade 5 showed significantly lower stereotyping that students in 3rd and 4th grade level. These results seem to indicate that students in higher grade levels stereotype less comparing to their peers in lower grade levels. This finding remarkably contradicts with the previous study findings which suggests that as age and grade level increases students' stereotyping are elevated too (Chambers, 1983, Miller et al., 2018). A probable explanation for our finding can be that students' exposure to a more complex science curriculum, as they progressed through their grade levels, reduced stereotyping. However, limitations in group homogeneity may affected the results in this case. In our sample, students from grade 5 represented the smallest group, compared to grade 4 and grade 3. We discuss this aspect in study limitations.

Visits to Museums and Science Laboratories

An interesting and novel finding from our study was related to students' visits to science museums. Students who indicated in their survey responses that they *visited science museums scored significantly higher in stereotyping indicators* than students who indicated on their survey answers that they have not visited science museums. This is a noteworthy finding, but further research on this area should be conducted to support such findings. It is possible that museums they visited focused on presenting scientists from the past centuries, and thus the scientists were predominantly white males which contributed to supporting students' perceptions about who scientists are. Science museums should make efforts to include contemporary scientists in their exhibitions and focus on representing a diversity of scientists (e.g., gender and ethnic representation, as well as various types of specialties in science).

However, findings related to students visiting a science laboratory did not show significant results. Students who visited a science laboratory did not show significant differences in their perception of scientists compared to students who did not visit a science laboratory. One possible explanation is that since a very low number of students from or sample visited a science lab, it is most likely that their sources of scientists' images came from other contexts (e.g., media, TV, books, cartoons) than visiting a science lab.

IMPLICATIONS

Findings from prior studies using "Draw-a-Scientist Test" (DAST) suggest that students see scientists predominantly as white, often unattractive men; one consequence may be that girls and minority students do not identify with science careers and feel that a science career is "not like me" (Losh et al., 2008; Wang, Eccles, & Kenny, 2013; Wong, 2015). Our research findings revealed that Romanian students from our sample had stereotypical images of scientists, in line with previous studies conducted in this area. Implications from our study could help educators and policy makers in Romania to develop science initiatives, similar to those implemented in other countries (i.e., U.S., UK) that support a strong STEM education, and implement a science curriculum that values diversity and research-based practices.

Studies show that both informal and formal science experiences can be a strong influence on students' perceptions of science and scientists (Jones et al., 2000). Studies that related students' out-of-school experiences with their perceptions of scientists, revealed that such experiences can help students develop more adequate perceptions about scientists and the nature of their work (Jarvis & Pell, 2002; Jones et al., 2000). Research findings suggest that students' scientific views and understanding of science evolve when they are given out-of-school opportunities to explore science *paired up with a rigorous formal science instruction* (Jarvis & Pell, 2002). As such, visits to science museums, zoos, botanical gardens, and participating in dialogues between peers can help students develop an understanding of science and

Students' Perception of Scientists and Their Work • **135**

provide opportunities to discuss stereotypes about scientists (Guberman &Van Dusen, 2001; Tunnicliffe, 2000). Hence, involving students in authentic science activities will provide them with valuable learning experiences, helping them to enhance their science content and views about the science careers. For instance, science summer camps, mentorship experiences with scientists, science magnet schools, STEM-focused programs in public schools, are a few examples of programs implemented throughout the United States. Similar programs can be adopted to Romania where the educational system provides very little support for students' STEM preparation at the elementary level and STEM-focused programs are needed.

Furthermore, teachers' role is significantly important in providing formal and informal science experiences to students addressing the role of science and scientists. Providing students with various instructional modes (i.e., active, inquiry-based) and immersive experiences (e.g., lab research experiences with a scientist), would facilitate students' conceptual understanding about the nature of science and scientists' work.

Additional research regarding attributes of *role models* in a given field can highly influence the perspective of observers about that field (Dasgupta, 2011). In several studies, students' representations of scientists reflected or specifically mentioned well-known scientists such as Albert Einstein and Newton (Finson et al., 2006; Türkmen, 2008). A recent study explored how the presentation of a role model can impact students' beliefs about success in science (Lin-Siegler et al., 2016). In this study, a group of 9th and 10th grade students read one out of three types of stories about renowned scientists describing (a) the scientist's intellectual struggles, (b) struggles in scientist's personal life, and (c) success in science career. Results revealed that students who read the struggle stories improved science learning, compared to those who read the success story (Lin-Siegler et al., 2016). Hence, adopting curriculum that would include biographies of scientists to represent diversity among scientists and a diversity of experiences in science, including scientists' struggles, can provide valuable learning tools for students about who scientists are and what is the nature of their work.

Limitations and Future Studies

One limitation of the current study could be related to students' demographic data and samples. Participants were all upper elementary school students (Grades 3–5) and all of them identified themselves as White-Caucasians (Table 8.1). Additionally, students' grade level differences did not meet the homogeneity of variance assumption as sample size in each group largely varied. There were few students from 5th grade ($n = 25$; 11.9%), compared to 4th grade ($n = 143$; 68.1%) and 3rd grade ($n = 42$; 20%). This may have influenced our comparative results regarding student grade levels with respect to perceptions of scientists.

Future studies could address these limitations and also focus on including systematic extensions to other jobs to assess where scientists "fit" as occupational incumbents. It could also be helpful to consider other student characteristics and relationship with the type/quality of drawings produced. For example, do high academic achievers depict scientists differently from less achieving students? Or, do students with low socio-economic-status (SES) depict professions, especially scientists differently than high SES students? Additional future studies could explore -in addition to demographic and cultural factors-the role of psychological factors, such as the impact of motivational beliefs (i.e., efficacy), or the effect of mindsets on students' depiction of scientists and domain identification.

APPENDIX A
Coding Rubric for the Draw-a-Scientist Test (DAST)

How many drawings included the following	Tally	Score
Personal Characteristics		
Laboratory coats		
Eyeglasses		
Facial Hair		
Pencils/pens in pocket		
Unkempt appearance		
Symbols of Research		
Test tubes		
Flasks		
Microscope		
Bunsen burner		
Experimental Animals		
Other		
Please list 'other' symbols of research		
Symbols of Knowledge		
Books		
Filing cabinets		
Other		

Students' Perception of Scientists and Their Work · **137**

	Tally	**Score**
Signs of Technology		
Solutions in glassware		
Machines		
Other		
Please list "other" symbols of technology		
Scientist's Specialty		
No specialty		
Yes		
Can't tell if it is a scientist		
How many drawings depicted Women and Men		
Drawing of men		
Drawing of women		
Drawing in which you can't tell if scientist is a man or woman		
Scientist's Racial or Ethnic Group		
Scientists who appear to be Caucasian/White		
Scientists who appear to be African-American, Hispanic or Native American		
Scientists who appear to be Asian or Asian-American		
Drawings in which racial/ethnic group of scientists in not evident		
Total Score		
Characterize the overall appearance as: *Eccentric*—Wild hair; unfashionable clothing; unkempt appearance; bloodshot eyes; *Sinister*—Violent explosions; evil facial expressions; animals crying or yelping for help; Frankenstein's monster type characters; captions with violent language; *Neutral*—Not necessarily positive or negative. *Positive*—Depicts the scientist in a non-traditional setting or using unusual or outdoor lab equipment.	**Notes**	

Note: The coding rubric in the current study was developed based on Mason, Kahle, & Gardner (1991) and Barman (1999).

APPENDIX B
Sample Students' Representations of Scientists
(Figures 8.1–8.5)

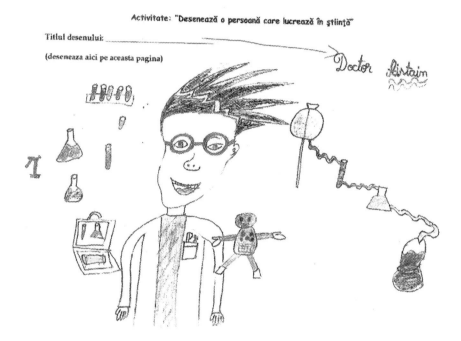

Translation for the drawing's title: "Doctor Einstein" (spelled by student as "Ainstain")

Figure 8.1 [Drawing ref. RO204]—Illustration of a scientist's personal characteristics.

Students' Perception of Scientists and Their Work ▪ **139**

Activitate: "Desenează o persoană care lucrează în ştiinţă"

Titlul desenului: _Omul stiintific_

Translation for the drawing's title: "The scientific person"

Figure 8.2 [Drawing ref. RO40]—Illustration of a scientist's specialty as chemistry.

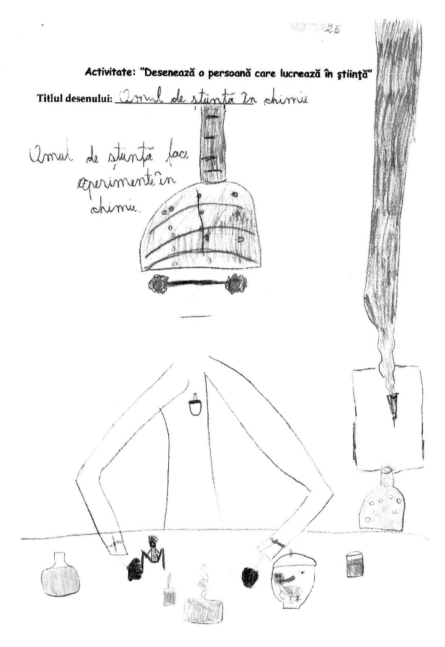

Translation for the drawing's title: "The chemist," and additional text: "Scientist performing a chemistry experiment."

Figure 8.3 [Drawing ref. RO25]—Illustration of a scientist's specialty as chemistry.

Students' Perception of Scientists and Their Work ▪ **141**

Translation for the drawing's title: "A doctor"

Figure 8.4 [Drawing ref. RO21]—Illustration of a scientist's specialty as medical doctor.

Translation for the drawing's title: "The geologist" and additional text: "My drawing is depicting a geologist that investigates a rock."

Figure 8.5 [Drawing ref. RO29]—Illustration of a scientist's female gender characteristics.

REFERENCES

Barman, C.R. (1999). Students' views about scientists and school science: Engaging K–8 teachers in a national study. *Journal of Science Teacher Education, 10*, 43–54.

Beardslee, D., & O'Dowd, D. (1961). The college-student image of the scientist. *American Association for the Advancement of Science, 133*(3457), 997–1001.

Bodzin, A., & Gehringer, M. (2001). Breaking science stereotypes. *Science and Children, 38*(8), 36–41.

Buldu, M. (2006). Young children's perceptions of scientists: A preliminary study. *Educational Research, 48*(1), 121–132.

Carreño, S., Palou, E., & López-Malo, A (2010). *Eliciting P–12 Mexican teachers' images of engineering: What do engineers do?* Proceedings of the ASEE Annual Conference and Exposition, Louisville, Kentucky.

Chambers, D. W. (1983). Stereotypic images of the scientist: The Draw-a-Scientist test. *Science Education, 67*(2), 255–265.

Cheryan, S., Plaut, V., Handron, C., & Hudson, L. (2013). The stereotypical computer scientist: Gendered media representations as a barrier to inclusion for women. *Sex Roles, 69*(1–2), 58–71.

Christidou, V., Bonoti, F., & Kontopoulou, A. (2016). American and Greek children's visual images of scientists. *Science & Education, 25*(5–6), 497–522.

Christidou, V., Hatzinikita, V., & Samaras, G. (2012). The image of scientific researchers and their activity in Greek adolescents' drawings. *Public Understanding of Science, 21*(5), 626–647.

Creswell, J. W. (2013). *Qualitative inquiry and research design: Choosing among five approaches.* Sage Publications.

Cruz López, C.C., Chavela Guerra, R.C., López-Malo, A., & Palou, E. (2011). *Eliciting Mexican high school students' images of engineering: What do engineers do?* Proceedings of the ASEE Annual Conference and Exposition, Vancouver, BC, Canada.

Dasgupta, N. (2011). In-group experts and peers as social vaccines who inoculate the self-concept: The stereotype inoculation model. *Psychological Inquiry, 22*(4), 231–246.

Dickson, J., Saylor, C., & Finch, A. (1990). Personality factors, family structure, and sex of drawn figure on the Draw-A-Person test. *Journal of Personality Assessment, 55*(1), 362–366.

Etzioni, A., & Nunn, C. (1974). The public appreciation of science in contemporary America. *Daedalus, 103*(3), 191–205.

Farland-Smith, D. (2012). Development and field test of the modified Draw-a-Scientist test and the Draw-a-Scientist rubric. *School Science and Mathematics, 112*(2), 109–116.

Finson, K. D. (2002). Drawing a scientist: What we do and do not know after fifty years of drawings. *School Science & Mathematics, 107*, 335–345.

Finson, K. D., Pedersen, J., & Thomas, J. (2006). Comparing science teaching styles to students' perceptions of scientists. *School Science and Mathematics, 106*(1), 8–15.

144 • M. M. THOMSON and Z. ZAKARIA

Flicker, E. (2003). Between brains and breasts-women scientists in fiction film: On the marginalization and sexualization of scientific competence. *Public Understanding of Science, 12,* 307–318.

Fort, D., & Varney, H. (1989). How students see scientists: Mostly male, mostly white, and mostly benevolent. *Science and Children, 26*(8), 8–13.

Funk, C. (2003). *VCU life sciences survey: Public values science but concerned about biotechnology.* Retrieved from http://www.vcu.edu/lifesci/images2/PublicValues.pdf

Griffith, A. L. (2010). Persistence of women and minorities in STEM field majors: is it the school that matters? *Economics of Education Review, 29,* 911–922.

Guberman, S. R., & Van Dusen, A. (2001). Children's investigations in a science center. Paper presented at the American Educational Research Association, Seattle, WA.

Halim, M. L. D., Ruble, D. N., Tamis-LeMonda, C. S., Shrout, P. E., & Amodio, D. M. (2017). Gender attitudes in early childhood: Behavioral consequences and cognitive antecedents. *Child Development, 88*(3), 882–899.

Hopwood, A. (2012). *Hosting professional scientists in the classroom: the effect on rural sixth graders' attitudes toward science,* Unpublished document.

Huber, R., & Burton, G. (1995). What do students think scientists look like? *School Science and Mathematics, 95*(7), 371–376.

Jarvis, T., & Pell, A. (2002). Effect of the challenger experience on elementary children's attitudes to science. *Journal of Research in Science Teaching, 39*(10), 979–1000.

Jones, M., Howe, A., & Rua, M. (2000). Gender differences in students' experiences, interests, and attitudes toward science and scientists. *Science Education, 84*(2), 180–192.

Kahle, J. B. (1988). Gender and science education II. *Development and Dilemmas in Science Education,* 249–265.

Karaçam, S. (2016). Investigating how the biographies of today's scientists affect 8th graders' scientist image. *EURASIA Journal of Mathematics, Science & Technology Education, 12*(8), 1971–1995.

Krajkovich, J., & Smith, J. (1982). The development of the image of science and scientists scale. *Journal of Research in Science Teaching, 19*(1), 39–44.

Lyons, J., & Thomson, S. (2006*). Investigating the long-term impact of an engineering-based GK–12 program on students' perceptions of engineering,* Proceedings of the ASEE Annual Conference and Exposition, Chicago, Illinois.

Losh, S.C., Wilke, R.A., & Pop, M. (2008). Some methodological issues with 'Draw-a-Scientist Tests' among young children. *International Journal of Science Education, 30*(6), 773–792.

Long, M., Boiarsky, G., & Thayer, G. (2001). Gender and racial counter-stereotypes in science education television: A content analysis. *Public Understanding of Science, 10*(3), 255–269.

Lin-Siegler, X., Ahn, J., Chen, J., Fang, F., & Luna-Lucero, M. (2016). Even Einstein struggled: Effects of learning about great scientists' struggles on high school students' motivation to learn science. *Journal of Educational Psychology, 108*(3), 314–328.

Mason, C., Kahle, J., & Gardner, A. (1991). Draw-A-Scientist test: Future implications. *School Science and Mathematics, 91*(5), 193–198.

Mead, M., & Metraux, R. (1957). Image of the scientist among high-school students. *Science, 126*(3270), 384–390.

Miller, D. I., Nolla, K. M., Eagly, A. H., & Uttal, D. H. (2018). The development of children's gender-science stereotypes: A Meta-analysis of 5 decades of US Draw-a-Scientist studies. *Child Development,* https://doi.org/10.1111/cdev.13039.

Miller, D., Eagly, A., & Linn, M. (2015). Women's representation in science predicts national gender-science stereotypes: Evidence from 66 nations. *Journal of Educational Psychology, 107*(3), 631–644.

Minogue, J. (2010). What is the teacher doing? What are the students doing? An application of the Draw-a-Science-Teacher test. *Journal of Science Teacher Education, 21*(7), 767–781.

Maoldomhnaigh, M., & Hunt, Á. ·(1988). Some factors affecting the image of the scientist drawn by older primary school pupils. *Research in Science & Technological Education, 6*(2), 159–166.

Monhardt, R. (2003). The image of the scientist through the eyes of Navajo Children. *Journal of American Indian Education, 42*(3).

National Research Council (2011). *Successful K–12 STEM education: Identifying effective approaches in science, technology, engineering, and mathematics.* National Academy Press.

National Research Council (2012) *A framework for K–12 science education: Practices, crosscutting concepts, and core ideas.* National Academy Press.

National Science Board (2016). *Science & engineering indicators 2016* (NSB Publication No. 2016-1). National Science Foundation.

National Science Foundation (2017). *Women, Minorities, and Persons with Disabilities in Science and Engineering: 2017.* Special Report NSF 17-310. Arlington, VA. Retrieved from: https://www.nsf.gov/statistics/2017/nsf17310/

Nix, S., Perez-Felkner, L., & Thomas, K. (2015). Perceived mathematical ability under challenge: a longitudinal perspective on sex segregation among STEM degree fields. *Frontiers in Psychology, 6* (530). https://doi.org/10.3389/fpsyg.2015.00530.

Organisation of Economic Cooperation and Development (2014). *Education at a Glance 2014: OECD indicators.*

Rodari, P. (2007). Science and scientists in the drawings of European children. *Journal of Science Communication, 6*(3), 1–12.

Ruiz-Mallen, I., & Escalas, M. (2012). Scientists seen by children: A case study in Catalonia, Spain. *Science Communication, 34*(4), 520–545.

Samaras, G., Bonoti, F., & Christidou, V. (2012). Exploring children's perceptions of scientists through drawings and interviews. *Procedia-Social and Behavioral Sciences, 46*, 1541–1546.

Steinke, J., Lapinski, M., Crocker, N., Zietsman-Thomas, A., Williams, Y., Evergreen, S., &Kuchibhotla, S. (2007). Assessing media influences on middle school aged children's perceptions of women in science using the Draw-a-Scientist test (DAST). *Science Communication, 29*(1), 35–64.

Thomas, M., Henley, T., & Snell, C. (2006). The Draw-a-Scientist test: A different population and a somewhat different story. *College Student Journal, 40*(1), 140–149.

Türkmen, H. (2008). Turkish primary students' perceptions about scientist and what factors are affecting the image of the scientists. *Eurasia Journal of Mathematics, Science & Technology Education, 4*(1), 55–61.

Tunnicliffe, S. (2000). Conversations of family and primary school groups at robotic dinosaur exhibits in a museum: what do they talk about? *International Journal of Science Education, 22*(7), 739–754.

Wang, M., Eccles, J., & Kenny, S. (2013). Not lack of ability but more choice: Individual and gender differences in choice of careers in science, technology, engineering, and mathematics. *Psychological Science, 24*(5), 770–775.

Wong, B. (2015). Careers "From" but not "in" Science: Why are aspirations to be a scientist challenging for minority ethnic students? *Journal of Research in Science Teaching, 52*(7), 979–1002.

CHAPTER 9

EXAMINING MOTIVATION AMONG ELEMENTARY-AGED AFRICAN-AMERICAN STUDENTS

A Review of Socio-Cognitive and Expectancy-Values Constructs

Quaneisha Smith, and Margareta M. Thomson

The purpose of the current research study is to examine in the existing literature various aspects of motivation related to African American boys at the elementary age (e.g., elementary school/primary school age). In the current research investigation, we are taking into consideration motivational constructs from the Social-Cognitive Theory (SCT) and Expectancy-Value Theory (EVT). The current literature review examines several seminal scholarly articles that focus on how various theories explain motivation for African American elementary-aged boys and the recommended strategies about how to help them overcome challenges associated with motivation.

Motivation and Engagement in Various Learning Environments, pages 147–160
Copyright © 2024 by Information Age Publishing
www.infoagepub.com
All rights of reproduction in any form reserved.

147

Historically and currently, African American boys have been perceived or described as underachievers. Oftentimes, they have been labeled as lazy, disengaged, or simply, unmotivated. Recent research suggests that many of these views and labels are misconceptions and current motivation theories help explain the complexity of factors associated with underperformance of African American boys in school. While there is limited research regarding motivation in African American elementary-aged boys, the scarce existing sources attempt at examining the relationship between academic achievement in black males and motivation.

The current literature review aims at exploring the perceived causes regarding *motivation* in African American boys and propose strategies that can be implemented to increase motivation. This literature review will also identify areas where further research is needed as well. One of the most analyzed, discussed and debated themes since the late 1980s has been related to young African American males and their social presence. Early research in this area, conducted by Garibaldi (1992) examined the current decline in the social, economic, and educational status of young African American males. Specifically, the study analyses data from 1987 in New Orleans showing that while 86% of the students were African American, Black males accounted for 58% of the non-promotions, 65% of suspensions, 80% of expulsions, and 45% of all dropouts. The study offers valuable recommendations that can be implemented when motivating black males to succeed in school. Most recommendations suggest that a common effort is needed to help African American male students succeed and gain recognition, by engaging not just the school personnel in education, but communities at large, business leaders, and parents as well (Garibaldi, 1992).

In his study *Motivation in African Americans*, Graham (1994) examined close to 140 studies comprising African American empirical literature on motivation. This research on the expectancy of success and self-concept of ability was reviewed to examine the hypothesis that African Americans have negative self-views about their competence. None of these assumptions were supported in the review. In fact, African Americans appear to maintain a belief in personal control, have high expectancies, and enjoy positive self-regard (Graham, 1994). Graham believes that "self" plays a major role in one's academic success. Self-efficacy, or the belief that one can be successful in a particular task or domain (e.g., to write an essay, or to build a robot), is a key psychological factor in motivation. The *self-efficacy* concept is similar to *expectancies*, a related motivational construct, which are the beliefs and judgments about one's capabilities that will successfully be able to engage and perform tasks successfully. Lastly, Graham's study also took into account teacher influences as a factor explaining why many African American males were underachieving. Teachers' expectations, attitudes or their perceptions regarding students' ability to succeed in a task have a

Examining Motivation Among Elementary-Aged African-American Students • **149**

great influence on students' performance (Bong, 2001; Schunk, Pintrich, & Meece, 2014).

Osborne (1999), in a similar study, examines the idea of identification with academics which is rooted in *self-concept* (i.e., self-efficacy and self-esteem), which greatly impacts individual performance and expectancy. Many theories attempt to explain why, despite all efforts, African American boys continue to lag behind their White counterparts. In Osborn's article, three prominent theories addressing the social and cultural factors that can inhibit academic excellence among these youth are examined. All three factors examined emphasize the barriers that prevent African American boys from incorporating academics as an important part of their self-concepts (Osbourne, 1999). In another study, Warren (2017) evaluates teachers' beliefs about the definition of empathy, the need to use empathy when working with African American boys in the classroom, and whether or not they use empathy when working with African American boys. Lastly, Asher's study (1979), takes a look at whether or not African American children comprehend more high-interest rather than low-interest reading material and whether or not the achievement gap between white and black children when interest reading material is used.

THEORETICAL FRAMEWORKS

The current study examines the topic of motivation among African American boys taking into consideration two major theoretical frameworks and related constructs relative to motivation and achievement. The two main theorical frameworks are briefly described below.

Expectancy-Value Theory (EVT)

In their study explaining the EVT, Wigfield & Eccles (1992) suggest that motivation for a given behavior or action is determined by two factors: *expectancy* and *value*. Expectancies are beliefs and judgments about one's capabilities to perform a task successfully. Values are individual beliefs about the reasons why they might engage in tasks. Expectancy answers the question "Can I do this task?" whereas, value answers the question, "Do I want to do this task and why?" As research suggests, in addition to teachers' anecdotal experiences, many African American boys are not motivated to complete tasks and do not expect to perform well on specific tasks or assignments because they do not expect to perform well and they do not value the task (Schunk, Pintrich, & Meece, 2014).

Task Value

One key motivational construct related to EVT framework is task value. This is defined in the literature as value as an incentive for engagement in academic activities. The four components of task value are, namely attainment value, intrinsic value, utility value and cost (Wigfield & Eccles, 1992). All value components have a powerful impact in how an individual approaches a task, perceives it and engages in the task.

Interest

Another key construct related to values, more specifically to intrinsic value (rather an individual in interested in a task due to personal interest) is interest. *Interest is* a motivational construct relevant in the interplay between motivation and learning and help explain certain motivation aspects in elementary-aged African American boys. A common belief is that students will learn and perform well if they are interested in what they are learning, and the activities presented to them are relevant. In contrast, when students are disinterested, they are less likely to perform well academically. Interest can be divided into three areas: the *personal interest* of the student, the *situational interest*, and interest in the materials used during an activity or an assignment.

Social-Cognitive Theory (SCT)

Another theoretical framework that can be used to explaining motivation is the Social-Cognitive Theory, proposed by Albert Bandura (1993). The SCT suggests that motivational processes influence both learning and performance, and learning occurs in a social context with a dynamic and reciprocal interaction of the student, environment, and behavior. A few motivational constructs associated with SCT and used in the current literature review, are the following:

Self-Efficacy

A key concept in the SCT is *self-efficacy,* which is an individual's belief in his or her capacity to perform behaviors necessary to produce specific performance achievements. Self-efficacy reflects confidence in the ability to exert control over one's own motivation, behavior, and social environment. Self-efficacy is greatly influenced by one's social environment and the behavior of others.

Teacher Influences

Another key motivational construct that impacts the motivation of elementary-aged African American boys is related to teacher influences. Teachers' instructional practices can affect student motivation in many ways.

Important aspects of instructional practices that can impact the motivation of African American boys are planning and decision making, grouping for instruction, teaching methods, use of models, and use of technology. In addition, the amount of empathy that teachers show African American boys can also have a positive or negative effect on their motivation.

EMERGENT THEMES IN THE LITERATURE

The motivational frameworks and related concepts described above, helped guide the formulation of study findings and explain some aspects related to motivation in African American boys. Furthermore, the current study, in light of findings, offers possible explanations for the key factors that impact motivation. The key findings and emergent themes found as a result of the current study are presented below.

Expectations

For many years the social, economic, and educational status of African American males has continued to decline according to research (Garibaldi, 1992). The study conducted in 1987 by Garibaldi, showed the staggering statistics about young African American males with respect to school attendance and academic performance. As the chair of a task force of community leaders and educators, Garibaldi was asked to review the situation of African American boys in the New Orleans Public Schools. The committee's goal was to look at the rates of school retention, suspension, explosion, academic achievement, grade attainment, school attendance, and participation in co-curricular activities. Prior to the committee's work, they viewed the precious academic year's data and solicited community input via a survey regarding how African American boys could be helped and supported.

When collecting data, the researcher learned that only 18% of African American boys scored in the highest quartile on the California Test of Basic Skills math achievement test. Furthermore, only 13% of African American boys scored in the highest quartile on the California Test of Basic Skill reading achievement test (Garibaldi, 1992). The results of the survey given to study participants, showed that 95% of the boys expected to graduate from high school. This shows that the African American boys that were a part of this study expected to do well in school. However, the African American boys, participants in the study, in their survey responses indicated that their teachers did not set high enough expectations and failed to provide the motivational support students needed. The results of the survey show that *teacher influences* heavily impact students' motivation and achievement.

152 • Q. SMITH and M. M. THOMSON

Without high expectations for African American boys and the belief that all students can succeed it is likely that their motivation will be impacted.

Instructional Influences

According to Schunk, Pintrich, and Meece (2014), there is a reciprocal influence between teachers and students. Many early studies of teaching effectiveness assumed that teachers' actions affected student motivation. The expectations that teachers have for their students and the belief that they are able to achieve are connected to the instructional practice of the teacher. In addition, instructional practices such as planning, grouping, effective teaching, the use of models, and technology, all impact student motivation. According to Garibaldi's study teachers play a critical role in reversing the negative effects of academic behaviors of African American boys. Other studies show similar findings, when teachers have internalized and projected the negative stereotypes surrounding African American boys (Todd, Thiem, & Neel, 2016).

Based on study findings, Garibaldi proposes some solutions and recommendations that would be helpful as it relates to the motivation of African American elementary-aged males. Garibaldi suggests that in the same way that society acknowledges athletic performance we should publicly recognize the successful academic experiences of young African American men which will raise their self-concept, self-esteem, and academic confidence. Moreover, "external influences that affect children's dispositions toward learning must be addressed by schools and teachers so that students who do perform at or above average are not ostracized, ridiculed, intimidated, physically assaulted, or belittled by their peers" (Garibaldi,1992, p.8). This shows that social cognitive factors have a profound impact on the motivation of young African American male students. It shows that the behavior and attitudes held by others, greatly impact the motivation of African American elementary-aged boys. Teacher influence plays a vital role in reversing the changing academic and social behaviors of African American males (Garibaldi, 1992). When teachers subscribe to internalizing and projecting the negative stereotypes and myths that are unfairly used to describe African American males, it makes it harder for African American elementary-aged boys to be successful (Garibaldi, 1992). Garibaldi suggests that African American males who are already successful in school must be challenged intellectually and receive positive reinforcement from their teachers. Additionally, the author lists more recommendations that can increase motivation among African American young students. Some of the suggestions are namely: students should be encouraged to participate in academic and athletic extracurricular activities, provide opportunities to engage in

Examining Motivation Among Elementary-Aged African-American Students • **153**

volunteer work and community service, be exposed to community leaders who can serve as role-models, be encouraged by teachers at an early age to attend college, hire more African American male teachers as they can mentor young male students, and ensure to include in classroom curriculum relevant resources to African American young male's personal and professional goals. Additionally, schools and communities should cooperate to help students succeed, such as, businesses can provide their employees with time to visit the elementary schools and volunteer, encourage parents to attend school conferences, and businesses could provide rewards and incentives for children of the employees when they are doing well in school (Garibaldi, 1992).

Socio-Cultural Factors

In the article *Motivation in African Americans* Graham reviews close to 140 reviews regarding African Americans and motivation. This review was organized around three assumptions regarding African Americans and motivation. First, research on achievement motivation was reviewed to examine the belief that African Americans lack certain personality traits necessary for achievement. Second, the empirical literature focuses on locus of control and the assumption that African Americans are less likely to believe in internal or personal control of outcomes. And lastly, research on the expectancy of success and self-concept of ability was reviewed to examine the hypothesis that African Americans have negative self-views about their competence. The last two assumptions mentioned above focus on the expectancy of success, motivational constructs related to and explained by the Expectancy-Value Theory. Most of the key motivational theories include expectancy of goal attainment as one of the important determinants of action (Graham, 1994). All studies in Graham's review were race comparative. Black and White students were presented with a task, and either before or after practice they are asked to predict how well they will do on the next activity. Following either manipulated or naturally occurring success or failure on that task, subjects may then be required to make one or more additional estimates about future performance (Graham, 1994). In addition, the students were given rating scales on which they rated themselves. The findings show that African American students in comparison to their White counterparts overestimated their future performance even when their current performance indicated otherwise. Graham believes that there is little evidence that supports that African American students have low expectancies, relative to either their outcomes or to their White counterparts. Graham concludes that both expectancies for future success and self-concept of ability among African American students remain relatively high even when achievement outcomes indicate otherwise. Given the limitations of the study, the findings described by Graham seem intriguing and more research needs to be conducted in this area.

In the article, *Unraveling Underachievement Among African American boys from an Identification with Academics Perspective*, Osbourne (1999) attempts to explain why African American boys continue to lag behind their White counterparts. This article is a literature review that addresses three theories that are the social and cultural factors that can inhibit academic excellence among these youth: Steele's stereotype threat model, Ogbu's cultural-ecological perspective, and Majors and Billson's "cool pose" theory. All three theories emphasize the barriers that prevent African American boys from incorporating academics as an important part of their self-concepts (Osbourne, 1999). According to Osbourne, factors deeply rooted in U.S. society keep students of color from viewing themselves as scholars, and thereby valuing academics personally. The lack of identification with academics has been shown to cause or contribute to poorer performance. Osbourne notes that several authors have argued that individuals are particularly likely to selectively devalue areas in which their group devalues. Influential factors such as teachers, school environment, and peers all play a part in impacting the motivation of a person. So, if factors around an African American elementary-aged student do not value achievement, it's a good chance that the student may not either.

Sociocultural factors negatively influence the ability of African American students to become and remain strongly identified with academics. Steele's theory of stereotype threat identifies negative stereotypes as a culprit in the academic underperformance of African American students. Steele's stereotype threat model argues that although all students experience anxiety in school situations, students who are members of minority groups for which negative group stereotypes concerning academic ability abound, suffer from even more anxiety. This is continued proof that for African American boys, their school environment and peers can impact their view of academics and eventually their academic achievement. Further, Osbourne examines how minority groups, due to various social influences, might consciously or unconsciously interpret school learning as a displacement process detrimental to their social identity, sense of security, and self-worth. Specifically, individuals identifying themselves as minority students (i.e., African American students) may have observed that even those among them who succeed in school are not fully accepted or rewarded in the same way that White students are accepted or rewarded. This, combined with peer pressure and cultural pressure not to "act White" keep African American boys from being able to identify with academics (Osbourne, 1999). Lastly, the "cool pose" view is one that has an interesting approach to masculinity that allows African American boys to cope and survive in an environment of social oppression and racism, including that found within U.S. schools. In his literature review, Osbourne provides possible solutions to this misidentification with academics among young African American males based on social and environmental factors. He suggests that we help students who are on the road to being disidentified with academics resist it. In addition, he recommends encouraging misidentified students to reidentify with academics by implementing a curriculum reform. The first type of curriculum reform suggested is a multicultural curriculum, which would help African American boys find their "place" in education and identify with academics (Osbourne, 1999). He proposes that another alternative would be to have special days, weeks, and months such as Black History Month where prominent African American can be highlighted. Also, providing a holistic approach to a multicultural curriculum, would help, such as relevant themes infused throughout the curriculum every day via literature, novels, music, art, math, science, social studies, and more. Furthermore, Osbourne proposes that African American males need for self-protective strategies should also be incorporated into the curriculum. The teaching of values such as cooperation, mutual respect, commitment, and love of family, race, community, and nation should also be incorporated.

Lastly and most importantly, a needed reform is related to the way schools implement remediation. Changing remediation practices will help improve African American boy's identification with academics. Though often well-meaning, the remediation focus in many schools increases the problem of stereotypes and disidentification. To students already struggling to overcome both overt and subtle messages that they might be intellectually inferior, remediation suggests that they are in dire peril and doomed to academic failure unless they receive help, further increasing stigma vulnerability and the likelihood of disidentification (Osbourne, 1999). Replacing the traditional model of remediation with a model of challenge would be the most helpful to African American boys. That means, providing young African American students with challenging schoolwork in a supportive, collaborative environment that conveys respect for their academic and social potential (Osbourne, 1999).

Socio-Emotional Factors

In his article, *Scale of Teacher Empathy for African American Males*, Warren (2015) focuses on how the intellectual, emotional, and social needs of Black males in the public school system are not being adequately addressed. Warren argues that when educating African American male students, schools should account for knowledge of the social, environmental, and historical contexts influencing the way black males experience school.

156 ▪ Q. SMITH and M. M. THOMSON

This is a missing component in schools and classrooms. Teachers with a different demographic background may not understand the social, emotional, and historical experiences of African American males (Warren, 2015). Studies show that early childhood adverse experiences, toxic stress and the impacts of racism affect people of color more than any other race. For example, studies show that Black children are three times more likely than their white peers to lose a mother by age 10 and Black parents are two times more likely to lose a child by the age of 30 (Shonkoff et al., 2021). Given the fact that Black students experience more deaths of family members and friends across the life and early in life "constitutes an added burden of stress and a major loss of the supportive relationships that can buffer the effects of adversity on health" (Shonkoff et al., 2021, p. 123).

In addition, the range of teaching and learning experiences offered by White teachers to Black students play an important role in how teachers influence students' motivation and achievement. Perception, racial bias, and racial stereotyping can significantly impair positive images of students of color. It has been determined that teachers tend to value and respond more positively to classroom behavior and learning preferences mirroring White cultural norms (Warren, 2015). Teacher empathy is theorized as essential to the work of teachers in multicultural classroom settings; however, empathy is subjective, based on the recipient or observer. Other studies and scholars in the field, conclude that empathy is essential when teaching African American boys, for raising academic outcomes and establishing productive student–teacher relationships (Azevedo et al., 2013).

Using the Scale of Teacher Empathy for African American Males (S-TEAAM) to measure teachers' empathy, Warren (2015) specifically examined the utility of efficacy as a professional disposition for White female teachers' interactions with their Black male students. Findings show that being an empathetic person and demonstrating empathy as a professional disposition are two different things. Most people believe that teachers are automatically empathetic and that may be true, but this does not mean that empathy is extended, or equally shown to students of all backgrounds within the classroom. According to Warren, teacher empathy looks like using what the teacher knows about the student to build relationships with them, on their terms. It also includes authentically sharing with students, being vulnerable, and demonstrating concern about the things that concern them.

The S-TEAAM survey study (Warren, 2015), included two specific questions: one set of questions was reliable for assessing teacher conceptions of empathy and the other set, teacher perceptions of their application of empathy with Black male students. The survey was completed by seventy-three practicing teachers. There were forty White participants, twenty-eight Black participants, and five participants that were labeled as other. In a snowball sampling method, the survey was given to school administrators, teachers, support staff personnel and other graduate school colleagues of the author. The recipients received a link in their email via Survey Monkey and were able to anonymously provide their answers. The first component measured the teacher's conceptual understanding of empathy. In this four-item component, teachers were asked to offer their opinion of whether empathy is a "necessary disposition for teachers" not only with Black boys, but also with Black children in general. The teachers respond to whether he or she believes empathy informs their personal relationships with Black male students (Warren, 2015). In the next five-item component, the teachers use of empathy in their teaching practices was measured. The questions inquire about the frequency teachers apply empathy to: their instructional planning, grading, discipline management, communication of academic and behavioral expectations, and the building of personal relationships with Black male students. Teachers were asked to describe how often they apply empathy when planning learning activities for groups of students that include African American male. Study findings indicated that teachers believe that empathy is a necessary characteristic of teachers of African American boys, however, they do not consistently implement it into their practice. These results are disheartening, leaving the reader to wonder why a teacher would believe that empathy is important and necessary, but not implement it in their practice. The lack of empathy can have a profound effect on African American boys and cause them to have a different view towards school and education. Teachers' beliefs about empathy must be followed up with appropriate instructional decisions that respond to the learning needs of students (Warren, 2015). While this survey provides some insight into whether or not teachers believe that empathy is important and whether or not they employ empathy when teaching African American boys, it has some limitations. One limitation is that the survey was unable to judge the ability of the teacher respondents to effectively engage in empathic concern and perspective taking (Warren, 2015). In addition, according to the survey teachers thought of themselves less likely to employ empathy within tasks that require less human interaction such as grading. Another powerful point that Warren makes is related to employing empathy even when grading assignments, urging educators to provide opportunities for individualized assignments in light of the social and cultural frames students encounter in completing homework. In this case, empathy may have greater significance and influence on how teachers carry out a "responsive task" (Warren, 2015). The results imply that there are discrepancies between how teachers conceive of empathy's importance as a professional disposition with Black students and what they do in the reality of their everyday work with Black students (Warren, 2015). In addition, empathy training as it relates to empathy for African American boys needs to be implemented in every school district.

158 ▪ Q. SMITH and M. M. THOMSON

Interest

Another motivational construct that heavily influences the motivation and achievement of African American boys is interest, or whereas, the lack of interest. In Asher's study, *Influence of Topic Interest on Black Children's and White Children's Reading Comprehension,* the researcher assessed whether black children comprehend more of high than low-interest reading material and whether performance discrepancy between white and black children, commonly found, is reduced in the high-interest condition. A second purpose of the study was to examine the degree of similarity between white and black children's interests (Asher, 1979). Asher acknowledges that there are many aspects that can impact the reading comprehension of students, but lack of student interest is definitely one of them. It's a known fact that students are less attentive to material that they are disinterested in, as well as when they have limited background knowledge about a topic they are not interested in. The study specifically looked at the contribution of topic interest to race differences in reading comprehension. Black children's reading achievement test performance is typically found to be lower than white children's performance, and the discrepancy increases as children grow older creating the achievement gap (Asher, 1979). Teachers acknowledge that most standardized tests are not culturally relevant to all students and White students are more likely to be interested in the topics included on those standardized tests.

Asher's study (1979) was conducted in a medium-sized midwestern city. Fifth-grade children were selected to participate because White and Black children's reading scores typically differ considerably at this grade level. The children were from seven classrooms in three different schools. In each classroom, all Black children and an equal number of White children were matched and randomly asked to participate. A total of 66 children, 19 White females, 19 Black females, 14 White males, and 14 Black males, were selected. Furthermore, Asher mentions that it would have been desirable to separate race from social class effects, social class information was not available for this study. The students that were a part of the study were from integrated schools versus schools where students were bused in (Asher, 1979). Standardized achievement test data from the Scholastic Testing Service Educational Development Series reading achievement test was used in this study and were available for 62 of the 66 students that were a part of this study. On this standardized test White children had an average score of 4.8, and Black children had an average score of 3.4 (Asher, 1979). The research method included assessing each child's interests with a picture rating technique. Specifically, the students were shown 25 color slides, each slide corresponded with a topic of interest (ex. Cats, airplanes, etc.). The research method also included testing reading performance with

Examining Motivation Among Elementary-Aged African-American Students • **159**

passages aligned with the topics that the students were most interested in. The children were given six passages, each in its own envelope, to read. The passages came from the Britannica Junior Encyclopedia (1970) and were presented to children in cloze format with the tenth word and every fifth word thereafter deleted. Children were told that they were to read each paragraph and decide what words were missing. Moreover, in a seventh envelope, the students were given rating scales in which they indicated on one to seven scales how much they would like to read more about each of the six topics. The tasks were administered in the classroom in two separate sessions, two weeks apart. Different experimenters administered the two sessions so that children would not perceive the connection between the interest assessment and the reading activity.

Study findings show that both Black and White students demonstrated better comprehension when reading high interest passages. The fact that Black children read better on high-interest material is encouraging given that the passages were in difficult standard English. The performance difference between Black and White students was not reduced on high-interest material. Black children's post reading preference ratings of high-interest material were as high as White children's ratings, yet Black children still comprehended less of this material (Asher, 1979). Other things may attribute to the reason why the children were not comprehending less such as lack of phonemic awareness, decoding deficiencies, and lack of fluency.

CONCLUDING REMARKS

The scholarly articles that were reviewed reveal that expectancy and value constructs, as well as motivational constructs from the social cognitive theory, represent key factors in the motivation of African American boys. While these scholarly articles were seminal works in the field, their findings are explained in the limitations that accompany the research conducted. Further research is needed in this area, particularly related to ever changing social cultural factors that greatly impacts our schools and everyday life.

REFERENCES

Asher, S. R. (1979). Influence of topic interest on Black children's and White children's reading comprehension. *Child Development, 50*(3), 686–690.

Azevedo R.T., Macaluso E., Avenanti A., Santangelo V., Cazzato V., Aglioti S.M. (2013). Their pain is not our pain: brain and autonomic correlates of empathic resonance with the pain of same and different race individuals. *Hum Brain Mapp, 34*(12), 3168–3181.

Bandura, A. (1993). Perceived self-efficacy in cognitive development and functioning. *Educational Psychologist, 29*, 117–148.

Bong, M. (2001). Between- and within- domain relations of academic motivation among middle and high school students: Self-efficacy, task values, and achievement goals. Journal of *Educational Psychology, 93*, 23–30.

Garibaldi, A. M. (1992). Educating and motivating African American males to succeed. *Journal of Negro Education, 61*(1), 4–11.

Gilliam, W. S., Maupin, A. N., Reyes, C. R., Accavitti, M., Shic, F. (2016). Do early educators' implicit biases regarding sex and race relate to behavior expectations and recommendations of preschool expulsions and suspensions? Stud. Brief, Yale Univ. Child Study Cent., New Haven, CT. Retrieved from https://medicine. yale.edu/childstudy/zigler/publications/Preschool%20Implicit%20Bias%20 Policy%20Brief _ final_9_26_276766_5379_v1.pdf

Graham, S. (1994). Motivation in African Americans. *Review of Educational Research, 64*(1), 55–117.

Osborne, J. W. (1999). Unraveling underachievement among African American boys from an identification with academic's perspective. *Journal of Negro Education, 68*(4), 555–565.

Schunk, D. H., Pintrich, P. R., & Meece, J. L. (2014). (4th ed.). *Motivation in education*: Theory, research, and applications. Pearson.

Shonkoff J. P., Slopen N., Williams D. R. (2021). Early childhood adversity, toxic stress, and the impacts of racism on the foundations of health. *Annual Review of Public Health, 1*(42), 115–134.

Todd, A. R., Thiem, K. C., & Neel, R. (2016). Does seeing faces of young black boys facilitate the identification of threatening stimuli? *Psychological Science, 27*, 384–393.

Warren, C. A. (2017). Scale of teacher empathy for African American males (S-TEAAM): Measuring teacher conceptions and the application of empathy in multicultural classroom settings. *The Journal of Negro Education, 84*(2), 154–174.

Wigfield, A., & Eccles, J. S. (1992). The development of achievement task value: A theoretical analysis. *Developmental Review, 12*, 265–310.

CHAPTER 10

RESEARCH EXPERIENCES FOR TEACHERS IN A COGNITIVE APPRENTICESHIP PROGRAM

Motivations, Emotions, and Instructional Changes

Margareta M. Thomson

THEORETICAL CONSIDERATIONS

Research has found that effective professional development (PD) has a direct impact on teachers' and students' development (e.g., Buck, 2003; Hanuscin & Musikul, 2007; Peters-Burton & Frazier, 2012). Additionally, teachers who, in particular, participated in inquiry-based PD programs have been shown to effectively increase the quality of their science instruction by implementing practices in ways that are similar to strategies used by scientists in their own research (e.g., asking research questions, formulating hypothesis, conducting repeated observations, making predictions). Professional

Motivation and Engagement in Various Learning Environments, pages 161–179
Copyright © 2024 by Information Age Publishing
www.infoagepub.com
All rights of reproduction in any form reserved.

161

162 ▪ M. M. THOMSON

development programs provide valuable opportunities to teachers from all grade levels to actively engage in experiences that can help improve their quality of teaching in addition to helping increase students' academic outcomes (Loucks-Horsely, Love, Stiles, Mundry, & Hewson, 2003; Seymour, Hunter, Laursen, & Deantoni, 2003). However, PD frequently requires teachers to make substantial modifications to their teaching. Consequently, teachers may have strong emotional reactions when their current practices are challenged (Darby, 2008; Pekrun & Schutz, 2007). Teachers may find interest in an educational innovation or conversely may feel incompetence and shame when they have initial difficulty implementing an innovation. Teachers' emotional reactions to PD can impact their motivation to implement strategies learned in PD. For example, a teacher may feel angry for being asked to provide time and effort to change his/her teaching practices and consequently feel unmotivated to implement the ideas learned during PD. Reciprocally, teachers' motivation can impact their emotions. When teachers feel motivated and excited to try new ideas, they feel pleased as they see students perform positively because their efforts.

The current research study investigated teachers' motivations, emotions and instructional practices due to their experiences in a novel PD immersive mentoring program, in which science teachers worked with scientists from different STEM areas in authentic research environments. The Control-Value theory (CVT) constituted the theoretical framework that supported the study's design in investigating teachers' motivations and emotions in relationship with instructional changes. In CVT, Pekrun (2000, 2006) proposed that, within educational settings, one's emotions and motivations are interrelated. In particular, CVT suggests that the specific emotions and motivations that individuals display in academic-related behavior will depend upon the extent to which they believe they have some amount of *control* and the extent to which they *value* the behavior (and related outcomes). According to CVT, if teachers perceive they do not have some *control* with respect to the implementation of the PD (e.g., they feel coerced to do so) and/or they do not see some *value* for the innovation, they will experience both negative emotions and low/no motivation to participate. The specific emotions that teachers experience, and their related motivations, will depend on the extent to which they perceive they have control and the extent to which they value the innovation. The key CVT components (Table 10.1) describe: types of object focus (i.e., outcome/prospective; outcome/retrospective, and activity), values associated with outcomes (i.e., positive and negative values), locus of control (i.e., high, medium, low), and type of emotions developed (i.e., positive and negative emotions).

Research has shown that teachers' perceptions of control and value are related in ways predicted by CVT (e.g., Papaioannou & Christodoulidis,

Research Experiences for Teachers in a Cognitive Apprenticeship Program • **163**

TABLE 10.1   The Control-Value Theory Model

Object focus	Appraisals		
	Value	Control	Emotion
Outcome/prospective	Positive (success)	High	Anticipatory joy
		Medium	Hope
		Low	Hopelessness
	Negative (failure)	High	Anticipatory relief
		Medium	Anxiety
		Low	Hopelessness
Outcome/retrospective	Positive (success)	Irrelevant	Joy
		Self	Pride
		Other	Gratitude
	Negative (failure)	Irrelevant	Sadness
		Self	Shame
		Other	Anger
Activity	Positive Negative	High	Enjoyment
	Positive/Negative	Low	Anger
	None	High/Low	Frustration Boredom

Source: Adapted from Pekrun, 2006

2007; Roth, Assor, Kanat-Maymon, & Kaplan, 2007). Teachers who had perceptions of agency (i.e., control), and who valued an innovation, were more willing to experience vulnerability (an emotional element) to implement reform efforts learned during PD. As teachers gained self-efficacy during the implementation (i.e., they believed they could successfully complete the required behaviors), they valued the reform, and they experienced more positive emotions. Consequently, they were more willing to take risks in implementing changes to their classroom practices. Indeed, teachers were further willing to take risks when they saw the potential positive outcomes (i.e., value) that the reform could provide. Darby (2008) found that teachers' feelings of fear were initiated when their professional identities were threatened which triggered perceptions of low control and low value. However, with supportive interactions from coaches and facilitators—in ways that increased their efficacy for performing the required behaviors—teachers' changed their attitudes more positively toward the reform. When teachers were given opportunities to collaborate (i.e., given control) they were more willing to take on the challenges related to the instructional changes.

CURRENT STUDY

In the current study, participants were all teachers and attended a Research Experience for Teachers (RET) program at a large university in the United States. Participants were K–12 teachers from different grade levels (i.e., elementary, middle-school and high-school). The duration of the PD program during the summer was of six weeks. During the PD teachers were hosted in science laboratories, working alongside science faculty to learn research in various areas (e.g., physics, biology). This PD model features a cognitive apprenticeship program in which teachers were mentored by the scientists, engaging in research projects conducted by the host lab, participating in seminars and mini conferences for the duration of the program, thus enhancing their science knowledge and research skills.

Research on participants' involvement in an RET or similar programs have suggested that the program greatly influenced teachers' thinking about teaching science and their teaching strategies (i.e., Dixon & Wilke, 2007; Smith & Southerland, 2007). Studies also suggested that participants' choices to implement changes in their teaching practices were related to the innovation of the program (i.e., "interest,") and how much teachers valued the elements of the program (Dixon & Wilke, 2007; Grove et al., 2009; Pop et al., 2010).

The goal of the current study was to investigate teachers' motivations and emotions about their RET program participation; how their emotions were related to their motivation for engaging in the RET program, and the instructional changes they made to their teaching practices due to program involvement. The following research questions guided our study:

1. What were teachers' reports of their emotions about the RET program, *before* and *after* attending the program? Specifically,
   a. what differences were reported between teachers from the elementary school level (EE) versus middle and high-school level (MH)?
   b. how do participants' responses about their emotions in the RET program varied based on demographic data such as age, gender, ethnicity, and years of teaching experience?
2. Generally, to what extent were teachers' emotions correlated to their (a) motivation for attending the RET program and (b) changes to their teaching practices?
3. Overall, how did teachers perceive their RET experiences within the context of their (a) motivation for attending the program, (b) emotions, and (c) changes to teaching practices via interviews?

METHODOLOGY

Participants

In the current study, a total of 90 teachers participated in the RET summer program at major research university in the United States. These 90 program teachers were contacted after their attendance and were invited to take part in the current study. Only 67 teachers responded to the study invitation, and thus completed the survey.

Survey Participants

An analysis of study's participants ($N = 67$) indicated that females represented 77.6% ($n = 52$) and males represented 22.4% ($n = 15$). Also, most participants were aged 26–30 years (21%, $n = 14$) or over 46 (37%; $n = 25$) and the range of teaching experience varied from one year to over 30 years, with the vast majority of participants (90%, $n = 60$) indicating that they had 1–10 years' experience in classrooms. With respect to grade levels, 51% of respondents ($n = 35$) indicated they were elementary school teachers (grade level 1–5). Middle school teachers (grade level 6–8) represented 18% ($n = 12$) of the total participants, and high school teachers (grade level 9–12) represented 30% ($n = 20$) of the total study participants. Thus, the combined number of middle and high school teachers (MH) represented 49% ($n = 32$) of the total study participants.

Comparative analysis by grade level, were performed by two groups: elementary level teachers (EE, $n = 35$) and middle & high school teachers (MH, $n = 32$). The decision to combine middle and high school teachers in one group is grounded theoretically. Middle school and high school teachers in the United States teach only science and hold a teaching certificate in one subject area (i.e., which is science, in this case); thus, they are specialized in one subject area. Elementary teachers are generalists; they hold a teaching certificate in elementary education (not in one subject area) and teach science in addition to other subjects (i.e., math, literacy, social studies).

Interview Participants

All survey participants agreed to participate in the follow-up interviews. A total of 12 participants were selected from the pool of survey respondents to be interviewed via telephone. Interviewees were selected to represent various demographics, such as grade level, gender, and teaching experience. The diversity of demographics represented by interviewees supported the collection of rich qualitative data.

Procedures

The study was conducted in two phases. First, online surveys were conducted in phase I, and then telephone interviews were conducted in phase II with selected participants.

Surveys: Phase I
All participants completed an online survey consisting of demographic items, and three additional questionnaires investigating participants' (a) *emotions* about their program experience, (b) *motivations* for engaging in the program (c) and *changes* to teaching practices due to their program attendance.

Interviews: Phase II
A total of 12 survey respondents were interviewed in the second phase of the study about their motivations and expectations of the program attendance, emotions related to their experiences and changes to teaching due to program involvement. Interview participants consented to have their interviews recorded. To protect participants' anonymity pseudonyms were assigned to each teacher. The in-depth, semi-structured interviews explored teachers' views about their experience with respect to their motivations, emotions, and changes to teaching practices related to PD. Two coders developed a coding scheme, first by independently coding sample interviews, then comparing notes. Once both coders reached complete agreement on the coding scheme interviews were coded.

Instruments

Emotional Survey
To indicate emotions about their RET program experiences, participants were asked to rate each of the 10 statements describing an emotion they experienced on a six-point Likert-scale (1 = "Not at all;" 6 = "Extremely") with respect to the extent they remembered feeling that emotion (e.g., excited, confident, disappointed) *before* and *after* their RET program participation. Four subscales measured participants' emotions for attending the RET program, as follows: (a) *Positive emotions before RET* (e.g., excited, inspired, determined, confident, contented); (b) *Negative emotions before RET* (e.g., disappointed, angry, overwhelmed, reluctant); (c) *Positive emotions after RET* (e.g., excited, inspired, determined, confident, contented); (d) *Negative emotions after RET* (e.g., disappointed, angry, overwhelmed, reluctant). With respect to each set of emotions, Cronbach's alphas were: *Positive emotions before RET*, .72; *Negative emotions before RET*, .60; *Positive emotions after RET*, .87; *Negative emotions after RET*, .56. Internal reliability coefficient for

the overall instrument measuring emotions before and after RET participation was .60.

Motivational Survey

Participants were asked to rate each of the 10 questionnaire items about their motivation for participating in the RET program. The four-point Likert-scale (1 = *Strongly disagree*, 4 = *Strongly agree*) asked participants to indicate specific reasons for attending the RET program (e.g., to gain science knowledge, to gain new teaching ideas) and report changes to their teaching practices (e.g., including more inquiry-based strategies in their teaching, more experiments). Two subscales measured participants' motivation for attending the RET program: (a) *Intrinsic incentives* (e.g., to gain new ideas for my classroom, to keep myself involved in the professional growth) and (b) *Extrinsic incentives* (e.g., to obtain certification/recertification, was mandated by school/district). The Cronbach's alpha for the overall instrument was .73; while the Cronbach's alphas obtained for the two subscales were .80 for *Intrinsic incentives* and .75 for *Extrinsic incentives*.

Instructional Changes Survey

Participants were asked to rate each item based on a four-point Likert-scale (1 = *Strongly disagree*, 4 = *Strongly agree*) to indicate what specific changes to their teaching practices they made due to their program experiences. Three subscales measured participants' reported changes to their teaching practices after attending the RET program: (a) *Changes to teaching style* (e.g., adopted a more student-centered approach in teaching); (b) *Changes to class instruction* (e.g., use of more collaborative activities in teaching); (c) *Changes to science thinking* (e.g., attending other programs to enhance science expertise). The Cronbach's alphas were .95 for the overall instrument, and for each subscale, Cronbach's alphas were: *Changes to teaching style*, .91; *Change to class instruction*, .93; and *Changes to science thinking*, .81. Overall, the Cronbach's alpha values for the three instruments and the obtained subscales demonstrated good internal consistency (Miller, 1995).

RESULTS

Teachers' Emotions

The study's first research question investigated the types of emotions teachers reported that they experienced *before* and *after* attending their PD involvement. Overall, survey results indicated that *before* their program attendance most participants felt "Excited" ($M = 4.61$; $SD = 1.1$), "Inspired" ($M = 4.12$; $SD = 1.2$), and "Determined" ($M = 4.10$; $SD = 1.2$). Remembered

168 ▪ M. M. THOMSON

emotions reported by the survey participants indicated that after the RET program involvement most participants felt "Excited" ($M = 5.01$; $SD = 1.1$), "Inspired" ($M = 4.97$; $SD = 1.0$), "Confident" ($M = 4.53$; $SD = 1.2$), and "Determined" ($M = 4.37$; $SD = 1.3$). Paired-Samples T-tests were conducted to see if teachers' remembered emotions changed from *before* their participation to *after* their participation. Results indicated significant differences between remembered emotions reported by all participants before and after their RET participation. Table 10.2 summarizes overall and comparative results of participants' reported emotions before and after RET attendance.

Significant differences between emotions felt before and after teachers' RET program participation were found with respect to particular reported emotions such as "Excited" ($t = -2.99$, $p < .005$), "Inspired" ($t = -6.15$, $p < .001$), "Confident" ($t = -4.71$, $p < .001$), and "Contented" ($t = -3.29$, $p < .005$). Particularly, significant differences were found with respect to EE teachers reported emotions before and after their RET participation regarding how much they were "Inspired" ($t = -4.85$, $p = .000$), "Confident" ($t = -3.51$, $p = .001$), and "Excited" ($t = -2.26$, $p = .030$) about their RET program participation. Significant differences were found for MSE teachers regarding their emotions before and after their RET participation with respect to being "Inspired" ($t = -3.82$, $p = .001$), "Confident" ($t = -3.09$, $p = .004$), and "Contented" ($t = -2.92$, $p = .006$).

Further comparative analysis for EE and MH teachers showed that emotions reported by the teachers before their RET participation were described as follows. The EE teachers reported their emotions before the program involvement, as: "Excited" ($M = 4.57$; $SD = 1.9$), "Inspired" ($M = 4.17$; $SD = 1.2$), and "Determined" ($M = 4.03$; $SD = 1.3$), and the MH teachers reported emotions they felt before their program participation were described as: "Excited" ($M = 4.66$; $SD = 1.0$), "Confident" ($M = 4.22$; $SD = 1.2$), and "Determined" ($M = 4.19$; $SD = 1.2$). Also, comparative analysis for the two subgroups showed that emotions reported by the teachers after their program participation were described by the EE teachers as: "Excited" ($M = 5.0$; $SD = 1.0$), "Inspired" ($M = 5.06$; $SD = 1.0$), and "Confident" ($M = 4.37$; $SD = 1.3$), and by the MH teachers as: "Exited" ($M = 5.03$; $SD = 1.2$), "Confident" ($M = 4.91$; $SD = 1.4$), and Inspired" ($M = 4.88$; $SD = 1.1$).

However, no significant differences were found between emotions reported by the EE and MH teachers, before and after their PD participation, except "Confidence." MH teachers felt more confident ($M = 4.22$; $SD = 1.2$) compared to EE teachers ($M = 3.57$; $SD = 1.1$) *before* the program involvement ($p = .03$). Such results are in line with most research in the field showing that elementary teachers in general hold less science teaching confidence than their middle and secondary peer teachers (Bryan, 2003). But more interestingly, however, there were no significant difference between emotions reported by the EE ($M = 4.91$; $SD = 1.4$) and MH group

TABLE 10.2 Teachers' Reported Emotions (before and after program attendance)

Emotions	EE teachers (n = 35)		MH teachers (n = 32)		Total (N = 67)	
	Emotions before RET Mean (SD)	Emotions after RET Mean (SD)	Emotions before RET Mean (SD)	Emotions after RET Mean (SD)	Emotions before RET Mean (SD)	Emotions after RET Mean (SD)
Exited	4.57 (1.9)	5.00 (1.0)*	4.66 (1.0)	5.03 (1.2)*	4.61 (1.1)	5.01 (1.1)*
Anxious	3.66 (1.4)	2.37 (1.4)	3.13 (1.2)	2.13 (1.4)	3.40 (1.3)	2.25 (1.4)
Inspired	4.17 (1.2)	5.06 (1.0)**	4.06 (1.3)	4.88 (1.1)**	4.12 (1.2)	4.97 (1.0)**
Disappointed	1.14 (.50)	1.46 (1.0)	1.31 (.64)	1.34 (.60)	1.22 (.57)	1.40 (.87)
Angry	1.17 (.51)	1.09 (.37)	1.13 (4.2)	1.16 (.62)	1.15 (.46)	1.12 (.50)
Overwhelmed	2.17 (1.5)	1.89 (1.1)	1.70 (.94)	1.66 (.86)	1.99 (1.06)	1.78 (1.04)
Determined	4.03 (1.3)	4.29 (1.3)	4.19 (1.4)	4.47 (1.3)	4.10 (1.2)	4.37 (1.3)
Reluctant	1.57 (.91)	1.43 (.85)	1.38 (.70)	1.19 (.47)	1.48 (.82)	1.31 (.70)
Confident	3.57 (1.1)	4.37 (1.3)**	4.22 (1.2)	4.91 (1.4)*	3.88 (1.2)	4.63 (1.2)**
Contented	3.86 (1.2)	4.20 (1.4)	3.78 (1.3)	4.47 (1.5)*	3.82 (1.2)	4.33 (1.4)*

$*p < .05$, $**p < .01$ (Paired Samples T-test); $N = 67$

170 • M. M. THOMSON

($M = 4.37$; $SD = 1.3$) with respect to confidence, *after* their PD program involvement ($p = .08$), which is a surprising result. This finding could lead to the assumption that both EE teachers and MH teachers, in the current study felt increased confidence after their PD program attendance, which is encouraging news for teaching research.

Comparative analysis (one-way ANOVA procedures) showed no significant differences with respect to emotions (i.e., *before* and *after* their PD program attendance) and participants' demographic data such as age, gender, ethnicity, years of teaching experience and which year/session they attended the PD program. This finding can suggest that factors external to the emotional component (i.e., demographics) are not related to teachers' changes in emotions, nor affected their emotions about their PD program attendance.

Teachers' Emotions, Motivation and Changes to Practices

Results for the second research question, which investigated whether teachers' reported emotions (both before and after their PD attendance) were associated with their (a) motivation for attending the program and (b) changes to their teaching practices, are presented below.

Before Program Attendance

Significant differences were found between teachers' ratings of positive emotions *before* their PD attendance and their ratings for intrinsic motivation for attending the program ($r = .263$, $p < .05$). This could suggest that teachers who felt positive emotions before their program participation (e.g., excited, inspired, determined) had intrinsic reasons for participating in the program (e.g., wanted to gain new ideas for teaching, or keep involved in the professional growth). On the other hand, teachers' ratings of negative emotions *before* their PD attendance were positively correlated to ratings of extrinsic motivation ($r = .247$, $p < .05$), possibly suggesting that teachers who were felt negative emotions about their program engagement (e.g., overwhelmed, anxious), attended the PD for extrinsic incentives (e.g., to obtain certification/recertification, or was mandated by school/district).

After Program Attendance

Furthermore, teachers' positive emotions *after* attending the PD program were positively related to changes to their (a) teaching style ($r = .434$, $p < .01$), (b) instructional strategies ($r = .371$, $p < .01$), and (c) science activities ($r = .438$, $p < .01$). This suggests that teachers who felt positive emotions before the PD program made changes to their teaching practices after their PD program attendance in areas such as teaching style and instructional strategies, as well as the types of science activities used in the classroom.

Research Experiences for Teachers in a Cognitive Apprenticeship Program • **171**

Interesting findings were revealed regarding correlations between positive emotions of teachers before and after their PD participation and/or negative emotions of teachers before and after their PD participation. Positive correlations were found between teachers' reports of positive emotions (e.g., excited, inspired) before and after their PD participation ($r = .570$, $p < .01$), suggesting that those teachers who reported positive emotions about their PD participation before the program involvement (e.g., being excited, inspired to participate in the PD program) they also reported positive emotions about their PD experiences after the program participation as well. Likewise, teachers' ratings of negative emotions before their PD participation were positively correlated to ratings of negative emotions after their PD participation ($r = .548$, $p < .01$), suggesting that negative emotions (e.g., overwhelmed, anxious) reported by teachers before the PD, were persistently reported by these teachers after the program participation as well. Results are presented in Table 10.3.

Teachers Perceptions of their Experiences

To answer the third research question, interviews were conducted which investigated teachers' emotions as related to their perceived PD experiences,

TABLE 10.3 Correlations Among Major Study Variables

Motivations		1	2	3	4	5	6	7	8	9
1	Intrinsic motivation (for RET)	1	.64	.27*	.30*	.25*	.26*	.05	.19	−.52
2	Extrinsic motivation (for RET)		1	−.24*	−.20	−.15	−.12	−.24*	.16	.25
3	Changes (to teaching style)			1	.84*	.87*	.19	.10	.43*	−.12
4	Changes (to class instruction)				1	.82*	.19	.15	.37*	−.12
5	Changes (to science thinking)					1	.23	.07	.43*	−.21
6	Positive emotions (before RET)						1	−.19	.57**	−.30*
7	Negative emotions (before RET)							1	−.12	.54*
8	Positive emotions (after RET)								1	−.40**
9	Negative emotions (after RET)									1

*$p < .05$, ** $p < .01$ (2-tailed); $N = 67$

172 • M. M. THOMSON

motivation for attending the PD program, and changes to their teaching practices. To best illustrate results from interviews, two case studies are presented, specifically one case study from the elementary teacher group (EE) and one case study from middle & high-school teacher group (MH). Nina (from the EE group) and John (from the MH group) are illustrative stories, chosen in this manuscript for the purpose to exemplify how PD experiences were influential in different individual cases. Nina, an elementary school teacher, recalls mainly negative emotions in her PD experiences, while John, a middle school teacher, recalls mainly positive emotions about his PD involvement.

Elementary School Teacher Case Report: Nina

Nina was a 5th grade teacher at the time she attended the PD program. She illustrates the desire to learn science with a scientist in the lab—a very new experience to her but felt negative emotions about such experience. She described her program experiences as connected to negative emotions, such as lack of confidence, and how negative emotions played an important role in her learning. In her interview, Nina stated that she wanted to attend the PD program so she would to be able to learn new things that would allow her to take back to class something valuable, such as the knowledge and skills learned in the program. However, learning new knowledge and skills would come to a certain cost for her; the program expectations and expertise level were overwhelming for her. As she explained, "I knew I'm going to learn a lot of science, get experience working with scientists, you guys told us what we would do; it was going to be fun, take all these back to our classrooms. I wasn't expecting how hard it was at that time, and the scientist level was so way out there. There was no pity on us."

Nina was one of the teachers who greatly emphasized her desire to learn (from the scientists and her peers) and saw herself as a life-long learner. Her description of emotions about the program involvement is extremely powerful. The intensity of the emotions as well as the range of emotions and behaviors she experienced, show how new learning environments can be intimidating for individuals. She felt 'very scared', afraid that she'll never 'get it', and cried for the first week: "In the beginning of the program, it was very scary, very scary; it was way, way over my head, and I think that's because the M. Lab, had that program the first time. I was among the first ones... I cried, I think for the first week or so and I thought, 'O my God, what are they talking about? 'I don't understand a thing.... I thought, 'I will never, ever get it.' My partner and I did a lot of research on our own, we would look up online about M. Lab, and just magnets and magnets, and that was very helpful. So, I learned a great deal."

Despite the fact that she experienced negative emotions before and during her PD involvement (i.e., anxiety, fear, low confidence), she placed a high value on her learning. After the program attendance, she felt positive emotions (i.e., joy) that she was able to have this opportunity to learn and challenge herself to a higher level. The positive values she associated with her learning allowed her to make changes in her classroom after the PD program attendance. In her interview, talking about the types of changes in teaching practices, Nina described that she was trying to use the same approach in her teaching science to elementary students as she witnesses the scientists interacting with teachers in the lab. Also, Nina mentioned that because of her program experiences she incorporated more research into her teaching, used more technology in class, and included more interactive activities (hands-on) and journal writings (similar to the daily PD program activities for teachers). According to her, "I tend to come back to how scientists do it at the M. Lab. I do take a lot of the things I saw, heard, experienced there; make sure kids know more; I give it back to them. I definitely try to research more, use technology more. I incorporate hands-on a lot, do hands-on, the book gives us some ideas, but I try to do more. There's also a "journal in" that I learned at the M. Lab, they're doing it at the museum. I try to encourage my kids to keep their journal as much as possible."

Middle School Teacher Case Report: John

John, a middle school teacher taught science to 6th and 7th grade students at the time he attended the PD program. Dan represents an illustrative story of teachers who felt mostly positive emotions before the PD and made significant changes in his professional advancement due to his program attendance. John mentioned in his interview that he felt confident about science teaching before and after the program, and as a result he became involved in other professional development programs making major progress in his professional growth. His primarily reasons for attending the PD program were the desire to stay engaged in his professional growth, to gain more content knowledge, and mainly to work with a scientist in an authentic laboratory setting. He explained, "In terms of summer opportunities, it looked like the most interesting one, worthwhile. The other ones seemed just a one [or] two-day workshop. I was always interested in interacting with scientists as opposed to programs that were run by people who weren't educators, or who weren't scientists. I don't know what they were.... But it just seemed to be a science [education]-type program. They would tell people how to teach, but yet, they weren't teachers themselves . . . this seemed to be not valid to me but [the RET] was more authentic."

One of the most valuable experiences for John (and for most MH teachers) in the program was the fact that he learned science in a laboratory, an authentic setting, side-by-side with a scientist. The professional growth and the unique experience of being able to work in a laboratory with a scientist, was expressed by John in his interview as follows: "[The] most valuable [experience to me], honestly was the professional growth since I've been involved in it. After 2 years of PD, I started to feel like [I was] heading in a different direction, doing something a little more unique, and I liked it. I started to become more involved in PD, helping in curriculum writing... I coordinated some workshops being delivered. I become more involved in teaching, not just classroom [teaching] but networking with other people and doing more than just teaching."

Emotions expressed by John were mainly positive about his program experiences, reporting feeling confidence before and after the PD program, having feelings of professional fulfillment, and feeling inspired by the program. As a result of his experiences, after attending the PD program, John continued to stay connected with the M. Lab's educational programs and got involved in various other science projects. He explained, "It's hard for me to isolate the PD experience by itself, I did it for two years, but then I've been involved with [the] Lab for 5–6 years, so for me it's all wrapped up—professional growth, fulfillment, and professional satisfactions... These feelings probably pertain to '[after] my PD involvement' versus comparing to 'in my PD involvement.' To me it has been a great experience and provided me with a lot of opportunities that I didn't have before. I definitely feel like a more accomplished teacher now than I was before the PD—that's for sure."

In fact, an extremely valuable experience for John when talking about his PD participation was the association of his PD experience with positive emotions (i.e., satisfaction, inspiration). Positive values associated by John to his program attendance were as well his engagements in future PD opportunities and developing a professional network. The positive emotions and values associated with his program experience brought changes not just at micro-level (i.e., science classroom teaching), but at a macro-level, such as expending his professional network and professional leadership engagement: "I was excited about this program because several opportunities that have come up since the RET program are related to my PD involvement. A couple of years after [the PD], I helped and have done some work with several people out of the M. Lab to put together this workshop that was delivered in San Francisco. And then, through that workshop, I met some people who applied and ended up being one of the four teachers in the U.S. funded to go to a similar type of workshop in Vienna, Austria. And then through that workshop, I met other people, other opportunities that have become available."

DISCUSSION

The current study investigated teachers' motivations and emotions, as related to instructional changes due to their experiences in a STEM-focused

Research Experiences for Teachers in a Cognitive Apprenticeship Program ▪ **175**

professional development program. Overall, study results showed that emotions played an important role in teachers' engagement in the PD program and triggered changes in teachers' thinking and implementation of their science teaching practices. Positive correlations were found among teachers' motivations and emotions about their PD experience, as well as changes to their teaching practices. Interview data provided more depth to understanding participants' views of their PD experiences. Findings generally suggest that participants' experiences in the program and changes they made after the program attendance were greatly influenced by the types of motives, they had for engaging in the program and the emotions they felt about the program. One of the most interesting findings was the intermix of motivations, emotions and cognitive elements (i.e., changes to teaching) expressed by the participants. Study results suggest that teachers' emotions and values about their PD experiences greatly influenced their learning of new knowledge and triggered positive changes in their classroom teaching.

Quantitative results indicated interesting results about confidence related to the two groups of teachers (EE and MH). The MH teachers felt significantly more confident before the program compared to the EE teachers. No significant differences between MH teachers and EE teachers in their confidence were reported after the PD attendance, possibly suggesting that they equally felt confident after the program attendance. Teachers' gains in science knowledge triggered positive emotions and later fostered changes in their teaching practices. Inspecting the mean score results showed that EE teachers increased their confidence to the level of the MH teachers. Such findings are affirming for science teacher PD programs and encourage the inclusion of EE teachers in the RET-like programs which commonly attract more middle and high school teachers due to high science expertise these programs request. Research in the field shows that many elementary teachers held negative attitudes toward science because they lack science knowledge and confidence (Poon, et al., 2012).

Moreover, quantitative analysis demonstrated that teachers' reports of positive emotions about the PD program, such as feeling excited and inspired, were correlated to changes in their teaching practices. Changes made by all teachers were related to their thinking about science teaching along with changes to their science instructional strategies. Therefore, what participants felt about the program, especially the novelty of the program, along with how much they valued the novelty of the PD program elements, may indicate to which extent teachers made changes to their teaching practice.

Positive emotions such as "Excited," "Inspired," and "Determined" were reported to be the most experienced emotions by all participants before and after their program involvement. This suggests that (a) teachers had high expectations going into their science-immersion experiences, (b) their expectations were met, and (c) they were looking forward to using the information they had gained. Also, significant increases in teachers' reported positive emotions before and after program participation such as feeling more " Inspired," "Confident" and "Excited" suggested that the science-immersion program increased their knowledge in perhaps profound ways, increased their efficacy to include science-immersion experiences for their students, and they were enthusiastic about implementing their new-found learning.

Qualitative data from the two case studies revealed in more depth how emotions are connected to values and outcome activity (i.e., changes to teaching practices). In line with CVT, participants articulated how positive values they associated with their PD attendance and were associated with positive outcomes of their program involvement (i.e., changes). While John's story illustrates how positive emotions can impact values and outcome activity, Nina's story shows that negative emotions can be a catalyst to positive values and positive outcomes as well. The qualitative data from Nina's case reveled how negative emotions (i.e., frustration, anxiety) played a significant role in motivating her (and similarly, other EE teachers) to overcome her lack of science knowledge, and tenaciously pursue learning. Nina's case study is an illustration of how negative emotions can be a catalyst for change and can lead to positive emotions at the end of the program, as well as positive outcomes (i.e., instructional changes in classroom). Negative emotions experienced in the beginning of the PD program amplified Nina's motivation for learning the science content and, by the end of the program, these achievements triggered positive emotions (satisfaction, confidence) and ultimately lead to changes in teaching practices. This is extremely important to become aware of and acknowledge for science education in general and for the PD program trainers. The power and intensity of the negative emotions can be responsible for increasing individuals' motivation to learn and succeed in a program if they have support for their learning. In the long run, participants' negative emotions (such as fear, anxiety) can develop into positive emotions and finally into positive outcomes.

One of the major findings of the study supported by the qualitative data was that the program prompted participants' positive values about PD involvement and therefore supported positive changes. Nina's descriptions of changes revolved around how she made instructional changes due to her PD experiences, and John's descriptions of changes revolved around professional growth (i.e., taking leadership in his field) due to his program involvement. Both, Nina and John suggested that the program experiences in the laboratory working with a scientist was extremely valuable in support of their own pedagogy and contributed to their change in thinking about science teaching. This may be due to the value of authentic PD experiences as well as the use of research-based PD strategies and techniques which allowed participants to model not just practices used in the lab by the scientist but also attitudes toward science. Such improvement in teachers' changes to their thinking about science and attitudes to science could be attributed to the duration of the PD program, one of the extremely valuable features of the program. Being involved in an authentic learning environment for a sustained duration allowed teachers to learn and process the new information (i.e., science knowledge, procedures, and relationships) in various ways and make more solid connections to their practices when applied in classroom teaching later. Research has shown that longer PD is more effective and results in more in-depth changes to teachers' thinking, planning, and delivering instruction compared to short term PD of just a few days, which is commonly developed for teachers due to lack of time and resources.

Limitations and Future Research

Limitations of this study can be due to several factors, such as (a) the relatively small number of participants ($N = 67$), and (b) retrospective accounts of participants. The total number of program attendees over the seven years period was in fact relatively small (90 teachers), and thus, had an impact on the size of the study participants ($N = 67$). With respect to retrospective accounts, participants could have memory of events and feelings that could result in inaccurate reconstructions of their PD experiences. Future research can address these limitations and expand our understanding of the blend of various psychological construct in a PD program. Findings from this study may lead to further research investigating cultural aspects of such constructs especially in long-term PD programs. Comparative cross-nation or international RET-like programs could investigate cultural aspects of emotions, motivations, and cognition in different contexts. This is of a great importance, considering the scarcity of research in this field, especially comparative studies (e.g., cross-national, or international RET-like programs) for teachers of all grade levels.

REFERENCES

Akerson, L.A., & Donnelly, L.A. (2008). Relationship among learner characteristics and preservice elementary teachers' views of nature of science. *Journal of Elementary Science Education, 20*(1), 45–58.

Buck, P. (2003). Authentic research experiences for Nevada high school teachers and students. *Journal of Geoscience Education, 51*(1), 48–53.

Darby, A. (2008). Teachers' emotions in the reconstruction of professional self-understanding. *Teaching and Teacher Education, 24,* 1160–1172.

Dixon, P., & Wilke, R. A. (2007). The influence of a teacher research experience on elementary teachers' thinking and instruction. *Journal of Elementary Science Education, 19*(1), 25–43.

Feldman, A., Divoll, K., & Rogan, A. (2007). *Research education of new scientists: Implications for science teacher education.* Unpublished manuscript. Paper presented at the Annual Meeting of the American Educational Research Association, Chicago, IL.

Grove, C., Dixon, P., & Pop, M. M. (2009). Research experiences for teachers: Influences related to expectancy and value of changes to practice. *Professional Development in Education, 35*(2), 247–260.

Guskey, T. R. (2003). Analyzing lists of the characteristics of effective professional development to promote visionary leadership. *NASSP Bulletin, 87*(637), 4–20.

Hanuscin, D.L., & Musikul, K. (2007). School's IN for summer: An alternative field experience foe elementary science methods students. *Journal of Elementary Science Education, 19*(1), 57–67

Hashweh, M. Z. (2003). Teacher accommodative change. *Teacher and Teacher Education, 19*(4), 421–434.

Lasky, S. (2005). A sociocultural to understanding teacher identity, agency, and professional vulnerability in a context of secondary school reform. *Teaching and Teacher Education, 21*, 899–916.

Lloyd, J. K., Bruaund, M., Crebbin, C., & Phipps, R. (2000). Primary teachers' confidence about understanding of process skills. *Teacher Development, 4*(3), 353–370.

Loucks-Horsley, S., Love, N., Stiles, K., Mundry, S., & Hewson, P. W. (2003). *Designing professional development for teachers of science and mathematics, 2nd edition.* Corwin Press, Inc.

Pekrun, R. (2000). A social cognitive, control-value theory of achievement emotions. In Heckhausen (Ed.), *Motivational psychology of human development.* Elsevier Science.

Pekrun, R. (2006). The control-value theory of achievement emotions: Assumptions, corollaries, and implications for educational research and practice. *Educational Psychology Review, 18*, 315–341.

Pekrun, K., & Schutz, P. A. (2007). Where do we go from here? Implications and future directions for inquiry on emotions in education, In Schutz & Pekrun (Eds,), *Emotion in education* (pp, 303–321). Academic Press.

Peters-Burton, E., & Frazier, W. M. (2012). Voices from the front lines: Exemplary science teachers on education reform. *School Science and Mathematics, 112(3)*, 179–190.

Pop, M. M., Dixon, P., & Grove C. (2010). Research experiences for Teachers (RET): Motivation, expectations, and changes to teaching practices due to professional development program involvement. *Journal of Science Teacher Education, 22*(2), 127–147.

Poon, C-L., Lee, Y-J., Tan, A-L., & Lim, S. S. (2012). Knowing inquiry as practice and theory: Developing a pedagogical framework with elementary school teachers. *Research in Science Education, 42,* 303–327.

Research Experiences for Teachers in a Cognitive Apprenticeship Program • **179**

Seymour, E., Hunter, A. B., Laursen, S. L., & Deantoni, T. (2003). Establishing benefits of research experiences for undergraduates in the sciences: First findings from a three-year study. *Wiley Interscience*. www.interscience.wiley.com

Smith, L. K., & Southerland, S. A. (2007). Reforming practice or modify reforms? Elementary teachers' response to the tools of reform. *Journal of Research in Science Teaching, 44*(3).

Zubrowski, B. (2007). An observational and planning tool for professional development in science education. *Journal of Science Teacher Education, 18*(6), 861–884.

CHAPTER 11

CASE STUDY

The Process Behind Developing an Environmental Education Program

Hannah M. A. Rickets, K. A. I. Nekaris, Marco Campera, and Muhammad Ali Imron

OVERVIEW

Environmental Education

The goal of environmental education (EE) is to create environmentally literate individuals that have the knowledge, attitudes, motivations, and skills needed to address complex conservation issues through pro-environmental behaviors (Athman & Monroe, 2001; Novo-Corti et al., 2018). Young children are often the chosen demographic of education programs due to the understating that pro-environmental opinions and attitudes form during early childhood (Asunta, 2003). Children introduced to EE at earlier ages are more likely to develop pro-environmental commitments and interests (Broom, 2017; Newton, 2001; Reibelt et al., 2017; Robertson, 2008). This chapter provides an overview of the process and rational behind developing an environmental education program for children at the Little Fireface

---

Motivation and Engagement in Various Learning Environments, pages 181–212
Copyright © 2024 by Information Age Publishing
www.infoagepub.com
All rights of reproduction in any form reserved.

Project, West Java, Indonesia, based on the Javan palm civet (*Paradoxurus musanga javanicus*). We share our justifications for the educational theories, learning content, teaching methods, learning styles, instructional activities, and evaluation methods used to develop the *Changing Minds* Javan palm civet program.

Environmental Education in Indonesia

The Indonesian archipelago consists of 17,000 islands, the largest being Sumatra, Java, Kalimantan, Sulawesi, and Papua (Embassy of Indonesia, 2017). Indonesia is one of seventeen global megadiverse countries that includes two geographical hotspot regions, classified as such due to their considerably high levels of endemism and habitat loss. These are: (a) Sundaland, which consists of the islands of Sumatra, Java, and Kalimantan, and (b) Wallacea, which consists of Maluku, the Lesser Sudan Islands, and Sulawesi (Mangunjaya & McKay, 2012; Von Rintelen et al., 2017). People's dependence on the environment is deep-rooted in the country's history, and includes utilising natural resources for construction materials, medicines, food, and agriculture. The natural environment also has religious and spiritual significance for many indigenous groups (Ichwandi & Shinohara, 2007).

As a result of an increasing global demand for natural resources including timber, coal, and palm oil, of which Indonesia is the largest producer, Indonesia lost over 38% of its primary forests between 2000–2012 (Margono et al., 2014). Approximately 1,282 species of flora and fauna are threatened, with habitat loss being the primary driver of population declines and extinction risks (Randall, 2018). Unsustainable wildlife trade is another significant threat to many species (Lee et al., 2005). The high prevalence of wildlife trade for bushmeat, pets, and the tourism industry both nationally and internationally is due to the lack of reinforcement of rules, penalties and quotas (Lee et al., 2005; Nijman et al., 2014; Nijman et al., 2015). Indonesia is making a concerted effort to mitigate its conservation challenges and develop a green economy in which socio-economic development is achieved without degrading the environment. This includes pledging to reduce CO_2 emissions by 29% by 2030, implementing suspensions on logging concessions, establishing protected areas, and introducing communities to EE (Anderson et al., 2016; Nomura, 2009; Walpole & Goodwin, 2001).

Indonesia's EE movement began during the 1960s under Suharto's authoritarian regime (Figure 11.1) and was first introduced into formal education settings at primary, secondary, and higher education levels (Nomura &Abe, 2005). During the 1970s Indonesian environmental NGOs started to emerge, including the Indonesian Forum for Environment (*Wahana Lingkum Hidup Indonesia*), in response to the rise in severity of conservation issues (Nomura, 2009). NGOs introduced EE into non-formal education settings

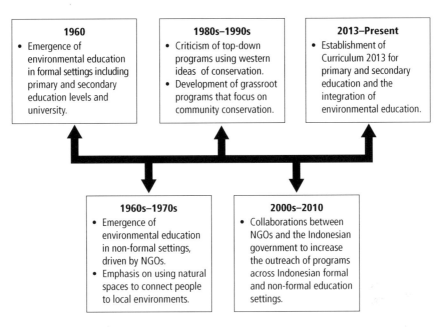

Figure 11.1 Indonesia's environmental education movement (adapted from Nomura, 2009).

and focused on getting people to connect with their local environments through outdoor activities (Nomura, 2007). Under Suharto's regime the content of EE programs was dictated by the government. Programs were heavily influenced by western ideas of conservation that did not represent the views and beliefs of the Indonesian people. This drastically changed after the ousting of Suharto in 1998, which lead to the political liberalisation of NGOs, and subsequently an increase in grassroot community-led EE programs (Nomura, 2009). In recent years focus has been placed on increasing the outreach of CE programs across Indonesia's islands. This has been assisted by the establishment of large-scale NGO organisations including the Environmental Education Network which is made up of over 200 organisations that collaborate with the Indonesian government on EE policies and programs (Nomura, 2007). Such collaborations have resulted in the integration of EE into primary and secondary education levels through the country's national curriculum, Curriculum 2013 (Parker, 2016; Rudy, 2015).

Javan Palm Civet

The Javan palm civet *(Paradoxurus musanga javanicus)*, endemic to Java and a sub-species of the of the Asian palm civet *(Paradoxurus musanga)*, is a relatively understudied species, with little known about its population dynamic, ecology, and behaviors (Birot et al., 2019). As such it has received limited conservation attention despite apparent threats including hunting, the pet trade, and the coffee industry (Roberts, 2020). At present, the Javan palm civet has not been given an IUCN status, however, due to its small geographic range and threats, it is likely the species will receive a Near Threatened status (Roberts, 2020).

The Little Fireface Project

The Little Fireface Project was established in 2012, in Cipaganti village, Cisurupan District, Garut Regency, West Java, Indonesia, in response to the threats facing the Critically Endangered Javan slow loris (*Nycticebus javanicus*; Nekaris, 2016; Nekaris, 2020). Cipaganti village lies at the foothills of Gunung Papandayan nature reserve (see Figure 11.2). The landscape surrounding the village is mosaic, including a contiguous forest, tree plantations, and agricultural fields containing crops such as tea, coffee, and tobacco. There are approximately 3000 people living in the village, the majority of which are ethnically Sundanese and Muslim.

The predominant occupations are farming and forestry, but also include shop sellers, teachers, and forest rangers (Nekaris, 2016). The literacy rate in the Garut district is approximately 99%, children are required to attend school until aged 12, but typically remain until aged 16 (Nekaris

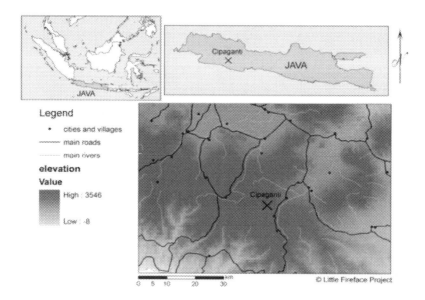

Figure 11.2 Map of Cipaganti, West Java (from Reinhardt and Nekaris, 2016).

et al., 2018). Attendance rates between boys and girls are not majorly different with approximately 98% of children attending primary school (ages 7–12), 75% attending junior secondary school (12–15), and 45% attending senior secondary school (15–18) (BPS, 2015; UNESCO, 2020). The main threats facing wildlife in this area include the high prevalence of hunting and encroachment into the surrounding forest and Gunung Papandayan nature reserve for timber and agricultural land resulting in forest loss and fragmentation (Nekaris, 2016; Rode-Margono et al., 2014); Prawiradilaga& Soedjito, 2013). West Java is known for its wildlife markets which take both legally protected and non-protected species from the wild at unsustainable levels to sell as pets, food, and for the tourism industry (Nijman &Nekaris, 2014). The project aims to teach children about the Javan slow loris and other local species through a range of activities within local environments (LFP, 2020). The project's outreach includes local schools and a twice weekly Nature Club (*Klub Alam*) which has been running since 2013 and is attended by up to 20–59 children between the ages of 8–12 (Nekaris, 2016). Several EE programs have been implemented in this time including *Slow Loris Forest Protector* in 2013 and *Building Bridges for Slow Loris Conservation* in 2018 (Holland, 2018; Nekaris et al., 2018).

METHODS

Our initial research, used to develop the program included a literature search on international education frameworks, Indonesia's national curriculum (Curriculum 13), and Indonesian EE resources using Google Scholar, Web of Science, and academic books. We used a purposive sampling approach (Palinkas et al., 2015), to search for Indonesian formal and non-formal EE resources that had successfully utilised the theories/methods specified in the international education frameworks and national curriculum. We focused particularly on UNESCO education frameworks as these have heavily shaped Indonesia's environmental policies and programs (Parker & Prabawa-Sear, 2019). We also liaised closely with educators at the Little Fireface Project to ensure our learning content and activities were relevant to the children and aligned with the educators current teaching practices to ensure an easy implementation.

DESIGN AND LAYOUT

The *Changing Minds* program consists of six civet stories (see Appendix), supplementary activities, and formative and summative evaluations. To ensure the program's successful implementation, we needed to integrate it into

TABLE 11.1 The Structure of the *Changing Minds* Program

Week	Activities
1	Welcome talk Pre-program essay: knowledge and attitude evaluation
2	Story 1: **The civet who helped the coffee farmer** Story 1: Coloring in sheet Story 1: Seed growing activity Behavioral and emotional engagement scoring
3	Story 2: **The civet who lost his mother** Story 2: Coloring in sheet Story 2: The smell trail activity Behavioral and emotional engagement scoring
4	Story 3: **The civets from different homes** Story 3: Coloring in sheet Story 3: Guess the adaptation activity Behavioral and emotional engagement scoring
5	Story 4: **The civet who made a friend** Story 4: Coloring in sheet Story 4: The do not disturb activity Behavioral and emotional engagement scoring
6	Story 5: **The civet who was saved** Story 5: Coloring in sheet Story 5: Name your favourite things activity Behavioral and emotional engagement scoring
7	Story 6: **The civet who had a dinner party** Story 6: Coloring in sheet Story 6: The civet detective game Behavioral and emotional engagement
8	Spreading the word activity Promise bracelet activity Behavioral and emotional engagement scoring
9	Post program essay: knowledge and attitude evaluation Certificate ceremony

the project's existing Nature Club structure. As such, the program will be conducted over nine weekly sessions, with a new story introduced every week (Table 11.1). To help educators feel confident with the learning content, we provided background information regarding the ecology, behaviors, taxonomy, and conservation challenges of Indonesia's civets.

When it came to the program's layout, we followed Golombisky and Hagen's (2013; See Figure 11.3) Three C's of Design, as follows:

1. **Captures** attention: We chose a bright green for the color scheme based on the subject matter (green for a terrestrial species). Bold

Case Study • 187

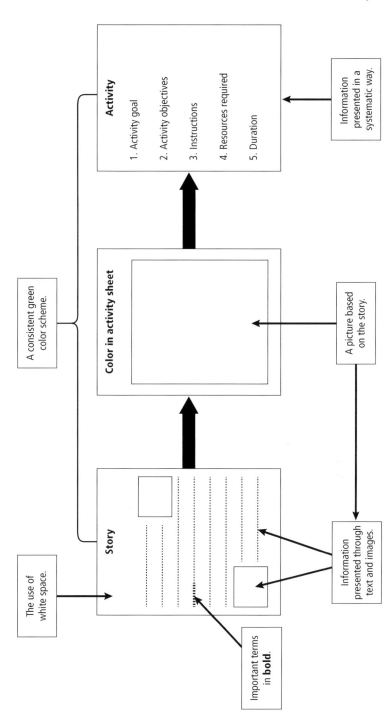

Figure 11.3 Three Cs of design. *Source:* Adapted from Golombisky and Hagen, 2013

188 ▪ H. M. A. RICKETS et al.

text is used to highlight important terms and concepts. To ensure information is clear, concise, and easy to read I made use of the white space on each page.

2. **Controls** eye movement across the page: Information is presented in a systematic way making it easy to follow and understand. The children will firstly be presented with a story, followed by supplementary activities that are broken down into activity goals and objectives, followed by instructions for achieving these.

3. **Conveys** information: Information regarding the Javan palm civet, and the program is presented through a variety of visual mediums including text, diagrams, pictures, and maps.

Developing Goals and Objectives

The 1977 Tbilisi Intergovernmental Conference Report (UNESCO, 1978), which utilises a holistic approach to education, recognising that individuals need to possess more than just an awareness and knowledge of conservation issues, was used as a framework for developing the programs overall goal and objectives (see Figure 11.4). These help structure teaching by outlining what the children are expected to achieve as a result of their participation in the program and how this will be accomplished.

To provide additional structure, more specific, measurable, and short-term goals and objectives with observable outcomes were developed for each activity session using the competency-based approach which has been utilised in Indonesian's Curriculum 13 and previous programs developed by the Little Fireface project (Holland, 2018; Nekaris et al., 2018). The competency-based approach centres around students demonstrating competencies (observable behaviors and skills) outlined in learning outcomes/goals, which are achieved by following the learning objectives (Misbah et al., 2019). In line with the approach, children will be required to master environmental knowledge, attitude, and skill competencies in order to achieve the programs overall goal; to develop the long-term interests, commitments, and behaviors required to protect the Javan palm civet.

We developed objectives that allow the children to demonstrate learning across the different levels of Bloom's cognitive and affective domains (Krathwohl et al., 1964; Krathwohl, 2002). Bloom's cognitive domain considers the knowledge and mental skills that contribute to learning. The domain is broken down into six hierarchical levels that increase in cognitive complexity, each level includes a set of behaviors and skills that need to be achieved to demonstrate learning at that level (see Figure 11.5; Forehand, 2005; Krathwohl, 2002). Through the cognitive domain, children have the opportunity to firstly build upon their lower-order thinking skills (remember, understand,

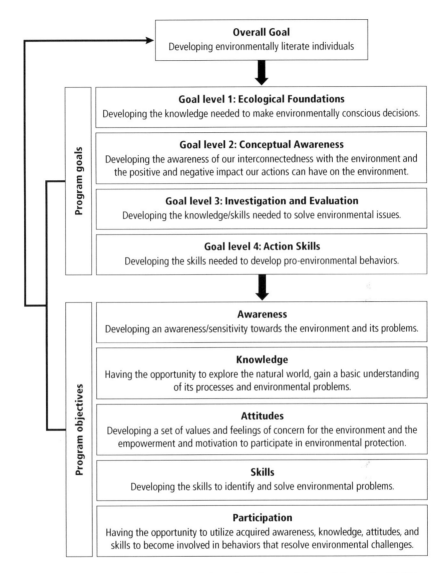

Figure 11.4 A holistic approach to education. *Source:* Adapted from the Tbilisi declaration 1977 (cited in UNESCO 1978).

apply) in response to concrete concepts such as how civets help farmers by dispersing their seeds. Once these skills have been achieved they can be used to advance to higher-order thinking skills (analyze, evaluate, create) in response to abstract concepts such as the emotional distress felt by civets in captive conditions (Krathwohl, 2002; Piaget, 1964).

190 ▪ H. M. A. RICKETS et al.

Create
Description: Ability to take information and generate new concepts or perspectives
Behaviors/Skills: Assemble, combine, create, design, modify
Example: Create a civet story using what you have already learned

Evaluate
Description: Ability to critique and justify information
Behaviors/Skills: Assess, decide, defend, judge, recommend
Example: Assess the benefits of reducing our use of single-use plastic

Analyze
Description: Ability to break down information into distinct parts and relationships
Behaviors/Skills: Compare, connect, criticize, differentiate, question
Example: Compare the impacts of deforestation on civets versus people

Higher-order thinking skills

Apply
Description: Ability to interpret information, by summarizing and describing it in their own words
Behaviors/Skills: Choose, demonstrate, modify, solve
Example: Demonstrate how we can help reduce the amount of litter found in the forest

Understand
Description: Ability to recognize and recall information
Behaviors/Skills: Define, describe, collect, examine, list, memorize
Example: List the types of food civets eat

Remember
Description: Ability to recognize and recall information
Behaviors/Skills: Define, describe, collect, examine, list, memorize
Example: List the types of food civets eat

Lower-order thinking skills

Figure 11.5 The six levels of the cognitive domain. *Source:* Adapted from Krathwohl, 2002

The affective domain involves learners' beliefs, values, emotions, and attitudes. The domain is broken down into five hierarchical levels, which increase in affective complexity, with each level including a set of behaviors and skills that must be met in order to demonstrate learning at each level (see Figure 11.6; Krathwohl et al., 1964; Savickiene, 2010). Emotional affinity, and values towards nature have been shown to influence positively people's long-term commitments and interests in conducting pro-environmental behaviors (Cheng& Monroe, 2012; Kals et al., 1999; Schultz, 2000). To address complex and multifaceted conservation challenges children require higher-order thinking skills including problem-solving and

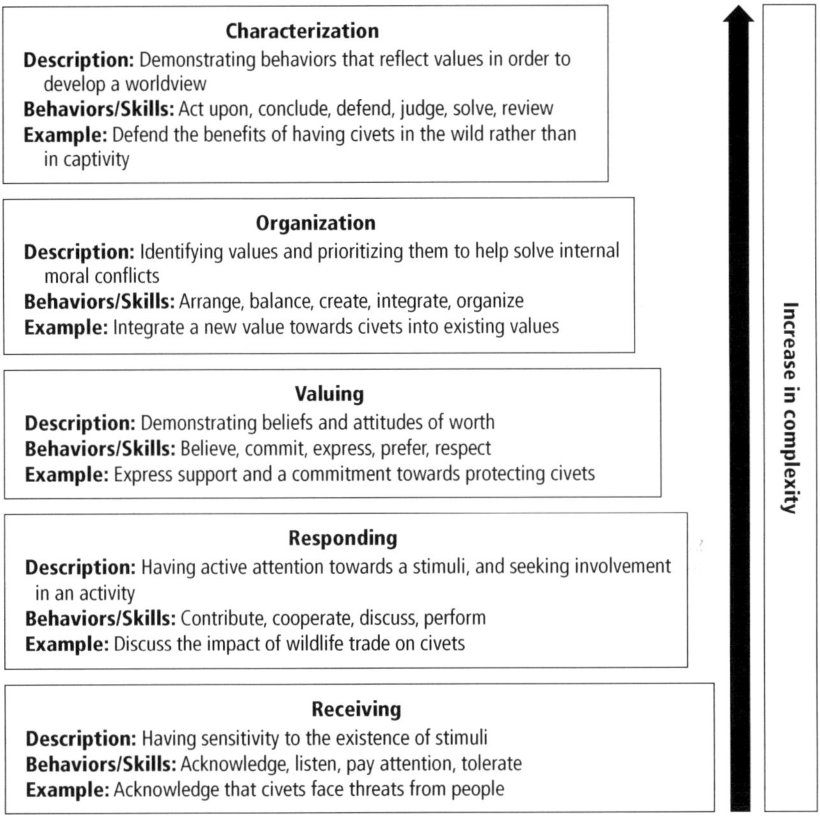

Characterization
Description: Demonstrating behaviors that reflect values in order to develop a worldview
Behaviors/Skills: Act upon, conclude, defend, judge, solve, review
Example: Defend the benefits of having civets in the wild rather than in captivity

Organization
Description: Identifying values and prioritizing them to help solve internal moral conflicts
Behaviors/Skills: Arrange, balance, create, integrate, organize
Example: Integrate a new value towards civets into existing values

Valuing
Description: Demonstrating beliefs and attitudes of worth
Behaviors/Skills: Believe, commit, express, prefer, respect
Example: Express support and a commitment towards protecting civets

Responding
Description: Having active attention towards a stimuli, and seeking involvement in an activity
Behaviors/Skills: Contribute, cooperate, discuss, perform
Example: Discuss the impact of wildlife trade on civets

Receiving
Description: Having sensitivity to the existence of stimuli
Behaviors/Skills: Acknowledge, listen, pay attention, tolerate
Example: Acknowledge that civets face threats from people

Increase in complexity

Figure 11.6 The five levels of the affective domain. *Source:* Adapted from Krathwohl et al., 1964

decision-making, as well as positive emotions and attitudes towards the natural world (Armstrong, 2017; Jacobson et al., 2015).

It is important to note that prior to developing our goals and objectives we needed to determine the children's current knowledge and perceptions towards civets (Larochelle et al., 1998). This information would help structure the learning content by identifying perceptions/attitudes that challenged our intended conservation messages. Through consulting with Little Fireface Project educators, we discovered that the children's' knowledge of civets is limited whilst perceptions are diverse. Many consider the civet a pest species, a commodity for the coffee industry, or a suitable pet (Cahill, 2020; Shepherd, 2008; Shepherd, 2012). To help counteract these negative perceptions and misconceptions, we decided to focus on teaching children about the ecological importance of wild civets for people as natural seed dispersers and pest killers (Nakashima et al., 2010; Subrata & Syahbudin, 2016).

LEARNING CONTENT

We decided to use storytelling as a method of introducing scientific knowledge in an engaging and culturally appropriate way. Our stories were written in English and Bahasa Indonesian, each with a different key civet concepts and conservation messages (Table 11.2). Storytelling has a long-standing place in many cultures and is used as a way to connect with people by sharing experiences, beliefs, and knowledge (Abrahamson, 1998; Greene, 1996). In Indonesia, storytelling has played a prominent role across all aspects of society. From its use as a peacebuilding strategy to address ethno-religious conflicts by promoting interfaith dialogue, to its use in education settings to improve literacy levels (Byron, 2016; Setyarini et al., 2018).

For educators, storytelling can be used to create a sense of wonder and excitement in which children are encouraged to think imaginatively and explore conservation concepts in culturally appropriate ways (Wells & Zeece, 2007). Creating stories with characters children can relate to and empathise with, whilst simultaneously introducing environmental concepts

TABLE 11.2 The Program's Six Stories Including Each Story's Message and Civet Concepts

Story	Message of the story	Concepts included in the story
The civet who helped the coffee farmer	Civets are very important to coffee farmers; they help their crops grow through seed dispersal and help them produce civet coffee.	• Ecological importance: seed dispersal • Ecology • Human-wildlife interactions
The civet who lost his mother	Civets can communicate with one another through scent marking.	• Behavior • Physiology
The civets from different homes	Civets have many adaptations which allow them to live in lots of different habitats.	• Adaptation • Human-wildlife interactions
The civet who made a friend	There are lots of misconceptions surrounding civets and how they behave around people. In fact they are very shy animals.	• Behavior • Conservation challenges • Human wildlife interaction
The civet who was saved	Civets do not do well in captivity. They belong in the wild.	• Behavior • Conservation challenges • Ecology • Human-wildlife interaction
The civet who had a dinner party	All civets are part of the family Viverridae. They are all omnivores and carry out seed dispersal.	• Ecological importance: seed dispersal • Ecology • Taxonomy

can help children to develop personal and enduring bonds with the characters and their conservation messages (Blizard &Schuster, 2007; Holland, 2018). Additionally, storytelling can promote the development of critical thinking skills as learners are encouraged to create, discuss, analyze, and question story content (Abrahamson, 1998; Nekaris, 2016).

We developed stories that are personally meaningful and relevant to the children and will therefore be engaging and enjoyable (Abrahamson, 1998; Payne, 2010). To achieve this, we have used non-extreme anthropomorphism which included basing the stories around civet characters that have names and express emotions. Studies have demonstrated that subtle levels of anthropomorphism—animals accurately drawn and depicted conducting species-specific behaviors—can assist in improving ecological knowledge, attitudes, and feelings of empathy towards animals due to their relatability (Beaumont et al., 2017; Kalof et al., 2016; McCabe & Nekaris, 2018). After consulting Little Fireface Project educators regarding our initial stories, we were advised that some were too anthropomorphic and could result the children developing anthropocentric attitudes (Ganea et al., 2014). For example, the "civet who made a friend" story focuses on the friendship between a civet and a young girl. The educators suggested that we reiterate that civets are wild animals as using the concept of friends may suggest that civets make suitable pets.

SUPPLEMENTARY ACTIVITIES

Our aim was to create activities which helped to reinforce the key messages in each story. For example, to reinforce the knowledge that civets play an important ecological role as seed dispersers, we designed a seed planting activity which included local plant species including coffee seeds (*Coffea arabica*) and persimmon seeds (*Diospyros kaki*), both of which are cultivated in Cipaganti village (Roberts, 2020). Coffee seeds have the added relevance of being a crop whose seeds civets eat and disperse (Shepherd ,2012; Subrata & Syahbudin, 2016). It was important for us to use materials that would be sustainable and have a low environmental impact. After consulting with Little Fireface Project educators, we decided to include activities that require the children to re-use waste materials, for example using plastic bottles as plant pots. Thereby helping to address one of Indonesia's most significant environmental issues–rubbish pollution (Parker & Prabawa-Sear,2019) whilst learning about the importance of keeping natural habitats pollution-free.

Our activities were developed in line with a range of teaching methods, learning styles, and instructional techniques to give children the opportunity to develop the knowledge, attitudes, skills, and behaviors specified in the goals and objectives (see Table 11.4). Activities were structured around a student-centred learning approach due to its familiarity with children through previous Little Fireface Project education programs and Indonesia's national curriculum (Holland, 2018; Rudy, 2015). The approach requires children to be actively involved in their learning through a range of instructional techniques including case studies, games, field trips, hands-on activities, and role-play (Roehl et al., 2013). In line with this approach educators take a supportive role, guiding and prompting children as they develop their critical thinking and creative skills individually or with peers (Nie et al., 2013; Ramdiah et al., 2018). For example, in the "guess the adaptation" game children will work in groups to match a scenario faced by a civet to the adaptation that would assist a civet in that scenario. Educators will guide learning by creating a group discussion in which they will encourage children to provide justifications for their answers.

To help the children develop conservation sensitivity and empathetic relationships with civets, we created activities that will take place in an outdoor setting (see Table 11.4; Crompton and Sellar, 1981; Dyment, 2005; Iozzi, 1989). Place-based outdoor education (PBOE) is an approach to learning which provides hands-on real-world experiences for children within their local outdoor settings (Lloyd et al., 2018). This approach promotes self-directed exploration and discovery, thereby encouraging learning in the cognitive and affective domains (Chalwa & Escalanta, 2007; Elder et al., 1998; Lloyd et al., 2018). For conservation, PBOE can encourage children to develop positive environmental attitudes and commitments towards protecting the species and its habitat due to them having personal meaning (Semken & Freeman, 2008; Sobel, 2004).

Additionally, PBOE can reinforce learning by placing information included in the stories into real-world context, thereby making it relevant and personally meaningful to the children (Llyod et al., 2018). For example, to accompany "the civet who helped the farmer" story, which tells the story of the relationship between a civet and a coffee farmer, we developed a "civet detective game" that would involve the children exploring local coffee plantations. Thereby placing the knowledge of civets as seed dispersers and producers of civet coffee into context to help enhance learning (Lugg, 2007). The activity will also give children the chance to take part in pro-environmental behaviors as they will be asked to pick up litter as they explore.

We wanted to ensure our activities gave children the opportunity to learn via different learning styles rather than using a more traditional single-style lecture approach that has consistently been shown to impact engagement and motivation levels negatively (Bender, 2017; Franquesa-Soler et al., 2018). The activities were developed in line with the VAK (visual, auditory, kinaesthetic, from Dunn and Dunn, 1978; see Table 11.3). Activities for visual learners include "name your favourite things" in which the children

TABLE 11.3 The VAK Model and Learning Methods

Learning	Description	Methods
Visual	Learners need to see information in order to process and understand it.	Prefer to be taught using pictures, video, graphs, maps, and diagrams.
Auditory	Learners need to hear and listen to information in order to process and understand it.	Prefer to be taught using lectures and group discussions.
Kinaesthetic	Learners need to be able to move about and manipulate objects in order to process and understand information.	Prefer to be taught using group work, experiments, role-play, and field trips.

Note: Model adapted from Dunn and Dunn (1978) and Gholami and Bagheri (2013)

TABLE 11.4 The Criteria We Used to Develop the Program's Activities

Criteria	Seed growing	The smell trail	Guess the adaptation	Do not disturb game	Name your favorite things	Civet detective game	Spreading the word	Promise bracelts
In line with program goal and objective	X	X	X	X	X	X	X	X
In line with the affective domain	X	X	X	X	X	X	X	X
In line with the cognitive domain: LOTS	X	X	X	X	X	X	X	X
In line with the cognitive domain: HOTS		X	X		X	X	X	
Transferable skills (communication/teamwork)		X	X				X	X
Demonstrate pro-environmental behaviors	X					X	X	X
Teaching method: student-centered active learning	X	X	X	X	X	X	X	X
Teaching method: place-based outdoor education	X					X		
Learning style: visual			X	X	X		X	
Learning style: auditory		X						
Learning style: kinaesthetic	X	X	X	X		X	X	X
Instructional technique: Hands-on activities	X					X	X	X
Instructional technique: games		X	X					
Instructional technique: case studies					X			
Instructional technique: role-playing				X				
Instructional technique: field trip	X					X		

Note: LOTS: Lower-order thinking skills; HOTS: Higher-order thinking skills

will be asked to write lists of items that make them happy to help them relate to the needs of civets. For auditory learners, activities include the "the smell trail" in which the children will have to guide a blindfolded member of their team using verbal instructions whilst they try to correctly identify scents. This activity will teach children about civet scent communication. For kinaesthetic learners, activities include the "do not disturb game" in which the children will try to sneak past the sleeping civet (a team member) and avoid being detected. The aim of the activity is to teach children how to behave around wild animals by physically acting out the behaviors.

To improve the likelihood of children developing long-term pro-environmental attitudes and behaviors, we looked to create activities that would be intrinsically motivating for them (Cetas & Yasué, 2017). Intrinsic motivations are behaviors that are driven internally due to an enjoyment or interest in an activity (Lanzini, 2014). In comparison to extrinsic motivations which are behaviors driven by rewards (monetary or non-monetary) or punishments (Pelletier et al., 1998). There are three underlying principles of intrinsic motivations that we used to develop the activities. (a) Autonomy: refers to people feeling like they have control over situations and was utilised in our program by developing activities that use a learner-centred teaching approach. (b) Competency: refers to people feeling like they can make a difference through positive feedback and encouragement. To achieve this, the children will be provided with encouragement through non-monetary extrinsic factors, including a civet protector bracelet and certificate which celebrate their completion of the program and signify their promise to protect civets. (c) Relatedness: refers to people feeling connected to the learning content due to its relevance (Cetas & Yasué, 2017). By focusing on a local species and it's conservation challenges we are ensuing our learning content and activities are relevant.

EVALUATION METHODS

To gain a detailed understanding of the impact of the program on children's knowledge and attitude towards civets, we have included both summative and formative evaluation methods. Whilst summative evaluations focus on determining the impact of a program on learning in terms of achieving program goals and objectives (Carlton-Hug & Hug, 2010; Jacobson & McDuff, 1997). Formative evaluations are used to track individual's progress towards achieving learning objectives and evaluate how they respond to the learning environments (Ozan & Kincal, 2017; Stiggins & DuFour, 2009). This information allows educators to make modifications to learning content, accordingly, helping to strengthen the quality of a program in terms of maximum engagement, enjoyment, and learning (Carlton-Hug & Hug, 2010).

Summative Evaluation

To determine whether the children have achieved the learning objectives, they will be asked to complete pre- and post-program essay stories to evaluate changes in knowledge and attitudes towards civets (Carleton-Hug & Hug, 2010). The children will be asked to write an essay in response to the statement "what do you know about the Javan palm civet?" We have used a neutral and unambiguous question to ensure the children express their knowledge and attitudes rather than what they think educators want them to write (Newing et al., 2011; Sorenson, 2019). Educators will use the six levels of the cognitive learning domain (see Figure 11.7) and the five levels of the affective learning domain (see Figure 11.8) as a framework to evaluate knowledge and attitudes (Nekaris et al., 2018; Sorenson, 2019). Educators will be able to determine which level of both domains the children have achieved learning in by comparing skills associated with each level to what the children have written. The pre-program essay will determine the children's initial knowledge and attitudes. Whilst the post-program essay will be conducted the week after completion so that knowledge and attitudes are still salient in the children's minds and easier to recall (Sorenson, 2019).

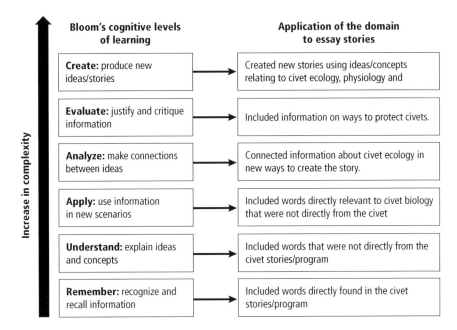

Figure 11.7 Levels of learning in the cognitive domain. *Source:* Adapted from Krathwohl, 2002 and Nekaris, 2016

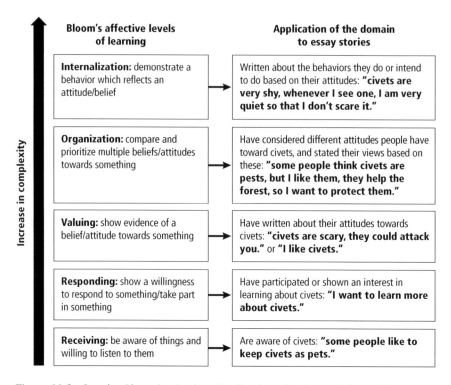

Figure 11.8 Levels of learning in the affective domain. *Source:* Adapted from Krathwohl et al., 1964 and Sorenson, 2019

Literacy rates in Cipaganti village are approximately 90%, therefore we believe essay writing is a developmentally appropriate evaluation method that will allow children to express their knowledge and attitudes in more depth than methods such as questionnaires (Nekaris, 2016). Additionally, we want to create an informal atmosphere in which the children do not feel like they are being examined or pressured to perform (Jacobson et al., 2015). Therefore, we decided against more formal test-style methods that are often used in Indonesian formal education settings (Gunawan, 2017; Ministry of Education and Culture, 2016).

Formative Evaluation

To evaluate how the children respond to the learning environments, behavioral engagement observations and affective engagement tests will be conducted throughout and upon completion of each activity (Carleton-Hug &Hug, 2010; Lee, 2014). Creating an engaging learning environment is essential in order to avoid the children becoming disengaged, disinterested, and unmotivated towards learning (Marks, 2000). We followed the Little Fireface Projects' current methods for collecting behavioral engagement observations as these are well-known and well-practiced within the Nature Club. Educators will be asked to observe and score the children's engagement behaviors in terms of levels of focus and participation using a 1–5 engagement scoring scale (Table 11.5). The higher the children score the more engaged they are in the activity. Observations will be conducted using a scan sampling method that involves recording group behaviors collectively at pre-determined intervals (every 10 minutes) throughout each activity (Altmann, 1974).

In addition to behavioral engagement, educators will evaluate the children's affective engagement levels (Appleton et al., 2008). Affective engagement refers to positive and negative emotional reactions towards activities, people, or settings. Positive emotional reactions may include liking, feeling a sense of belonging, being happy, or being interested. Whereas negative emotional reactions include disliking, being sad, and being bored (Lee, 2014). To evaluate affective engagement, the children will be asked to rate their level of agreement using a 5-point Likert scale from strongly agree to strongly disagree on six statements after completing each activity. These statements are, (a) I liked this activity, (b) I felt happy during this activity, (c) I felt stressed during this activity, (d) I felt bored during this activity (e) This activity was easy, and (f) I want to do this activity again. We chose an odd number scale that included a neutral mid-point as some children may feel neutral towards a statement and therefore will not be forced to choose a side (Newing et al., 2011). To determine their overall affective engagement the educators will add up the frequency of each response given to each statement. We decided that this evaluation will be learner-centred as it gives the children the opportunity to be directly involved in evaluating the program which is in line with the active learning approach (Armbruster et al., 2009). Additionally, educators may find it challenging to accurately record the children's emotional responses, particularly if these aren't visually expressed (Grogan et al., 2014).

TABLE 11.5 The Scale to Determine the Children's Engagement Levels	
Engagement score	Behavior
1	The child has left the classroom.
2	The child is moving around the classroom and not focusing on the activity.
3	The child is sitting still and not focusing on the activity.
4	The child is focusing on the activity but not actively participating.
5	The child is focusing on the activity and actively participating.

CONCLUSION

By working collaboratively with educators at the Little Fireface Project and using international and national education frameworks, we have created a program we hope will be implemented on a long-term basis. Thereby helping to bring greater support for Javan palm civet conservation by providing children with the knowledge, attitudes, and skills needed to become environmentally conscious individuals (Jacobson et al., 2015).

Our decision to choose the endemic Javan palm civet was not only due to the threats the species faces, but because we want to maximise learning opportunities in both the cognitive and affective domains by creating personally meaningful and relevant learning content; therefore it was important to choose a local species familiar to the children (Payne, 2010; Piaget, 1964). Focusing on local species to improve environmental knowledge and attitudes is an approach that has been successfully conducted by EE programs around the world. From Lake Alaotra, Madagascar where attention has been placed on the locally endemic Alaotra gentle lemur (*Hapalemur griseus alaotrensis*; Maminirina et al., 2006). To Yucatan state, Mexico, home of the black howler monkey (*Alouatta pigra*), a Mexican flagship species (Franquesa-Soler et al., 2020).

Our program demonstrates a diverse range of educational theories, teaching methods, learning styles, and instructional techniques that are not only applicable to Indonesia but to EE programs around the world (Hungerford & Peyton, 1994). Environmental education is important now more than ever as global biodiversity is threatened with a sixth mass extinction (Ceballos et al., 2015). By introducing EE from a young age, educators can help to raise generations of children that have the knowledge, attitudes, and skills required to address conservation challenges and protect the natural world (Jacobson et al., 2015; Maltese & Tai, 2010).

APPENDIX
The *Changing Minds* Program's Six Civet Stories Written in English

Story: The Civet Who Helped the Farmer

It was night-time in the forest, and Lala the civet was wide awake and ready to explore. Civets are nocturnal which means they sleep during the day and are awake at night. Not long after she had started her journey, she came across a large field filled with coffee plants. She noticed the plants were covered in bright red cherries and she was very excited, cherries were her favourite snacks! She started to eat them right away.

As the sun began to rise the farmer came down to the fields to inspect his coffee plants. He was excited to see Lala eating the cherries. Once Lala has eaten the cherries, she will spread the cherry seeds across the fields in her poo! These seeds will grow into new coffee plants. This process is called seed dispersal.

After Lala had left the farmer noticed all the coffee beans in her poo. He became very excited because it meant he could make his favourite coffee. This is a special coffee made from coffee beans that have been eaten by civets and partially broken down in their stomachs by molecules called enzymes. The farmer knew he could sell this coffee for a lot of money as people all around the world wanted to try it. He knew the secret to making the best civet coffee was to collect the poo from happy and healthy civets that live in the wild.

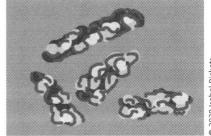

Civets and coffee farmers have a very special relationship called a mutualistic relationship. A mutualistic relationship is where both the farmer and civets' benefit. The farmer benefits because the civets disperse cherry seeds and help his crops grow. He can also use their poo to make and sell civet coffee. Civets like Lala benefit because they get to eat the cherries. This means it is important that civets always remain in the wild.

Story: The Civet Who Lost His Mother

Yiyi and his mother were walking through the forest at night looking for food. This was Yiyi's first trip away from home and he was excited to start exploring the forest. As they walked along the forest floor Yiyi became distracted by all the new sights and sounds. So distracted that he had forgotten to check which path his mother had taken and now he was lost!

Just as Yiyi was starting to get scared he smelt a familiar scent. He followed the smell to a nearby tree and recognised the scent as his mother's! His mother had been leaving scent marks for him to follow. Just like how humans recognise each other and communicate by speaking, civets communicate through smell.

Every civet has their own unique scent which is made in a part of the body near their tail called the perineal gland. Civets use these scents to let other civets know who they and mark their territories. Their wet noses help them locate a scent from far away.

Yiyi followed this mother's scent down the path but soon the path split and he didn't know which direction to go! Suddenly he smelt a new scent coming from a branch in a tree down one of the paths. He climbed up the tree and along the branch to the scent and took a big sniff with his wet nose. This scent belonged to an unfamiliar male civet. He had accidentally walked into another civet's territory which could be dangerous, especially

for a young civet all alone, so he decided to take the other path.

He began to worry that he would never find his mother before sunrise. Just then he caught his mother's scent again! This meant he was on the right path. He found his mother's scent on some rocks by the edge of a stream. This scent was very fresh which meant she was close by. He looked up there she was smiling at him from the other side of the stream. He had arrived home just in time as the sun was coming up and it was time for him to go to bed!

Just like humans, civets have their own special way of communicating with each other, they are very clever animals!

Story: The Civets From Different Homes

Layla was waking up in the forest, and Esther was waking up in the nearby town. They had made plans to meet at their usual spot; the forest edge. It was a long walk so they set off straight away. Civets can live in many different habitats, including forests, plantations, and around towns.

This is because they have lots of adaptations that help them live in different places. Adaptations are something all animals including humans have. An adaptation can be a part of the body, a process inside the body, or a behavior. Layla and Esther's adaptations will help them reach their meeting point.

Half way into their journeys they began to feel hungry. Both Layla and Esther can use a body adaptation to help them find food. This body adaptation is their curved claws! In the forest Layla uses her claws to help her climb to the top of trees where the best mangos are found. In the town Esther's claws help her climb buildings to hunt for rats and mice. Her claws make her the best pest killer!

Along the way Layla and Esther face many dangers. Luckily they can release a scent from their body which smells very bad. They use this scent to scare off animals that may attack them! This is a process adaptation. In the forest Layla comes across a hungry snake who is looking for his next meal! Luckily Layla knows how to escape! She releases her scent and the snake quickly slithers away. In the town Esther has accidentally bumped into a group of people. They try to touch her and she gets scared, so she releases her scent to make sure they stay back.

There is one last hurdle they need to overcome before they reach the meeting point! For Layla the meeting point is on the other side of a plantation. To get to the other side she has learnt to use water-pipes as a bridge! Esther just has to cross two buildings before she reaches Layla. It's too far to jump so she uses wires

and pipes as a bridge! Civets are clever, they have learnt to use man-made structures as bridges. This is a behavior adaptation.

Layla and Esther have finally met! They have used their adaptations to help them survive two very different habitats. In all the habitats where civets live, people live too! People and civets need to live peacefully alongside each other.

Story: The Civet Who Made a Friend

It was late at night and Wita was wide awake. She couldn't sleep so she decided to go and sit outside and get some fresh air. As she sat outside, she noticed something coming towards her. As it came into the light she realised it was a civet! She had never seen a civet before, but she had heard stories about them. They would attack people and steal their livestock. She was so frightened she ran back inside and hid under her blanket.

The next night she lay in bed wide awake when suddenly she heard a rustling from outside her window. She tuned on her bedroom light and slowly went to the window. There was the civet again! He was balancing on a wire frozen in fear. The light had scared him, and he was now trying to turn around and run away. But the cable was so wobbly it looked like he was going to fall! Wita ran across the room and switched off the light. But when she came back to the window the civet was gone.

When she had looked at him, she hadn't seen a scary animal that wanted to attack her. Instead she saw a very shy and scared animal. Maybe the reason he had been so scared was because he thought she was going to attack him! That thought made her sad, she didn't want the civet to fear her.

Every night for the next week Wita sat by her window and waited for the civet to come back. At first there was no sign of him, and she was worried she had scared him off forever. But then as the week went on, he started appearing! She quietly watched him as he balanced on wires and jumped across buildings chasing after mice and rats. She decided to call him Dendi since he had become her special night-time friend. She was no longer afraid of him, and he was no longer afraid of her! Civets are very shy animals that don't attack people. Next time you see a civet don't be scared, it won't hurt you. Just keep your distance because they are wild animals.

Story: The Civet Who Was Saved

Civets are sometimes taken from the wild to be sold as pets. This is what happened to Zaldo when he was a baby. In the wild Zaldo was a very happy civet, he spent his days exploring the forest with his mother and searching for his favourite foods including mongos and kasemak.

But in captivity Zaldo became very sick. His owners did not know his favourite foods and they kept him up during the day to play. But the daytime is when he would normally be sleeping! Most of all he missed running through the forest and climbing trees with his mother.

One day one of the children of the owners noticed how sick Zaldo was and knew they had to do something to make him better. So him and his father took Zaldo to the Little Fireface Project. The people at the Little Fireface project explained to them the reason Zaldo was sick was because civets are not meant to be kept as pets. He decided the best thing to do for Zaldo was to give him to the Little Fireface Project and they would find him the best place to recover.

A few weeks later Zaldo was well enough to be released back into the wild. As soon as he was released, he ran all the way back home where his mother was waiting for him! Together they wandered through the forest feeding on

all the foods he had missed. He was so happy to once again have all this space to play and explore. Zaldo was very grateful to the family for taking him to the Little Fireface Project, he would always remember their kindness. Even years later when he was all grown up and now a father, he would tell his baby the story of the family who saved his life.

Civets do not do well as pets; they are wild animals that should be able to live happy and healthy lives in the wild.

REFERENCES

Abrahamson, C. E. (1998). Storytelling as a pedagogical tool in higher education. *Education, 118*(3), 440–452.

Altmann, J. (1974). Observational study of behavior: Sampling methods. *Behaviour, 49*(3/4), 227–267.

Anderson, Z. R., Kusters, K., McCarthy, J., & Obidzinski, K. (2016). Green growth rhetoric versus reality: Insights from Indonesia. *Global Environmental Change, 38*, 30–40.

Appleton, J. J., Christenson, S. L., & Furlong, M. (2008). Student engagement with school: Critical conceptual and methodological issues of the construct. *Psychology in the Schools, 45*(5), 369–386.

Armbruster, P., Patel, M., Johnson, E., & Weiss, M. (2009). Active learning and student-centred pedagogy improve student attitudes and performance in introductory biology. *CBE—Life Sciences Education, 8*(3), 203–213.

Armstrong, P. (2017). *Bloom's Taxonomy.* Available at: https://programs.caringsafely .org/wp-content/uploads/2019/05/Caring-Safely-Professional-Program -Course-Development.pdf. (Accessed: November 2021).

Asunta, T. (2003). *Knowledge of environmental issues. Where pupils acquire information and how it affects their attitudes, opinions, and laboratory behaviour.* Faculty of Education of the University of Jyvaskyla.

Athman, J. A., & Monroe, M. C. (2001). Elements of effective environmental education programs. In A. Fedler (Ed.), *Defining best practices in boating, fishing, and stewardship education* (pp. 37–48). Recreational Boating and Fishing Foundation.

Beaumont, E. S., Mudd, P., Turner, I. J., & Barnes, K. (2017). Cetacean frustration: The representation of whales and dolphins in picture books for young children. *Early Childhood Education Journal, 45*(4), 545–551.

Bender, W. N. (2017). *20 strategies for increasing student engagement.* Learning Sciences International.

Birot, H., Campera, M., Imron, M. A., & Nekaris, K. A. I. (2019). Artificial canopy bridges improve connectivity in fragmented landscapes: The case of Javan Slow Lorises in an agroforest environment. *American Journal of Primatology, 84*(4), 1–10.

Blizard, C. R., & Schuster, R. M. (2007). Fostering children's connections to natural places through cultural and natural history storytelling. *Children, Youth and Environments, 17*(4), 171–206.

Broom, C. (2017). Exploring the relations between childhood experiences in nature and young adults' environmental attitudes and behaviours. *Australian Journal of Environmental Education, 33*(1), 34–47.

Byron, A. S. (2016). Interfaith dialogue to de-radicalize radicalization: Storytelling as peacebuilding in Indonesia. *Journal of Living Together, 2–3*(1), 1–11.

Cahill, C. (2020). [Un]becoming a resource: Translating the nature of civets in Indonesia. *Ethnos, 85*(1),100–117.

Carlton-Hug, A., & Hug, J. W. (2010). Challenges and opportunities for evaluating environmental education programs. *Evaluation and Program Planning, 33*, 159–164.

Case Study • **207**

Ceballos, G., Ehrlich, P. R., Barnosky, A. D., García, A., Pringle, R. M., & Palmer, T. M. (2015). Accelerated modern human–induced species losses: Entering the sixth mass extinction. *Science Advances, 1*(5), 1–5.

Cetas, E. R., & Yasué, M. (2017). A systematic review of motivational values and conservation success in and around protected areas. *Conservation Biology, 31*(1), 203–212.

Chalwa, L., & Escalanta, M. (2007). *Student gains from place-based education.* Available at: https://www.colorado.edu/cedar/sites/default/files/attached-files/CYE_FactSheet2_Place-Based%20Education_December%202010_0.pdf

Cheng, J. C. H., & Monroe, M. C. (2012). Connection to nature: Children's affective attitude toward nature. *Environment and Behavior, 44*(1), 31–49.

Crompton, J. L., & Sellar, C. (1981). Do outdoor education experiences contribute to positive development in the affective domain? *The Journal of Environmental Education, 12*(4), 21–29.

Dunn, R. S., & Dunn, K. J. (1978). *Teaching students through their individual learning styles. A practical approach.* Prentice Hall.

Dyment, J. E. (2005). Green school grounds as sites for outdoor learning: barriers and opportunities. *International Research in Geographical & Environmental Education, 14*(1), 28–45.

Elder, J., Basnage, M., Caswell, K., Danish, J., Dankert, B. and Kay, J. (1998). *Stories in the Land: A Place-Based Environmental Education Anthology.* Great Barrington, MA: The Orion Society.

Embassy of the Republic of Indonesia Washington DC (2017). *Facts and figures.* Available at: https://www.embassyofindonesia.org/index.php/basic-facts/ (Accessed November 2021)

Forehand, M. (2005). Bloom's taxonomy: Original and revised. In M. Orey (Ed.), *Emerging perspectives on learning, teaching, and technology* (pp. 47–56). The University of Georgia.

Franquesa-Soler, M., Barraza, L., & Serio-Silva, J. C. (2018). Children's learning preferences for the development of conservation education programs in Mexican communities. *The Journal of Educational Research, 112*(1), 28–37.

Franquesa-Soler, M., Jorge-Sale, L., Aristizabal, J. F., Moreno-Casasola, P., & Serio-Silva, J. C. (2020). Evidence-based conservation education in Mexican communities: Connecting arts and science. *PloS one, 15*(2), 1–18.

Ganea, P. A., Canfield, C. F., Simons-Ghafari, K., & Chou, T. (2014). Do cavies talk? The effect of anthropomorphic picture books on children's knowledge about animals. *Frontiers in Psychology, 5*(283), pp. 1–9.

Gholami, S., & Bagheri, M. S. (2013). Relationship between VAK learning styles and problem-solving styles regarding gender and students' fields of study. *Journal of Language Teaching and Research, 4*(4), 700–705.

Golombisky, K., & Hagen, R. (2013). *White space is not your enemy: A beginner's guide to communicating visually through graphic, web & multimedia design.* Taylor & Francis.

Greene, E. (1996). *Storytelling: Art and technique* (3rd ed.). ABC-CLIO.

Grogan, K. E., Henrich, C. C., & Malikina, M. (2014). Student engagement in after-school programs, academic skills and social competence among elementary school students. *Child Development Research, 2014*(2), 1–9.

Gunawan, I. (2017). Indonesian Curriculum 2013: Instrumental management, obstacles faced by teachers in implementation and the way forward. *Advances in Science, Education and Humanities Research, 128,* 53–63.

Holland, L. (2018). *Building bridges: Conserving the Slow Loris through conservation education and outreach via social media.* MSC thesis. Oxford Brookes University. Available at: https://www.dropbox.com/sh/2w9jjg8ntg8qhpr/AABMoeYW ySgDvy9Rb00h8fzEa/2017-2018/L.%20Holland%202018?dl=0&preview=L.+ Holland+2018 Dissertation.pdf&subfoldernavtracking=1. (Accessed: November, 2021)

Hungerford, H. R., & Peyton, R. (1994). *Procedures for developing an environmental education curriculum: A discussion guide for UNESCO training seminars on environmental education* (revised). UNESCO-UNEP, International Environmental Education Program. Available at: http://unesdoc.unesco.org/ulis/index.html. (Accessed: November 2021).

Ichwandi, I., & Shinohara, T. (2007). Indigenous practices for use of and managing tropical natural resources: A case study on Baduy community in Banten, Indonesia. *Tropics, 16*(2), 87–102.

Iozzi, L. A. (1989). What research says to the educator: Part one: Environmental education and the affective domain. *The Journal of Environmental Education, 20*(3), 3–9.

Jacobson, S. K., & McDuff, M. (1997). Success factors and evaluation in conservation education programmes. *International Research in Geographical & Environmental Education, 6*(3), 1–18.

Jacobson, S. K., McDuff, M. D., & Monroe, M. C. (2015). *Conservation education and outreach techniques* (2nd ed.). Oxford University Press.

Kalof, L., Zammit-Lucia, J., Bell, J., & Granter G. (2016). Fostering kinship with animals: Animal portraiture in humane education. *Environmental Education Research, 22*(2) 203–228.

Kals, E., Schumacher, D., & Montada, L. (1999). Emotional affinity toward nature as a motivational basis to protect nature. *Environment and Behavior, 31,* 178–202.

Krathwohl, D. R. (2002) A revision of Bloom's taxonomy: An overview. *Theory Into Practice, 41*(4), 212–218.

Krathwohl, D. R., Bloom, B. S., & Masia, B. B. (1964). *Taxonomy of educational objectives, Book II. Affective domain.* David McKay Company, Inc.

Lanzini, P. (2014). The effects of rewards on spillover in environmental behaviours: Monetary vs praise rewards. *Proceedings from the 50th Societas Ethica Annual Conference 2013. Climate Change; Sustainability; and an Ethics of an Open Future.* The Netherlands, 22–25 August. Soesterberg: Linköping University Electronic Press, pp. 163–177.

Larochelle, M., Bednarz, N., Garrison, J., & Garrison, J. W. (Eds). (1998). *Constructivism and education.* Cambridge University Press.

Lee, J. S. (2014). The relationship between student engagement and academic performance: Is it a myth or reality? *The Journal of Educational Research, 107*(3), 177–185.

Lee, R. J., Gorog, A. J., Dwiyahreni, A., Siwu, S., Alexander, H., Paoli, G. D., & Ramono, W. (2005). Trade and implications for law enforcement in Indonesia: A case study from North Sulawesi. *Biological Conservation, 123,* 77–488.

Case Study · **209**

Little Fireface Project (LFP). (2020). *Nature club (Klub Alam)*. Available at http://www.nocturama.org/en/klub-alam/ (Accessed: November 2021)

Lloyd, A., Truong, S., & Gray, T. (2018). Place-based outdoor learning: More than a drag and drop approach. *Journal of Outdoor and Environmental Education, 21*(1), 45–60.

Lugg, A. (2007). Developing sustainability-literate citizens through outdoor learning: Possibilities for outdoor education in higher education. *Journal of Adventure Education & Outdoor Learning, 7*(2), 97–112.

Maltese, A. V., & Tai, R. H. (2010). Eyeballs in the fridge: Sources of early interest in science. *International Journal of Science Education, 32*(5), 669–685.

Maminirina, C. P., Girod, P., & Waeber, P. O. (2006). Comic strips as environmental educative tools for the Alaotra region. *Madagascar Conservation & Development, 1*(1), 11–14.

Mangunjaya, F. M., & McKay, J. E. (2012). Reviving an Islamic approach for environmental conservation in Indonesia. *Worldviews, 16*, 286–305.

Margono, B. A., Potapov, P. V., Turubanova, S., Stolle, F., & Hansen, M. C. (2014). Primary forest cover loss in Indonesia over 2000–2012. *Nature Climate Change, 4*, 730–735.

Marks, H. M. (2000). Student engagement in instructional activity: Patterns in the elementary, middle, and high school years. *American Educational Research Journal, 37*(1), 153–184.

Mathur, M., & Hameed, S. (2016). A study on behavioural competencies of the Z generation. *International Conference on Management and Information Systems,* 63–71.

McCabe, S., & Nekaris, K. A. I. (2018). The impact of subtle anthropomorphism on gender differences in learning conservation ecology in Indonesian school children. *Applied Environmental Education & Communication, 18*(1), 1–12.

Ministry of Education and Culture. (2016). *Competency assessment standards for primary and secondary schools.* Available at: https://bsnp-indonesia.org/standar-penilaian-pendidikan/ (Accessed: November 2021)

Misbah, Z., Gulikers, J., Dharma, S., & Mulder, M. (2019). Evaluating competence-based vocational education in Indonesia. *Journal of Vocational Education & Training,* 1–28.

Nakashima, Y., Inoue, E., Inoue-Murayama, M., & Sukor, J. A. (2010). High potential of a disturbance-tolerant frugivore, the common palm civet *Paradoxurus hermaphroditus* (Viverridae), as a seed disperser for large-seeded plants. *Mammal Study, 35*(3), 209–215.

Nekaris K. A. I. (2016). The Little Fireface project: Community conservation of Asia's Slow Lorises via ecology, education, and empowerment. In M. Waller (Ed.), *Ethnoprimatology. Developments in primatology: Progress and prospects* (pp. 259–272). Springer.

Nekaris, K. A. I., McCabe, S., Spann, D., Ali, M. I., & Nijman, V. (2018). A novel application of cultural consensus models to evaluate conservation education programs. *Conservation Biology, 32*(2), 466–476.

Nekaris, K. A. I., Shekelle, M., Wirdateti, Rode-Margono, E. J., & Nijman, V. (2020). *Nycticebus javanicus. The IUCN Red List of Threatened Species 2020.* Available at:

https://www.iucnredlist.org/species/39761/86050473. (Accessed: November 2021).

Newing, H., Eagle, C. M., Puri, R. K., & Watosn, C. W. (2011). *Conducting research in conservation: A social science perspective.* Routledge.

Newton, B. J. (2001). Environmental education and outreach: Experiences of a federal agency: Lessons learned by NRCS conservationists about the effectiveness of various education and outreach techniques can help scientists communicate better with the general public. *BioScience, 51*(4), 297–299.

Nie, Y., Tan, G. H., Liau, A. K., Lau, S., & Chua, B. L. (2013). The roles of teacher efficacy in instructional innovation: Its predictive relations to constructivist and didactic instruction. *Educational Research for Policy and Practice, 12*(1), 67–77.

Nijman, V., & Nekaris, K. A. I. (2014). Traditions, taboos and trade in Slow Lorises in Sundanese communities in Southern Java, Indonesia. *Endangered Species Research, 25*(1), 79–88.

Nijman, V., Spaan, D., Rode-Margono, E. J., & Nekaris, K. A. I. (2015). Changes in the primate trade in Indonesian wildlife markets over a 25-year period: Fewer apes and langurs, more macaques, and slow lorises. *American Journal of Primatology, 79*(11), 1–13.

Nijman, V., Spaan, D., Rode-Margono, E. J., Roberts, P. D., & Nekaris, K. A. I. (2014). Trade in common palm civet *Paradoxurus hermaphroditus* in Javan and Balinese markets, Indonesia. *Small Carnivore Conservation, 51*, 11–17.

Nomura, K. (2009). A perspective on education for sustainable development: Historical development of environmental education in Indonesia. *International Journal of Educational Development, 29*, 621–627.

Nomura, K. (2007). Democratisation and environmental non-governmental organisations in Indonesia. *Journal of Contemporary Asia, 37*(4), 495–517.

Nomura, K., & Abe, O. (2005). The environmental education network in Indonesia. In K. Nomura & L. Hendarti (Eds.), *Environmental education and NGOs in Indonesia* (pp. 125–137). Yayasan Obor Indonesia.

Novo-Corti, I., García-Álvarez, M. T., & Varela-Candamio, L. (2018). The importance of environmental education in the determinants of green behaviour: A meta-analysis approach. *Journal of Cleaner Production, 170*, 1565–1578.

Ozan, C., & Kincal, R. Y. (2017). The effects of formative assessment on academic achievement, attitudes toward the lesson, and self-regulation skills. *Educational Sciences: Theory & Practice, 18*(1), 85–118.

Palinkas, L. A., Horwitz, S. M., Green, C. A., Wisdom, J. P., Duan, N., & Hoagwood, K. (2015). Purposeful sampling for qualitative data collection and analysis in mixed method implementation research. *Administration and Policy in Mental Health and Mental Health Services Research, 42*(5), 533–544.

Parker, L. (2016). Religious environmental education? The new school curriculum. *Environmental Education Research, 23*(9), 1249–1272.

Parker, L., & Prabawa-Sear, K. (2019). *Environmental education in Indonesia: Creating responsible citizens in the global south?* Routledge.

Payne, P. G. (2010). Remarkable tracking, experiential education of the ecological imagination. *Environmental Education Research, 16*(3–4), 295–310.

Pelletier, L. G., Tuson, K. M., Green-Demers, I., Noels, K., & Beaton, A. M. (1998). Why are you doing things for the environment? The motivation toward the environment scale (mtes) 1. *Journal of Applied Social Psychology, 28*(5), 437–468.

Piaget, C. (1964). PART 1 Cognitive in children: Piaget development and learning. *Journal of Research in Science Teaching, 2,* 176–186.

Prawiradilaga, D. M., & Soedjito, H. (2013). Conservation challenges in Indonesia. In P. H. Raven, N. S. Sodhi, & L. Gibson (Eds.), *Conservation biology: Voices from the tropics* (pp. 134–141). John Wiley & Sons, Ltd.

Ramdiah, S., Abidinsyah, H., & Mayasari, R. (2018). Problem-based learning: Generates higher-order thinking skills of tenth graders in ecosystem concept. *JPBI (Jurnal Pendidikan Biologi Indonesia), 4*(1), 29–34.

Randall, J. A. (2018). *Endangered species: A reference handbook.* ABC-CLIO.

Reibelt, L. M., Richter, T., Rendigs, A., & Mantilla-Contreras, J. (2017). Malagasy conservationists and environmental educators: Life paths into conservation. *Sustainability (Switzerland), 9*(2), 1–15.

Reinhardt, K. D., & Nekaris, K. A. I. (2016). Climate-mediated activity of the javan slow loris, *Nycticebus javanicus. AIMS Environmental Science, 3*(2), 249–260.

Roberts, P. D. (2020). *The Asian palm civet: Fundamental baseline findings in ecology, captive husbandry and effects of trade in civet coffee.* PhD Thesis. Oxford Brookes University. Available at: https://docs.google.com/document/d/194zUhzYGEI0 9LxL68Quf2U06MsrWIrjdjY-csCasJg/edit. (Accessed: November 2021).

Robertson, J. S. (2008). *Forming pre-schoolers' environmental attitude: Lasting effects of early childhood environmental education.* Royal Roads University. MSc thesis. Available at: https://viurrspace.ca/bitstream/handle/10170/58/Robertson%2c%20Jim .pdf?sequence=4&isAllowed=y (Accessed: November 2021).

Rode-Margono, E. J., Nijman, V., Wirdateti, W., & Nekaris, K. A. I. (2014). Ethology of the critically endangered javan slow loris *Nycticebus javanicus* E. Geoffroy Saint-Hilaire in West Java. *Asian Primates, 4*(2), 27–41.

Roehl, A., Reddy, S. L., & Shannon, G. J. (2013). The flipped classroom: An opportunity to engage millennial students through active learning strategies. *Journal of Family & Consumer Sciences, 105*(2), 44–49.

Rudy, P. C. (2015). The perspective of curriculum in Indonesia on environmental education. *International Journal of Research, 4*(1), 77–83.

Savickiene, I. (2010). Conception of learning outcomes in the Bloom's Taxonomy affective domain. *Quality of Higher Education, 7,* 37–59.

Schultz, W. (2000). Empathizing with nature: The effects of perspective taking on concern for environmental issues. *Journal of Social Issues, 56,* 391–406.

Semken, S., & Freeman, C. B. (2008). Sense of place in the practice and assessment of place-based science teaching. *Science Education, 92*(6), 1042–57.

Setyarini, S., Muslim, A. B., Rukmini, D., Yuliasri, I., & Mujianto, Y. (2018). Thinking critically while storytelling: Improving children's HOTS and English oral competence. *Indonesian Journal of Applied Linguistics, 8*(1), 189–197.

Shepherd, C. R. (2008). Civets in trade in Medan, North Sumatra, Indonesia (1997–2001) with notes on legal protection. *Small Carnivore Conservation, 38,* 34–36.

Shepherd, C. R. (2012). Observations of small carnivores in Jakarta wildlife markets, Indonesia, with notes on trade in Javan ferret badger *Melogale orientalis* and

212 ▪ H. M. A. RICKETS et al.

on the increasing demand for common palm civet *Paradoxurus hermaphroditus* for civet coffee production. *Small Carnivore Conservation, 47,* 38–41.

Sobel, D. (2004). *Place-based education: Connecting classroom and community.* The Orion Society.

Sorenson, K. (2019). *Education for primate conservation in Northeast Madagascar: Methods in place-based education.* Oxford Brookes University. MSc thesis. Available at: https://www.dropbox.com/sh/2w9jjg8ntg8qhpr/AABdVD-pMAgw31KicJ51 Aabga/2018-2019?dl=0&preview=K.+Sorenson+2019.pdf&subfoldernav tracking=1. (Accessed: November 2021).

Stiggins, R., & DuFour, R. (2009). Maximizing the power of formative assessments. *Phi Delta Kappan, 90*(9), 640–644.

Subrata, S. A., & Syahbudin, A. (2016). Common palm civet as a potential seed disperser of important plant species in Java. *AIP Conference Proceedings, 1744*(1), 1–4.

United Nations Educational, Scientific and Cultural Organisation. (1978). Final report of intergovernmental conference on environmental education. Organized by UNESCO in cooperation with UNEP. *Tbilisi,* USSR, 14–26 October 1977.

United Nations Educational, Scientific and Cultural Organisation. (2020). *Indonesia: Education and literacy.* Available at: http://uis.unesco.org/en/country/id. (Accessed: November 2021)

Von Rintelen, K., Arida, E., & Häuser, C. (2017). A review of biodiversity-related issues and challenges in megadiverse Indonesia and other Southeast Asian countries. *Research Ideas and Outcomes, 3,* 1–16.

Walpole, M. J., & Goodwin, H. J. (2001). Local attitudes towards conservation and tourism around Komodo National Park Indonesia. *Environmental Conservation, 28*(2), 160–168.

Wells, R., & Zeece, P. D. (2007). My place in my world: Literature for place-based environmental education. *Early Childhood Education Journal, 35*(3), 285–291.

CHAPTER 12

ENHANCING STUDENTS' ENGAGEMENT IN LEARNING SCIENCES THROUGH PROJECT-BASED SCIENCE

Using Digital Technologies Support

Miriam Kenyeres and Irina Pop-Pacurar

Progress in science and digital technologies have revolutionized the way educators should approach their instruction. Driven by the desire to enhance students' involvement in the learning of sciences, numerous types of research have been carried out: from integrated teaching through STEM (Shahali et al., 2017) to the introduction of digital technologies in the teaching-learning activities and so forth (Haleem et al., 2022). Starting from the question of how an educator can ignite students' engagement in studying sciences, the main focus of this chapter is to highlight and present psychological and contextual factors embedded in a didactic framework based on Self-Determination Theory, which contributes to promoting

---

Motivation and Engagement in Various Learning Environments, pages 213–243
Copyright © 2024 by Information Age Publishing
www.infoagepub.com
All rights of reproduction in any form reserved.

learners' involvement in the study of science. The main question of this chapter is: how can inquiry-based learning (IBL) and project-based learning (PBL), combined in the form of project-based science (PBS), supported by the medium of digital technology, can increase students' engagement toward learning sciences? Using a psychological and pedagogical perspective throughout this chapter, we first detail how motivation promotes students' involvement in learning activities, how it is related to engagement, and how both can be stimulated through the medium of Self-Determination Theory (Ryan & Deci, 1985). Next, we outline and propose a pedagogical approach based on project-based science (PBS) supported by digital technologies (DTs), adequate for enhancing students' interest in learning sciences. Finally, we provide suggestions for activities based on inquiry-based learning, project-based learning, and digital technologies that can be used in designing teaching approaches for learning sciences.

CONCEPTUAL FRAMEWORK OF ENGAGEMENT: A SELF-DETERMINATION THEORY APPROACH

What is Student's Engagement?

Studies regarding understanding, defining, and promoting students' engagement have captured the interest and curiosity of educational psychologists, researchers, and practitioners in education. Wellborn, in 1991, asserted that engagement could be illustrated by a student's active involvement in a learning activity. In 1992, Newmann defined engagement as "the learner's psychological investment in an effort directed toward studying, understanding, or mastering the knowledge, skills, or crafts that academic work is intended to promote."

How Can Engagement be Promoted Among Students?

Over time, numerous theories that enhance the involvement of students in learning activities have been discussed and stated. In 1985, Deci and Ryan elaborated the Self-Determination Theory (SDT), which relates to innate psychological needs and external conditions that influence a person's motivation. However, how is motivation related to engagement? According to Reeve (2012), motivation is considered a private, unobservable construct that precedes engagement, which is an observable behavior. Russell et al. (2005), stated that: "Motivation is about energy and direction, the reasons for behavior, why we do what we do. Engagement describes the energy in

Enhancing Students' Engagement in Learning Sciences • **215**

Figure 12.1 Interdependence between motivation, engagement, outcomes and context of learning (adapted from Reeve, 2012)

action, the connection between person and activity." Studies addressing the problem of fostering students' involvement in learning concluded that engagement is the outcome of motivation, and motivation is the source of the former. Skinner et al., in 2009, asserted that engagement is the external manifestation of a person's motivation which sustains involvement in the learning activities. According to Reeve (2012), engagement, motivation, context, and outcomes are established in a relationship in which each element influences the other (Figure 12.1).

Hence, SDT provides a motivational foundation for students' engagement. According to Ryan and Deci, the necessities underlying the development of motivation are three basic psychological needs: *autonomy*, "choice, acknowledgment of feelings and opportunities for self-direction," and "a sense that one's actions are self-determined or self-authored" (Deci & Ryan, 2002, p. 8), *competence*: "feeling effective in one's interactions with the social environment and experiencing opportunities to exercise and express one's capacities" (p. 7), and *relatedness* as «caring for and being cared for by others, having a sense of belongingness both with other individuals and one's community" (p. 7). Students experience autonomy when they perceive choice over their actions, meaning they have freedom in choosing how they involve and fulfill the tasks (Reeve, Nix, & Hamm, 2003). Students feel competent when they are successful and accomplish an activity or a task, in which they are involved (Deci, 1975). Last, but not least, students experience "relatedness" when they fulfill the need to establish both close friendships (strong relationships) and peer group affiliations (relationships based on shared interests and activities; Ryan, 1993). In a research review, Reeve concluded that friendships and peer affiliations with already engaged students promoted a higher sense of belonging in school, which, in turn, fostered engagement (Reeve, 2012). Therefore, SDT states the motivational resources a student both needs and possesses. Moreover, satisfying these psychological needs, leads to the energization of involvement and fulfills the psychological nutrients that the daily life events need to be psychologically, physically and socially well (Reeve, 2012). Based on this Theory, educators can adapt their instructional approach to facilitate students' engagement in learning.

Why Does Engagement Matter?

Engaged students put effort, persist in the learning challenges, and develop skills, social behavior, and adjustments. According to Freeman et al., in 2014, the key to knowledge building depends on students' involvement.

Hence, how can students' engagement in learning sciences be promoted following SDT and outlining a conducive learning context?

In this chapter we propose a pedagogical approach adapted for the study of sciences, that follows the three major concepts from SDT, that ignite students' motivation: autonomy, competence, relatedness, taking into account the learning context (Figure 12.2).

AN IBL FRAMEWORK: ENGAGING STUDENTS IN LEARNING SCIENCE THROUGH IBL

What Is Inquiry Based-Learning (IBL)?

As science is an evolving domain, the question of how students should be actively involved in the learning process is still debated. Inquiry-based learning (IBL) is a pedagogical approach adequate for teaching science and making

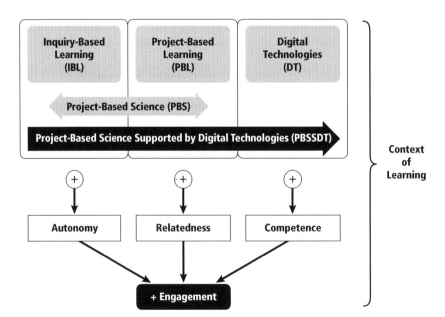

Figure 12.2 A pedagogical approach for enhancing students' engagement in learning sciences.

Enhancing Students' Engagement in Learning Sciences • **217**

students active agents in their learning progress. IBL is an alternative to traditional science teaching and is a set of knowledge and practices that guide the instructional process (Lazonder & Harmsen, 2016). Dewey introduced the concept in the first half of the 20th century (Dewey, 1938). He considered that students should learn how to think and act scientifically. Similar to science, the IBL approach is governed by a research question or a topic, the answer to which is discovered using scientific methods: investigations using computer simulations, virtual labs, tangible materials, or existing databases (Lazonder & Harmsen, 2016). National Research Council, in 1996, defined inquiry as: "an iterative, student-centered learning process that involves making observations; posing questions; examining books and other sources of information to see what is already known; planning investigations; reviewing what is already known in light of experimental evidence; using tools to gather, analyze, and interpret data; proposing answers, explanations, and predictions; and communicating the results (p. 23)." Therefore, using inquiry learning in science implies the involvement of students in activities scientists use, such as:

- formulating questions,
- hypothesizing,
- designing investigations,
- collecting and analyzing data,
- communicating results and
- justify the explanations (National Research Council, 1996).

According to Bybee, 2002, inquiry-based learning supports the development of new scientific knowledge. Starting from the scientific investigation carried out by scientists, IBL enhances the acquisition of skills to carry out scientific processes and the knowledge related to these processes. In teaching-learning sciences, IBL is considered identical to scientific inquiry, which starts with a scientifically oriented question and is based on mind-on and hands-on activities. According to Llewellyn, (2013), scientific investigation can exist only in the form of "minds-on" activity (which relies on documentation and the use of various resources, including the web). However, the combination of "minds-on" and "hands-on" type activities is more suitable. Hands-on activities include experiments or demonstrations and are any teaching and learning science activity in which students observe or manipulate objects individually or in small groups (Millar & Abrahams, 2009).

How Can the IBL Approach Be Integrated Into Learning Sciences?

Adopting inquiry-based science instruction implies conducting experiments, demonstrations, or observations in addition to a literature review

(Millar & Abrahams, 2009). Pop-Păcurar (2013) states "the experiment is a research method designed to discover, confirm or deny truths both in the natural and social sciences. As a didactic method, it involves intentionally provoking some processes and phenomena to study them. The research experiment has the role of familiarizing students with the approach of scientific investigation: posing the problem, documenting, formulating hypotheses, developing an experimental plan, conducting the experiment, recording and processing data, formulating conclusions, and arguing them."

The demonstration is considered a didactic method by means of which reality is explored. Its knowledge is based on the artificial experimentation of original situations, of natural phenomena, which cannot be studied in their natural state due to the inaccessibility or the much too large scale. The specificity of this method consists in using substitutes for reality (Bocoș, 2013).

Observation is another teaching method used in inquiry-based learning. Observation can be guided by the teacher towards the learning objectives, or unguided observation, in which the student engages autonomously in collecting information and exploring reality. In the second case, the observation results are heterogeneous but have strong formative potential. Exploring reality through observation may involve the analysis of figures, tables, diagrams, microscopic preparations, simulations, and others (Pop-Păcurar, 2013).

Why Can IBL Be Related to SDT and Foster Students' Engagement in Science?

IBL exists in several forms, depending on the autonomy offered to the learners and the degree of intervention of the teachers. According to Martin-Hensen, 2002, there are at least three scenarios of learning through investigation:

- *Structured investigation*: the research activity is centered around the educator: he gives the students the problem/question to be solved, as well as a plan or methods to guide its solution;
- *Guided investigation:* the research activity involves the distribution of the tasks, at each stage, between the teacher and the students: the teacher gives the students the problem/question to be solved, and the students identify the plan to solve it;
- *Open investigation* the research activity is centered on the student, with the teacher's interventions being reduced to a minimum: the students formulate the question or the problem to be solved, as well as the plan to solve it;

Therefore, depending on the investigation type, the idea of autonomy attributed to learners is a characteristic of IBL. Considering the philosophy of SDT, it is recommended to integrate guided or open inquiry in learning activities to promote student's engagement toward science.

Moreover, achieving a task, answering a science-orientated question, or obtaining a result, can enhance the level of competence a student experiences and, hence, foster a positive attitude towards science.

What Are the IBL Phases?

Over time, several learning models based on IBL have been proposed. In 2006, Bybee et al. proposed a five-step cyclic model of teaching-learning that supports and builds on inquiry-based learning (Figure 12.3). The five-stage learning model (Engage-Explore-Explain-Elaborate-Evaluate) assumes:

1. *(Engagement)* Engaging students in learning. Students involve in activities that promote curiosity and elicit prior knowledge. In this phase, learners formulate their questions that can be approached scientifically. The search and identification of the answer to this question is made through investigation;
2. *(Exploration)* Exploring the initial question. Students use hands-on activities: collecting evidence (most often in the form of experimental data), or utilizing minds-on activities: documentation, for gathering information;
3. *(Explanation)* Explaining the phenomenon or phenomena that determined the question. Students, based on the evidence collected, formulate and explain: definitions, rules, or principles, therefore, providing an answer to the initial question based on the research they have made;

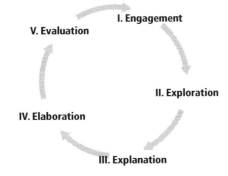

Figure 12.3 Five-stage learning model for implementing IBL (adapted from Bybee et al., 2006)

4. *(Elaboration)* Transferring the acquired knowledge. Learners apply the definitions, rules, principles, and laws identified, as well as elements of previously assimilated procedural knowledge, in new tasks;
5. *(Evaluation)* Evaluating and reflecting on their learning style. Students reflect on the investigative process they have carried out and evaluate their work (including the practical activity) and the results obtained.

Another approach proposed by Pedaste et al., 2015, posits that inquiry entails the sequence of the following phases:

1. *Orientation phase:* students are anchored in the subject by identifying and exploring the problem or the situation. The main focus of this phase is arousing and harnessing students' interest.
2. *Conceptualization phase:* students define the problem and gather information to generate the research question(s) or the hypothesis.
3. *Investigation phase:* students orient depending on the outcome of the second phase. If the outcome was a question, they proceed with the exploration sub-phase, where they collect data to answer the question. If the learners formulated a hypothesis, they design an experiment and gather data. The collected data are then interpreted.
4. *Conclusion phase:* students reflect on the first stated questions or hypothesis and consider whether the conducted investigations answer these.
5. *Discussion phase:* students communicate their results to peer students or other people and reflect on their learning process. This phase does not occur at the end, but in parallel with the others (Figure 12.4).

PROMOTING STUDENTS' ENGAGEMENT IN LEARNING SCIENCES THROUGH PROJECT-BASED SCIENCE

What is Project-Based Learning (PBL) and Project-Based Science (PBS)?

IBL is a pedagogical approach that can be implemented in several forms and embeds different teaching methods, for example, project-based learning (PBL). PBL is not a novel pedagogical approach. It was implemented in the second half of the 20th century by Dewey, the implementer of IBL (Dewey, 1986). PBL is considered an innovative learning approach that engages learners in pursuing knowledge by asking and following questions that have aroused their interest. "Students drive their learning through inquiry, as well as work collaboratively to research and create projects that

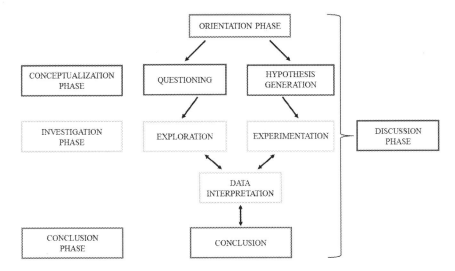

Figure 12.4 Inquiry-based learning framework (adapted from Pedaste et al., 2015)

reflect their knowledge" (Bell, 2010). Learners are challenged to search for information in different sources than the "classic ones" (textbooks or notebooks) to find an answer to the questions formulated (Akgun, 2013). In the context of teaching and learning science, a type of PBL was introduced: project-based science. Blumenfeld et al., in 2000, described project-based science as follows: "Students need opportunities to construct knowledge by solving real problems through asking and refining questions, designing and conducting investigations, gathering, analyzing, and interpreting information and data, drawing conclusions, and reporting findings (p.150)." Therefore, starting from the definitions assigned to PBL and PBS, it is considered that PBS is a particular type of inquiry-based learning where learners integrate, apply and construct their learning collaborating in creating solutions and concrete artifacts to complex problems (Guo et al., 2020).

How Can PBS Be Implemented in Teaching-Learning Science?

The steps for implementing PBS in learning activities are similar to IBL. The uniqueness of this pedagogical approach is that the investigation activities are completed with the construction of a product, a concrete "artifact" which illustrates the assimilated knowledge. The final product is often presented using videos, photographs, sketches, reports, models, and other collected artifacts (Holubova, 2008). The phases of implementing PBS in learning activities are:

1. Learners start with a driving question or a problem that needs to be solved.
2. Students participate in authentic inquiry processes to explore the driving question.
3. Students, teachers, and community members collaborate in activities to find an answer to the initial question or problem.
4. Students use learning technology to find solutions while engaged in inquiry.
5. Learners create an artifact, a tangible product that addresses the driving question (Krajcik & Blumenfeld, 2006).

According to Krajcik & Blumenfeld, (2006), "in project-based science (PBS), students engage in authentic, meaningful problems that are important to them and that are similar to what scientists do. A project-based science classroom allows students to explore phenomena, investigate questions, discuss their ideas, challenge the ideas of others, and try out new ideas." To ignite students' interest and improve students' engagement in learning sciences, Blumenfeld et al., in 1991, highlighted some crucial factors that influence PBS activities:

1. The subject of the research should be novel, topical, and relatable for learners (for example, subjects concerning personal health, community concerns, current events, and others);
2. The subject should challenge the students in the research process;
3. The activity should have a closure (construction of an artifact);
4. The learners should have control over the process and freedom over project performance regarding the activities carried out and the final product;
5. The activities should create a collaborative working space; learners should have the opportunity to exchange ideas with peer students.

Blumenfeld et al., in their research, concluded that PBS is a teaching-learning approach which ensures the fulfillment of all three attributes or psychological needs: *autonomy, competence,* and *relatedness,* stated in SDT. In a PBS activity, where learners choose or are attributed a relevant subject, they gain the freedom to make decisions regarding the research process and final product. Finding answers to initial questions and creating a final product enhance the feeling of competence. Having the opportunity to work with peer students, learners experience relatedness. Thus, all three basic psychological that are the basis of motivation according to SDT, are fulfilled. As a result of this, the chances of students getting involved in an activity based on PBS in learning science are very high.

PROMOTING STUDENTS' ENGAGEMENT TOWARD LEARNING SCIENCE THROUGH PBS AND DIGITAL TECHNOLOGIES

Project-based science designs a pattern for involving learners in studying science by supporting their autonomy, competence, and relatedness needs. However, besides the desideratum to fulfill these psychological needs, it is crucial to place all the activities in the context of learning.

What is the Context of Learning?

The context of learning or the learning environment is represented by the conditions in which instructional activities facilitate knowledge acquisition (Balsam & Tomie, 2014). De Figueiredo, in 2005, asserted that it is a set of circumstances relevant to knowledge acquisition. For instance, a classroom, a lecture, a laboratory assignment, a shared project, or a website facilitating the knowledge-building process.

What Is the Role of Learning Context in Enhancing Engagement?

According to Reeve, 2012, the learning environment is critical in pursuing knowledge because it can either support or thwart the inner motivational resources a student has. In 2007, Lam et al., proposed six components of instructional motivating contexts: 1. challenge, 2. real-life significance, 3. curiosity, 4. autonomy, 5. recognition, and 6. evaluation. In their study, the more the teachers proposed challenging activities with real-life significance, offered autonomy in fulfilling the tasks and also recognized their results, the more the intrinsic motivation of students aroused.

Considering contemporary students' needs, interests, and goals, it is imperative to create learning contexts where they can express themselves. Most of the students in the present day represent Generation Z, meaning they were born after 1995. This generation has several assigned terms, according to Dolot, 2018: iGeneration, Gen Tech, Online Generation, and C Generation (c-from connected, connected to the internet or computerized, or communicating). Children born in this period were raised in an era when the most profound changes in digital technology were made: the appearance of the world wide web, the internet, smartphones, laptops, and others. These changes also influence the world of education, which is currently undergoing a second revolution. Digital technologies (DTs), represented by computers, mobile devices, and digital media, should transform how we approach

Why Use Digital Technologies?

Several studies have reported a decline in students' involvement in learning science, the leading cause being the old-fashioned way science is taught (Rocard et al., 2007). In the knowledge acquisition process, it is essential to know how the main actors of the process work and think. Some characteristics of the digital natives, learners belonging to Generation Z, are: they can easily switch between the real and virtual world and perceive them as complementary; they have instant access and the possibility to check the information they need; they are able to share the information quickly and they can express their opinion using different means (Dolot, 2018). Since 2003, Levin and Bruce have emphasized the importance and benefits of integrating digital technology into the teaching-learning process. Embedding DTs in teaching science facilitates inquiry, communication, construction, and expression. Regarding the inquiry process specific to science, DTs simplify searching, finding, and interpreting data. DTs sustain communication by enabling the presentation of data through audio, visual, or audio-visual forms and support the creation of a collaborative space. DTs regarding construction facilitate the production of different artifact; last, technologies regarding expression sustain the creation of aesthetic and artistic products (Akgun, 2013).

Moreover, recent studies concluded that the introduction of DTs in lessons create a learning environment that: captures students' interest through the vastness of accessible materials and experiences; provides autonomy for exploring, analyzing, observing, and building their knowledge; stimulates their creativity; provides various up-to-date sources of information and enable multisensory learning experiences (Venegas & Proaño, 2021).All these features of DTs support the implementation of PBS in science lessons, thus completing the previously proposed framework, which aims to fulfill the basic psychological needs and considers the learning context adapted to the needs of contemporary students.

How Do DTs Support PBS and Enhance Students' Engagement in Learning Sciences?

According to Akgun, 2013, technology, in this chapter, referred to as digital technology, "is an indispensable component of any science or project-based activity." Embracing digital advancements in inquiry-based

Enhancing Students' Engagement in Learning Sciences • **225**

instruction improves students' interest and learning in science and nurtures knowledge acquisition by allowing them to investigate as scientists do in the real world. In PBS learning, DTs support students in the knowledge-building process through:

- accessing, collecting, and interpreting scientific data and information;
- providing tools for learners to visualize and analyze scientific data;
- allowing collaboration and sharing of information;
- planning and testing models;
- creating multimedia artifacts that illustrate students' knowledge; (Krajcik & Blumenfeld, 2006)

Moreover, according to Dogan and Robin, 2015, learners can use spreadsheets, databases and participate in virtual worlds or simulations that ignite their curiosity and interest. Also, they are able to clarify abstract concepts or misconceptions through DTs. Guzey, in 2010, have stated that DTs are practical tools that allow students to test hypotheses and regulate their learning process. ChanLin, in 2008, highlights the importance of using DT to support intrinsic motivation by creating opportunities for learners to explore knowledge and design artifacts within a collaborative space.

How Can DTs Supplement or Complement the Existing Face-to-Face PBS Learning?

As stated previously, the inquiry-based approach is realized by utilizing practical work, including experimentation, observation, testing, and demonstration. However, inadequate equipment and facilities in the science laboratories are still the main hindrances to teaching and learning science (Wolf, 2009). DTs represent a solution that can cover this lack. They comprise many forms: simulations, augmented reality, educational gaming, and online laboratories.

Simulation
This type of technology allows students to involve and carry out experiments that are impossible to be performed in the classroom due to lack of equipment, time, or because they are too dangerous. According to Akpan and Andre (2000), "Simulations promote learning about what-ifs and possibilities, not about certainties." The main advantage of this type of DT is that it supports science learning by allowing learners to manipulate both the real and virtual worlds. For example, students may practice and learn about animal dissection, natural/scientific phenomena, ecosystem models, and others (Renken et al., 2016).

226 ▪ M. KENYERES and I. POP-PACURAR

Augmented Reality (AR)

It is a type of software working on smart devices that can reproduce and project digital items, such as organs or systems, onto the actual image produced by the camera. VR (virtual reality) programs allow students to create 3D artifacts illustrating different phenomena or objects related to science (Vahidy, 2019).

Educational Gaming

Online games promote *learning by doing*. Students can play different roles, for example, a physicist, doctor, or nurse, to exercise their ability to act, practice their knowledge, or make connections between different subjects. Educational gaming covers different topics and can increase students' engagement through immediate feedback and through the achievements they earn by playing the game. Games are usually challenging and promote learners' involvement in knowledge acquisition (Kärkkäinen & Vincent-Lancrin, 2013).

Online Laboratories

Are an innovative technology representing a way to increase training of experimental learning. The main features of online laboratories are lower-cost access (they can be accessed using only the internet) and flexible access (they can be accessed anytime and anywhere). Online laboratories increase students' learning and engagement by providing a way to a wide range of laboratory tools they can practice on. Online laboratories are a good complement or substitute for school science laboratories, especially in those lacking of equipment (Kärkkäinen & Vincent-Lancrin, 2013).

PRACTICAL EXAMPLES OF ACTIVITIES FOR ENHANCING STUDENTS' ENGAGEMENT TOWARD SCIENCE THROUGH PROJECT-BASED SCIENCE SUPPORTED BY DIGITAL TECHNOLOGIES (PBSSDT) APPROACH

The next section of the chapter will present examples of different activities based on PBS and DTs and the extent to which they can engage students in learning science.

Gizmos and Scratch Platform

Gizmos (www.gizmos.explorelearning.com) is an online learning platform that allows the simulation of specific experiments in Mathematics, Science, or STEM cases, as well as the virtual performance of some practical activities (online laboratories; Figure 12.5).

Enhancing Students' Engagement in Learning Sciences • **227**

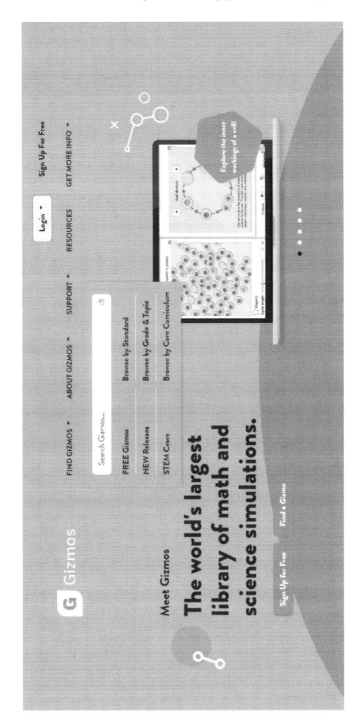

Figure 12.5 ExploreLearning Gizmos. © ExploreLearning.

This platform is a paid one and requires the creation of an account. Creating an account offers the free trial version, free of charge for 30 days, in which various activities suitable for students of all grades can be accessed. For complete and unlimited access is necessary to request a purchasing info. By accessing the STEM cases section, teachers have at their disposal several case studies that combine information from Mathematics, Biology, Chemistry, and Physics, which are adapted to different grades for students. These STEM cases can be used as a source of inspiration for the adaptation and integration of technology in the study of sciences, following the proposed pedagogical approach: PBSSDT.

As an example, the case study "Water contamination." This activity embeds notions from Physics, Chemistry, and Biology and is adapted for elementary and middle school students. It engages learners in studying human impact on the environment and the impact of a polluted environment with heavy metals on human health. Students play the role of a civil engineer who investigates the problems at the water treatment plant that cause the spread of Legionnaires' disease (Figure 12.6).

In this activity, firstly, students are introduced to the subject. They learn about pollution sources and physical water treatment: how it works, and its stages. Later, they formulate hypotheses about how water should be adequately treated to be potable. Students test the hypotheses by simulating various experiments. In the end, they obtain results from their experiments and interpret them according to their stated hypotheses (Figure 12.7).

This example of an activity based on investigation supported by digital technologies can be introduced in a project-based science with the theme *Human-Nature Relationship*. Students have the opportunity to consult different sources of information to emphasize the negative impact human activities can have on nature. Through this platform, learners can experience and study the impact of human activities on water quality. In order to fit into the pedagogical framework proposed by us, the final product of this activity can be the presentation of an animation that illustrates the human-nature relationship, for example, using the Scratch platform.

Scratch (www.scratch.mit.edu) is a free online-platform that stimulates students' creativity and possibility to collaborate in a common working space to illustrate different relationships, phenomena or aspects through programd animations (Figure 12.8).

Labster Platform and EON-XR

Labster (www.labster.com/) is another online platform used for virtual simulating and experimenting in sciences. It is presented as an immersive learning environment where students can practice laboratory skills and

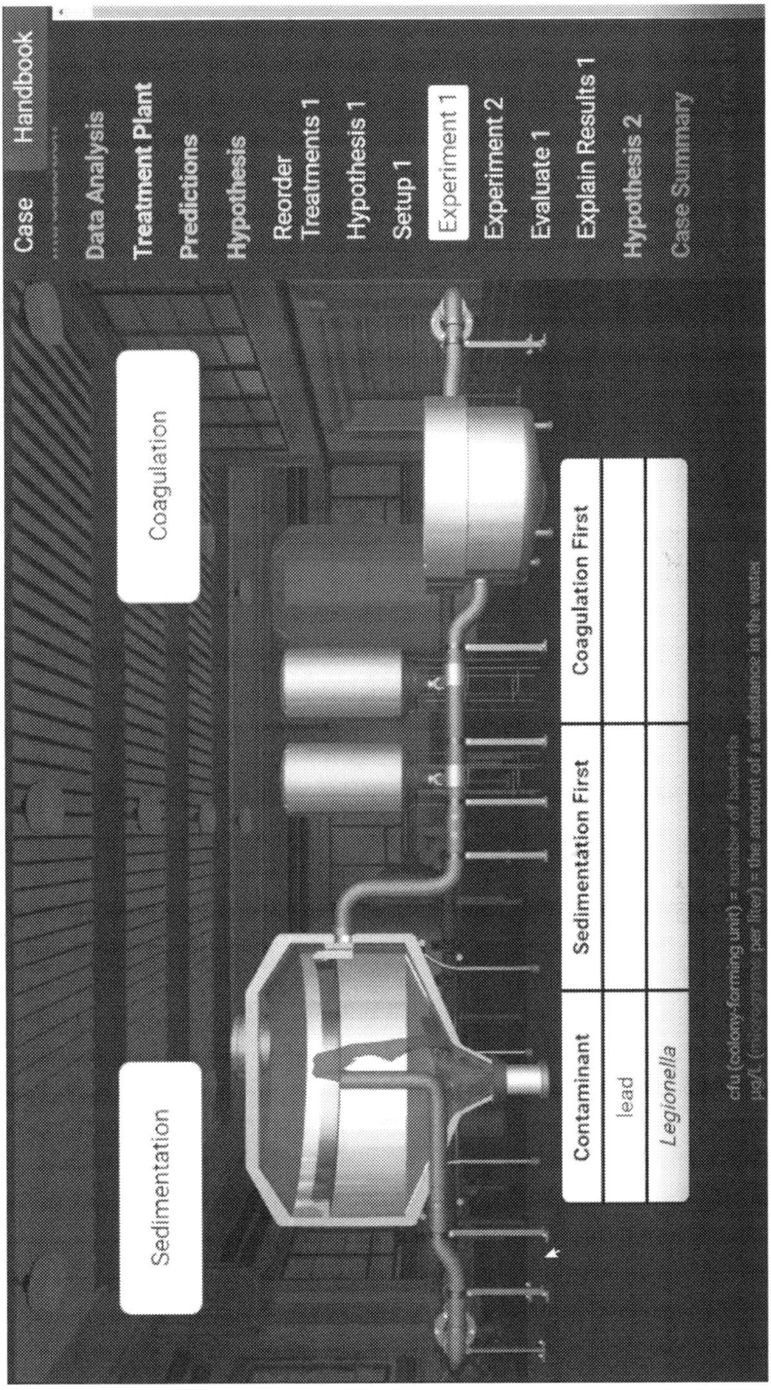

Figure 12.6 STEM case, ExploreLearning Gizmos, [Water contamination]. © ExploreLearning

230 ▪ M. KENYERES and I. POP-PACURAR

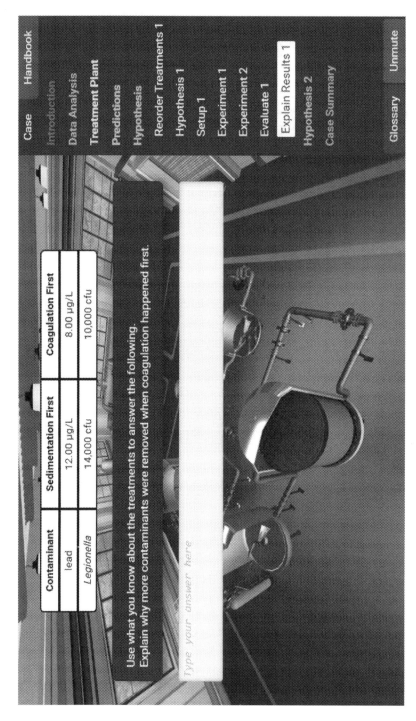

Figure 12.7 Testing hypotheses and interpreting results on "Water contamination" case ExploreLearning Gizmos, [Water contamination]. © ExploreLearning.

Enhancing Students' Engagement in Learning Sciences ▪ **231**

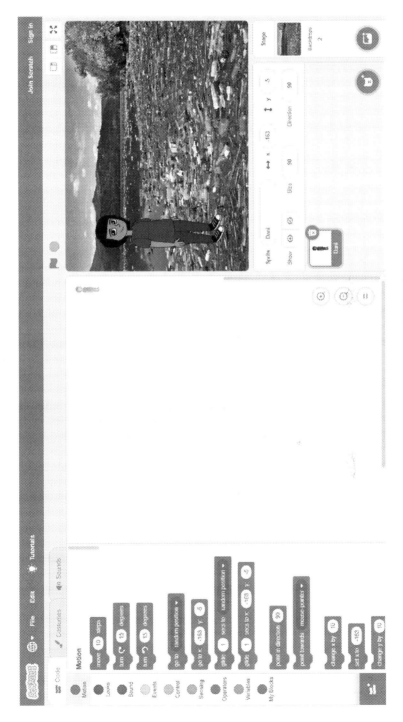

Figure 12.8 Scratch platform for creating animations (*Source*: www.scratch.mit.edu)

visualize theory. The platform aims at higher-level education students (high school, professional, or university). It offers course packages with a wide range of themes (Figure 12.9).

Labster requires the creation of an account. Creating an account offers the free trial version, free of charge for 30 days. For complete and unlimited access is necessary to request a purchasing info, the platform being a paid one. An example of an activity that can be carried out using Labster, following the proposed PBSSDT approach, is: "Carbohydrates: The sugars that feed us." Learning about the carbohydrates, high school students can discover through this platform how is the molecular structure of the most common carbohydrates (for example, glucose and fructose). They can find out the primary sources of sugars and how these are digested. Last but not least, learners can predict and investigate the effect of carbohydrates on the body, by testing and recording the amount of blood glucose (glycemia) resulting from different foods (Figure 12.10).

To illustrate and create a product to explain the research results, students can use EON-XR (www.eonreality.com/platform; see Figure 12.11). EON-XR is a platform that allows learners to create 3D artifacts in VR (virtual reality). Using EON-XR, students are able to collaborate and create, for example, a 3D lesson to exemplify the sugars' digestion pathway.

Figure 12.9 Labster platform (*Source:* www.labster.com)

Enhancing Students' Engagement in Learning Sciences ▪ 233

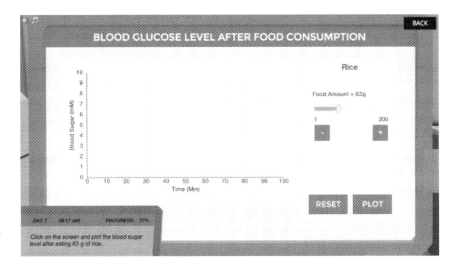

Figure 12.10   Testing blood glucose level on Labster platform (*Source:* www
.labster.com)

Students can record a lesson in order to explain the process and results. They can add annotations using a 3D model from the library or to build one themselves, importing 3D assets from the Sketchfab library (Figure 12.12).

This platform can be accessed from a laptop or computer, but it can also be accessed from a mobile device. The most excited feature of EON-XR is that the created models can be visualized in real world, in a 3D form with the help of a mobile device (Figure 12.13).

Any grade student can access EON-XR. It offers a free trial that consists of creating five free 3D lessons and access to up to four thousand 3D/360 assets. The subscription prices can be consulted at enterprise pricing and packages.

PhET Platform and Evernote Application

Another suggestion for enhancing students' engagement in learning science following the PBSSDT approach is using the platform PhET (www.phet.colorado.edu/). PhET offers learners interactive simulations in Science and Mathematics (Figure 12.14). It is a free access platform, suitable for any grade student that does not require creating an account. PhET encourages learning science by experimenting with different hypotheses and demonstrating various phenomena, often inaccessible in the real world.

PhET can be used in a learning activity related to the subject of natural selection and the genetic transmission of characters, for example. In this type of activity, firstly, students are familiarized with the subject. After this,

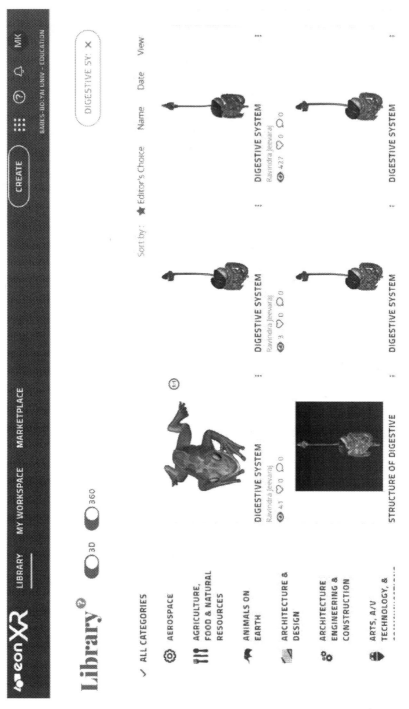

Figure 12.11 EON-XR platform (*Source:* www.eonreality.com/platform)

Enhancing Students' Engagement in Learning Sciences ▪ **235**

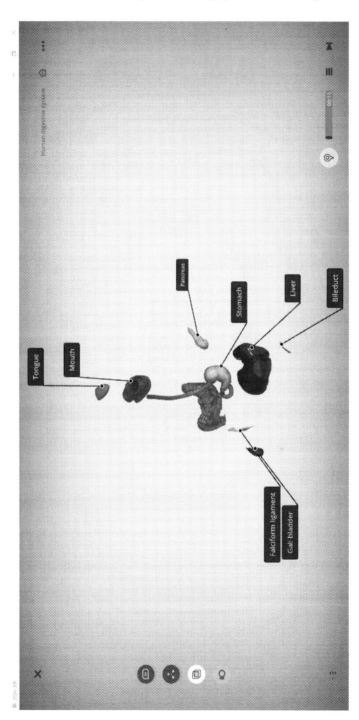

Figure 12.12 Creating a 3D model or lesson with EON-XR (*Source:* www.eonreality.com/platform)

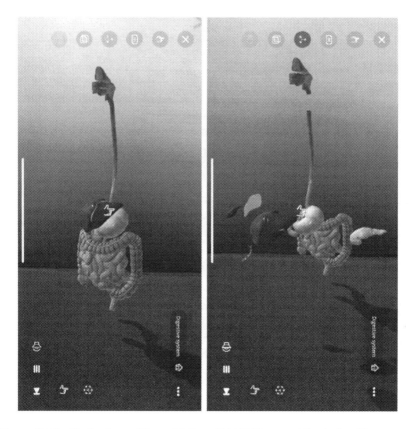

Figure 12.13 Projecting a 3D model from EON-XR on mobile device (*Source:* www.conreality.com/platform)

working in groups, they can formulate hypotheses regarding natural selection and test them by the mean of PhET. Learners can consider various variables they can test and can record the results in different forms. Moreover, students can trace the pattern in which genetic characters are transmitted using the pedigree generated by the platform (Figure 12.15 and 12.16).

To collaborate and create a final product of the research activity, students can use the Evernote application. This app is free and allows creation of a collaborative working-space where learners can communicate and exchange ideas in real time, they can record the data and present it in various forms: as tables, graphics, or sketches. Moreover, Evernote has other different and important features such as tracking plans for different tasks, work chat and possibility of creating notebooks for subjects.

Enhancing Students' Engagement in Learning Sciences ▪ **237**

Figure 12.14 PhET platform (*Source:* www.phet.colorado.edu)

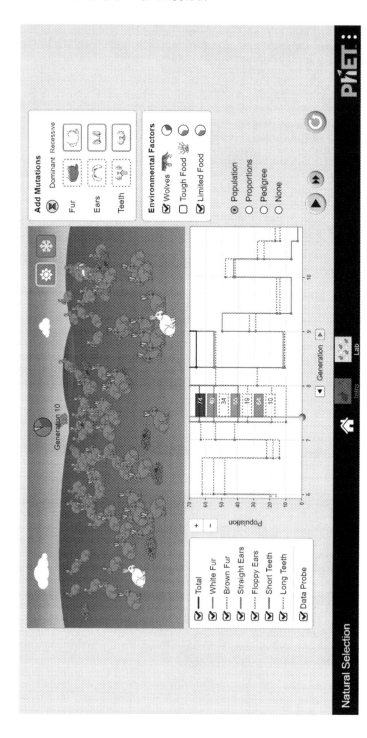

Figure 12.15 Testing the effect of various environmental factors on natural selection using PhET (*Source:* www.phet.colorado.edu)

Enhancing Students' Engagement in Learning Sciences • **239**

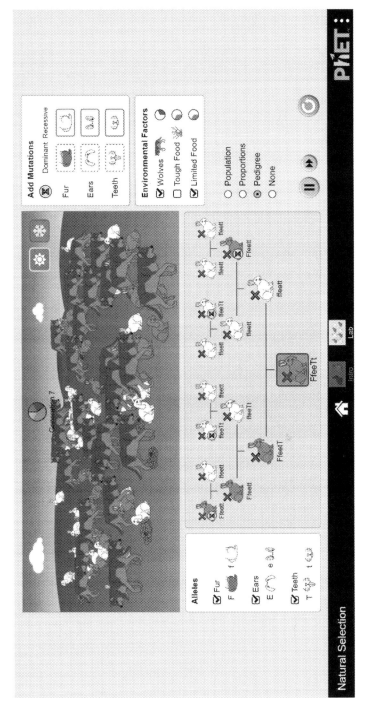

Figure 12.16 Tracing the pattern in which genetic characters are transmitted using PhET (*Source:* www.phet.colorado.edu)

CONCLUSIONS AND FUTURE RECOMMENDATIONS

This chapter was guided by the question: "How can teachers arouse students' interest in the study of science?" As was emphasized previously, stimulating students' interest in studying science leads to their active involvement in learning and contributes to the knowledge-construction process. Starting from the theory stated by Deci and Ryan (1985), Self-Determination Theory, we proposed a didactic framework that is based on the idea that the fulfillment of the three basic psychological needs: autonomy, competence, and relatedness, has a positive effect on motivation and, implicitly, on the engagement of students in learning. This framework converges the following learning types: IBL (inquiry-based learning) (a learning type similar to the research carried out by scientists) and PBL (project-based learning), which applied in the context of science teaching can be found in the form of PBS (project-based science). In the didactical framework proposed by us, PBS is supported by digital technologies (DTs). The integration of digital technologies in the teaching-learning process is connected to their progress and to the needs of generation Z (Dolot, 2018). The ways in which digital technologies can substitute or complement "classical" teaching contribute to the harness of interest of students and their engagement in learning. In conclusion, to promote student engagement in learning science, it is essential to deploy learning activities that embrace digital advancements and adopt project-based science instruction that fulfills students' need for autonomy, competence, and relatedness.

APPENDIX
Web Sources of Illustrations

www.gizmos.explorelearning.com
www.scratch.mit.edu
www.labster.com/
www.eonreality.com/platform/
www.phet.colorado.edu/

REFERENCES

Akgun, O. E. (2013). Technology in STEM project-based learning. In *STEM Project-Based Learning*, 65–75.

Akpan, J. P., & Andre, T. (2000). Using a computer simulation before dissection to help students learn anatomy. *Journal of Computers in Mathematics and Science Teaching, 19*(3), 297–313.

Balsam, P., & Tomie, A. (2014). *Context and learning*. Psychology Press.

Enhancing Students' Engagement in Learning Sciences • **241**

Bell, S. (2010). Project-based learning for the 21st century: Skills for the future. *The Clearing House, 83*(2), 39–43.

Blumenfeld, P. C., Soloway, E., Marx, R. W., Krajcik, J. S., Guzdial, M., & Palincsar, A. (1991). Motivating project-based learning: Sustaining the doing, supporting the learning. *Educational Psychologist, 26*(3–4), 369–398.

Blumenfeld, P., Fishman, B.J., Krajcik, J., Marx, R.W., & Soloway, E. (2000). Creating usable innovations in systemic reform: scaling up technology-embedded project-based science in urban schools. *Educational Psychologist, 35*(3), 149–164.

Bocoş, M.D. (2013). Instruirea interactivă. Repere axiologice și metodologice, *Editura Polirom* (Interactive Teaching. Axiology and metdodology. *Iasi: Polirom*)

Bybee, R. W. (2002). *Learning science and the science of learning: science educators' essay collection*. NSTA Press.

Bybee, R. W., Taylor, J. A., Gardner, A., Van Scotter, P., Powell, J. C., Westbrook, A., & Landes, N. (2006). The BSCS 5E instructional model: Origins and effectiveness. *Colorado Springs, Co: BSCS, 5*, 88–98.

ChanLin, L. J. (2008). Technology integration applied to project-based learning in science. *Innovations in Education and Teaching International, 45*(1), 55–65.

Collins, A., & Halverson, R. (2010). The second educational revolution: Rethinking education in the age of technology. *Journal of Computer Assisted Learning, 26*(1), 18–27.

de Figueiredo, A. D. (2005). Learning contexts: A blueprint for research. *Interactive Educational Multimedia*, 127–139.

Deci, E. L. (1975). *Intrinsic motivation*. Plenum Press.

Deci, E. L., & Ryan, R. M. (1985). *Intrinsic motivation and self-determination in human behavior*. Plenum Press.

Dewey, J. (1938). *Experience and education*. Collier.

Dewey, J. (1986). Experience and education. In *The educational forum*, 241–252.

Dogan, B., & Robin, B. (2015). Technology's role in STEM education and the STEM SOS model. In *A Practice-Based Model of STEM Teaching*, 77–94.

Dolot, A. (2018). The characteristics of Generation Z. *E-mentor, 74*(2), 44–50.

Freeman, S., Eddy, S. L., McDonough, M., Smith, M. K., Okoroafor, N., Jordt, H., & Wenderoth, M. P. (2014). Active learning increases student performance in science, engineering, and mathematics. *Proceedings for the National Academy of Sciences of the United States of America, 111*, 8410–8415.

Guo, P., Saab, N., Post, L. S., & Admiraal, W. (2020). A review of project-based learning in higher education: Student outcomes and measures. *International Journal of Educational Research*.

Guzey, S. S. (2010). *Science, technology, and pedagogy: Exploring secondary science teachers' effective uses of technology*.

Haleem, A., Javaid, M., Qadri, M. A., & Suman, R. (2022). Understanding the role of digital technologies in education: A review. *Sustainable Operations and Computers*.

Holubova, R. (2008). Effective teaching methods—Project-based learning in physics. *US-China Education Review, 12*(5), 27–35.

Kärkkäinen, K., & Vincent-Lancrin, S. (2013). *Sparking innovation in STEM education with technology and collaboration: A case study of the HP Catalyst Initiative*.

Krajcik, J. S., & Blumenfeld, P. C. (2006). *Project-based learning*, 317–334.

Lam, S. F., Pak, T. S., & Ma, W. Y. (2007). Motivating instructional contexts. *Issues in the Psychology of Motivation*, 115–132.

Lazonder, A. W., & Harmsen, R. (2016). Meta-analysis of inquiry-based learning: Effects of guidance. *Review of Educational Research, 86*(3), 681–718.

Levin, J. A., & Bruce, B. C. (2003). Technology as media: A learner centered perspective. In Y. Zhao (Ed.), What should teachers know about technology? *Perspectives and Practices*, 45–51.

Llewellyn, D. (2013). *Differentiated science inquiry*. Corwin Press.

Martin-Hansen, L. (2002). Defining inquiry. *The Science Teacher, 69*(2), 34.

Millar, R., & Abrahams, I. (2009). Practical work: Making it more effective. *School Science Review, 91*(334), 59–64.

National Research Council. (1996). *National science education standards*. National Academy Press.

Newmann, F. M. (Ed.). (1992). *Student engagement and achievement in American secondary schools*. Teachers College Press.

Pedaste, M., Mäeots, M., Siiman, L. A., De Jong, T., Van Riesen, S. A., Kamp, E. T., Manoli, C. C., Zacharia, Z. C., & Tsourlidaki, E. (2015). Phases of inquiry-based learning: Definitions and the inquiry cycle. *Educational Research Review, 14*, 47–61.

Pop-Păcurar, I. (2013). Dezvoltări în didactica biologiei–fundamente şi cercetări pentru optimizarea învăţării prin activităţi individuale şi de grup, colecţia Didactica activă, *Editura Paralela 45, Piteşti* (Didactics of Biology—theory and research on effectiveness of group and individual learning activities, *Pitesti: Paralela 45*).

Reeve, J. (2012). A self-determination theory perspective on student engagement. In *Handbook of research on student engagement*, 149–172.

Reeve, J., Nix, G., & Hamm, D. (2003). Testing models of the experience of self-determination in intrinsic motivation and the conundrum of choice. *Journal of Educational Psychology, 95*, 375–392.

Renken, M., Otrel-Cass, K., Peffer, M., Girault, I., & Chioccarello, A. (2017). Simulations as Scaffolds in Science Education. *Springer briefs in educational communications and technology*.

Rocard, M., Csermely, P., Jorde, D., Lenzen, D., Walberg-Henrikson, H., & Hemmo, V. (2007). *Science education now: A renewed pedagogy for the future of Europe*. Brussels: European Commission: Directorate-General for Research.

Russell, J., Ainley, M., & Frydenberg, E. (2005). *Issues digest: Motivation and engagement*. Canberra, Australia: Australian Government: Department of Education, Science and Training.

Ryan, R. M. (1993). Agency and organization: Intrinsic motivation, autonomy and the self in psychological development. In J. Jacobs (Ed.), *Nebraska symposium on motivation: Developmental perspectives on motivation* (pp. 1–56).

Ryan, R. M., & Deci, E. L. (2002). An overview of self-determination theory: An organismic-dialectical perspective. In E. L. Deci & R. M. Ryan (Eds.), *Handbook of self-determination research* (pp. 3–33). University of Rochester Press.

Shahali, E. H. M., Halim, L., Rasul, M. S., Osman, K., & Zulkifeli, M. A. (2016). STEM learning through engineering design: Impact on middle secondary students' interest towards STEM. *EURASIA Journal of Mathematics, Science and Technology Education, 13*(5), 1189–1211.

Skinner, E. A., Kindermann, T. A., Connell, J. P., & Wellborn, J. P. (2009). Engagement and disaffection as organizational constructs in the dynamics of motivational development. In K. R. Wentzel & A. Wigfield (Eds.), *Handbook of motivation at school* (pp. 223–246). Taylor & Francis.

Vahidy, J. (2019). Enhancing STEM learning through technology. *Technology and the curriculum.*

Venegas, G., & Proaño, C. (2021). Las TIC y la formación del docente de educación superior. *Dominio de las ciencias 7,* 575–592.

Wellborn, J. G. (1991). *Engaged and disaffected action: The conceptualization and measurement of motivation in the academic domain.* Unpublished doctoral dissertation, University of Rochester, Rochester.

Wolf, T. (2009). Assessing student learning in a virtual laboratory environment. *IEEE Transactions on Education, 53*(2), 216–222.

ABOUT THE EDITOR

Margareta M. Thomson, PhD is a full professor in educational psychology at North Carolina State University. Her research, funded by major federal agencies, such as the National Science Foundation (NSF) and the National Institutes of Health (NIH), investigates teacher and student motivation with the aim of improving instructional practices and student outcomes. Additionally, she mentors doctoral students and teaches courses in educational psychology and related areas. Dr. Thomson is a recipient of several prestigious professional awards, including the U.S. Fulbright Scholar Award and the University Faculty Scholar Award.

Webpage: https://ced.ncsu.edu/people/mmpop/

Motivation and Engagement in Various Learning Environments, page 245
Copyright © 2024 by Information Age Publishing
www.infoagepub.com
All rights of reproduction in any form reserved.

ABOUT THE CONTRIBUTORS

Berry Billingsley, Professor of Science Education and Director of LASAR Centre, Canterbury Christ Church University. Dr. Billingsley established the LASAR (Learning about Science and Religion) Research Centre in 2009 and it has become an established and vibrant hub for research that uses epistemic puzzles and collaboration through co-creation to bring people together for conversations about the nature, application, and communication of knowledge. LASAR Centre focuses in encouraging and supporting explorations of Big Questions that bridge multiple knowledge compartments. Dr. Billingsley has an interest in research co-creation with teachers and practitioners and is interested in its impact on helping young people to successfully navigate the borders between different knowledge compartments in education by developing their epistemic insight (knowledge about knowledge, especially knowledge about disciplines and how they interact). Her interests include Epistemic Insight, young people's engagement in science, artificial intelligence, Big Questions bridging science, religion and the wider humanities and also the communication of science and technology news in the media. Dr. Billingsley's first career was with the BBC where she produced and presented television and radio programs including BBC World Service's 'Science in Action', BBC TV's 'Tomorrow's World' and BBC Education's 'Search out Science'.

Micaha Dean Hughes, a doctoral student in the Educational Psychology program in the Teacher Education and Learning Sciences department at North Carolina State University. Her research interests include community-

---

Motivation and Engagement in Various Learning Environments, pages 247–252
Copyright © 2024 by Information Age Publishing
www.infoagepub.com
All rights of reproduction in any form reserved.

248 • About the Contributors

engaged approaches to educational equity and access in STEM education, college recruitment and K–12 outreach practices for women and minoritized students in STEM, mathematical identity development for adolescents and young adults, and culturally sustaining STEM outreach assessment and evaluation. Micaha received her Master of Science in STEM (Science, Technology, Engineering and Mathematics) Education degree from the University of Kentucky College of Education, and her Bachelor of Science in Integrated Strategic Communication (Public Relations) from the University of Kentucky College of Communication and Information Studies. She worked as an undergraduate engineering recruiter and K–12 outreach director for five years prior to beginning her doctoral program.

Marco Campera, a Lecturer in Conservation and Biodiversity at Oxford Brookes University. He worked on conservation projects in Indonesia and Madagascar. His interests include conservation biology, agroforestry, sustainability, animal ecology, and conservation education.

Katherine Chesnutt, PhD serves as the Director of the Empowering Teacher Learning (ETL) Project at Appalachian State University. This research is examining the impacts of using online, competency-based micro-credentials for teacher professional learning on teachers and students in rural, high-need schools. Chesnutt has experience in STEM education research, external evaluation, and teacher professional learning that focuses on autonomous, self-directed learning for educators.

Stefan Colley, Project Manager, Canterbury Christ Church University. Stefan has worked in Widening Participation and Outreach for eight years, with an extensive background in Higher Education Data analysis with Teacher Education and Outreach to under-represented groups. He has managed several large-scale Outreach projects and Programmes for the Canterbury Christ Church University writing, co-ordinating, delivering sessions and overseeing data collection and analysis against comparator groups of these projects, often working with Senior Academics from the university's LASAR Research Centre. Stefan oversees the day-to-day project management and delivery of the Uni Connect programme collaborating with universities. He represents the university at national and international conferences speaking about Widening Participation, best practice and specifically how to engage the most disadvantaged students raising both aspiration and attainment.

Megan Ennes, PhD is the Assistant Curator (Professor) of Museum Education in the Florida Museum of Natural History at the University of Florida. A former museum educator, her research focuses on how museums can support the science interests and career aspirations of underrepresented groups through family programming and civic engagement. She also con-

About the Contributors • **249**

ducts research on how to help museum educators and scientists more effectively engage in climate change communication with the public. Dr. Ennes has a PhD in Science Education from North Carolina State University.

M. Gail Jones is Alumni Distinguished Graduate Professor of Science Education and Senior Research Fellow, Friday Institute for Educational Innovation at NC State University, Raleigh, North Carolina. Dr. Jones teaches preservice and inservice teachers and conducts research on teaching and learning science, concepts of size and scale, and the development of science career aspirations. She serves as the Co-Editor in Chief of the *International Journal of Science Education*. Dr. Jones' research group is currently identifying factors and strategies to enhance science career aspirations and studying new approaches to convergence science education.

Miriam Kenyeres has her first degree in Biochemistry and two MA degrees in Biology. Currently, she is a PhD student in the field of Educational Sciences at the Faculty of Psychology and Educational Sciences, Babes-Bolyai University, Cluj-Napoca. Her research focuses on interventions that enhance the acquisition of procedural knowledge and competencies targeting this type of knowledge through the study of Biology in middle school. She is particularly interested in identifying digital technologies and practical activities carried out in the laboratory and in nature that facilitate students' engagement in learning and developing procedural skills.

Pamela M. Huff is a recent doctoral graduate of the North Carolina State University in the Department of STEM Education. Her area of interest is in understanding secondary science teacher's perception of science equipment, facilities, and teacher autonomy in the context of North Carolina charter schools. In addition, Dr. Huff's research is focused on the unique challenges of teaching science in secondary charter schools during the COVID–19 pandemic.

Muhammad Ali Imron, faculty member at the Universitas Gadjah Mada, Indonisia. His passion is to find a possible new balance between human and nature with the emphasis on wildlife in Indonesia. He has conducted various research projects in Sumatra, Kalimantan and Java as well as the Lesser Sunda Islands in Indonesia.

Finley I. Lawson, Lead research Fellow Outreach and Schools' Partnership, LASAR Centre, Canterbury Christ Church University. Finley joined LASAR in 2017 having previously worked in schools for 10 years as an educational support worker and Religious Studies specialist. He is interested in the dialogue between STEM, Religion, and the wider humanities, and how this can be fostered in school curricula. His current research examines the impact

250 • About the Contributors

of developing students' epistemic insight through Informal Science Learning via philosophical questions and he leads on the development of co-created research with teachers and schools. His broader interests focus on the impact of epistemic insight pedagogy on students' and teachers' navigation of a compartmentalized curriculum and the extent to which interdisciplinary learning and teaching opportunities can build epistemic agency. This includes understanding the role of co-creating research as professional development. Additional research interests include understanding how the development of epistemic agency can influence student recruitment, retention and progression within HE. In addition to his faculty role he has recently submitted his PhD in theology. The thesis applies current scientific understanding of the holistic nature of the world to our theological metaphysics, in particular in relation to discussions of divine and human personhood.

Daniel Macher is a psychological-technical assistant at the research group of Educational Psychology at the University of Graz (Austria), where he also finished his Masters degree and Ph.D. Dr. Macher's research interests lie in learning and instruction. Thus, he did research on restricting factors for learning like anxiety and its bifold influence on learning strategies and learning success as well as on facilitating factors like motivation. Furthermore, he is strongly interested in psychological methodology with a focus on structural equation modelling.

Anna Nekaris, a Professor of Anthropology at Oxford Brookes University and the University Lead for Public Engagement of Research. She is a member of the IUCN Primates specialist group, and directs the Little Fireface Project, a charity working to conserve Asian and African lorises. Her interests include conservation biology, taxonomy, toxinology, and conservation education. Regarding the latter, she built a school in Java, Indonesia, and founded a Nature Club in the area where she runs a long-term project on slow loris ecology and conservation.

Oana Negru-Subtirica, Associate Professor of Psychology in the Psychology department at Babes-Bolyai University, Romania. Dr. Negru-Subtirica's research expertise is in the area of academic motivation, professional motivation and student development. She teaches graduate and undergraduate courses in Psychology, Motivation and Educational Psychology. She is the recipient of prestigious research awards, like Erasmus, and has numerous research publications in high ranked international journals.

Catherine Noonan, PT, DPT, PCS, CEIM, is a board-certified specialist in pediatric physical therapy, infant massage educator, and former associate professor in the Doctor of Physical Therapy program at Campbell Univer-

About the Contributors • **251**

sity. She is currently pursuing a PhD in Education: Learning, Design, and Technology from North Carolina State University. Her primary research interests center around human development, including child development, maternal development, disability, rehabilitation, technological influences, and supports for families with young children.

Manuela Paechter, PhD is a professor of Educational Psychology at the University of Graz (Austria). She studied psychology at the Technical University of Darmstadt (Germany) and the University of Hull (UK) and received her Ph.D. from the Technical University of Braunschweig. Her research interests focus on learning and instruction in different age groups starting from early childhood to adult learning and education. Learning occurs within a complex interaction of a learner's personal characteristics, attitudes, and experiences with characteristics of the learning environment and the wider societal context. Within this framework she investigates facilitating and restricting factors for learning including learner characteristics as well as characteristics of the learning environment. In her research she also employs psychophysiological methods like ECG and shows how research in educational psychology may profit from the inclusion of psychophysiological measures.

Irina Pop-Pacurar, Associate Professor in the Science Education and Teacher Training Department at Babes-Bolyai University, Romania. Dr.Pop-Pacuar teaches undergraduate and graduate courses in Science Education, Methods courses in Biology, and teacher training related courses. Additionally, she is an award-winning science textbook author, and has published numerous articles and books.

James Percival, a senior lecturer in education at Oxford Brookes University in the UK. After studying history and political philosophy to postgraduate level, he worked for a decade in Oxfordshire primary schools where he became a curriculum leader. In 2003 James moved into Higher Education where he taught the humanities to trainee teachers, and history and sociology of education modules to both undergraduates and postgraduates. His research interests are shared between history pedagogy and the sociology of education.

Quaneisha D. Smith is a Reading Interventionist and a Nationally Board-Certified Elementary School Teacher. She has been teaching for 23 years. She is the owner of Elite Virtual Tutoring Services, LLC, and the founder of For Girls Like Quaneisha Mentoring Program. Quaneisha has Bachelor's degrees in Elementary Education and African American Studies. She also has Master of Education degrees in Literacy and Learning Design and Technology. She is passionate about seeing all children achieve academic

252 ▪ About the Contributors

success, especially African American children. She has devoted her life to impacting the academic success of and the lives of the students that she teaches, tutors, or mentors. She has a particular interest in discovering how to motivate African American boys to achieve academically.

Margareta M. Thomson, Full Professor of Educational Psychology at North Carolina State University. Dr. Thomson's research expertise is in the area of teacher and student motivation, motivational beliefs and STEM learning. She teaches graduate and undergraduate courses in Educational Psychology, Motivation and Research Methods. She is the recipient of prestigious research awards, like NSF, NIH and U.S. Core Fulbright and has numerous publications in top-tier journals.

Hannah Rickets is a science communication field specialist and graduate of Oxford Brookes University with a 1st class master's degree in Primate Conservation. Her thesis focused on developing environmental education programs for wildlife NGOs and has since been published in the Oxford Brookes Canopy journal. Since graduating, she worked as an Account Executive at a global healthcare comms agency where she managed the communications for a global pharmaceutical company. She has spent several months working in Sierra Leone at Tacugama Chimpanzee Sanctuary where she developed 3 environmental education programs and trained local educators on how to teach these to their students.

Zarifa Zakaria, is an educational researcher and a graduate of the Educational Psychology program at North Carolina State University. Dr. Zakaria's research interests are in student and teacher development, motivation, and online learning environments. In addition to research, she has K–5 teaching experience, and college level teaching in Educational Psychology, as well as research experience in federal funded research projects.

Printed in the United States
by Baker & Taylor Publisher Services